Reading Enhancement And Development

Seventh Edition

Rhonda Holt Atkinson
Central Missouri State University

Debbie Guice Longman
Southeastern Louisiana University

THOMSON

™

HEINLE

Australia • Canada • Mexico • Singapore • Spain • United Kingdom • United States

THOMSON

HEINLE

Reading Enhancement and Development

Rhonda Holt Atkinson & Debbie Guice Longman

Publisher: Michael Rosenberg
Acquisitions Editor: Stephen Dalphin
Sr. Developmental Editor: Michell Phifer
Director of Mktg., Higher Ed.: Lisa Kimball
Executive Mktg. Manager: Ken Kasee
Production Editor: Jeff Freeland

Sr. Manufacturing Coordinator:
  Mary Beth Hennebury
Compositor: Forbes Mill Press
Cover Designer: Ha Nguyen
Printer: Edwards Brothers

Printed in the United States
1 2 3 4 5 6 7 8 9 10   06 05 04 03 02

For more information contact Heinle, 25 Thomson Place, Boston, Massachusetts 02210 USA, or you can visit our Internet site at http://www.heinle.com

For permission to use material from this text or product contact us:

Tel   1-800-730-2214
Fax   1-800-730-2215
Web   www.thomsonrights.com

Atkinson, Rhonda Holt.
  Reading enhancement and development / Rhonda Holt Atkinson, Debbie Guice Longman.— 7th ed.
      p. cm.
  Includes bibliographical references and index.
  ISBN 0-15-506243-3
   1. Reading (Higher education) 2. Developmental reading. 3. Study skills. I. Longman, Debbie Guice. II. Title.

LB2395.3 .A85 2002
428.4'071'1--dc21   2002074316

Contents

| Chapter 3 | Reading | 63 |

Chapter 4   Memory and Test-Taking   97

Chapter 5   Vocabulary Development   141

Chapter 8	**Reading and Thinking Critically**	**221**

Chapter 9	**Reading in the Information Age**	**255**

Chapter 10	Reading Graphics	285

Chapter 11   *Sample Chapter*   325

READ List of Readings

Preface

In one of our favorite movies, *A League of Their Own,* the character portrayed by Tom Hanks says, "It's supposed to be hard. If it wasn't hard, everyone would do it. The 'hard' is what makes it great." We have worked hard on this edition of READ and hope that it will help enhance and develop your reading abilities. Although a book cannot be everything to everyone, we have worked to make READ, seventh edition, clear and concise and yet have it contain the information you need to achieve academic success.

Reading Enhancement and Development (READ) has five central purposes:

- READ identifies the reading skills necessary for good comprehension and vocabulary development.

- READ shows students how to develop the ability to monitor their own comprehension: To do so, instruction goes beyond simply defining skills to exploring why and how specific reading strategies are developed. As a result, readers not only learn, but also understand the mental processes involved in reading.

- READ applies reading theory to developmental reading instruction based on metacognition, whole-brain learning, schema theory, whole language, and the reading-writing connection.

- READ matches teaching methods and materials to the backgrounds and knowledge of today's postsecondary students. Practical, relevant instruction applied to content-specific text information provides students with learning strategies that last.

As teachers who are also avid readers, we emphasize the importance of recreational reading as a device for building comprehension and vocabulary. We hope that READ encourages students to become lifelong readers and learners.

New to This Edition

Today's postsecondary students face new learning challenges both inside and outside the classroom. Learning is no longer confined to buildings, but now occurs in cyberspace as well. Increased demands to assimilate information quickly from a variety of sources have changed the academic environment and the kinds of skills required for success. New content and features in READ reflect those changes.

- New essays, stories, and other text information reflect the diversity of materials from which today's students must read and learn.
- Two new chapters: Vocabulary Development and Reading in the Information Age.
- Extensive changes in vocabulary sections with new selections for 90 percent of the chapters.
- Revision of the content in more than 75 percent of the exercises.
- Streamlined content and exercises to make the text easier to read and use.
- New Internet activities.

Key Features

READ, seventh edition, contains many of the same features found in earlier editions, including:

- Reading strategies taught in context
- High-interest student readings
- Emphasis on critical thinking and active learning
- Timed readings for speed practice
- Chapter map and outline exercises that show students how to organize information in right- and left-brain formats
- Write to Learn exercises that emphasize reflective writing on reading content
- Expanded applications of the SQ3R learning strategy
- Vocabulary development pretests and posttests
- Chapter review and summary exercises

READ Supplements

A wide variety of supplements are available with this text to assist you in teaching this course and to promote student involvement and learning.

- *Instructor's Manual.* Revised for this new edition, the Instructor's Manual contains suggestions for instruction and sample exams.
- *Transparency Masters.* More than 50 transparency masters accompany and enhance material in the text, including sample chapter pages and student handouts.

Acknowledgments

Many people have helped us make READ a success through the years. Our continued appreciation goes to Clark Baxter for his sound advice and constant support during our years with West Publishing. We appreciate the work of our editorial and production team at Heinle and Heinle: Stephen Dalphin, Michell Phifer, and Jeff Freeland, who helped make READ, seventh edition, a reality. As always, we appreciate the understanding support of our families and our colleagues at our respective universities. Their assistance enables us to work together on a regular basis while maintaining full-time jobs and managing other family responsibilities. In the transition period from one publisher to another . . . to another, one constant has remained: Robin Gold of Forbes Mill Press. Robin's stability, cheerful encouragement, and ever-growing professional expertise were major factors in the successful revision of this text. Thank you, Robin!

Last, but certainly not least, we thank the following reviewers whose comments have helped shape READ through the years:

Seventh edition reviewers: Susan Blair, Jefferson State Community College; Vicki Fehr, Hardin-Simmons University; JoAnn Forrest, Prairie State College; Diane Kostelny, Okaloosa-Walton Community College; David Londow, DeAnza College; Francis Moran, Front Range Community College; and Fran Turner, Shelton State Community College.

Previous edition reviewers: Judith E. Olson, Sam Houston State University; Jacqueline Shehorn, West Hills Community College; Alyssa K. Emerson, West Hills Community College; Teri M. Gibson, Metropolitan Community College; Sheryl Thompson, California State University –Northridge; J. D. Nalepka, Jackson Community College; Marcia Gilder Orcutt, University of Hartford; Marion Van Nostrand, Northeastern University; Beverley Wickersham, Central Texas Community College; Barbara Beauchamp, County College of Morris; Katherine W. Black, South Carolina State University; Marilyn Bowers, Waiters State Community College; Vicki Butler, Chemeketa Community College; Debra A. Demers, Buffalo State College; Barbara S. Doyle, Arkansas State University; Harold Dreyer, Mankato State University; Georgia A. Fertig, Coastal Carolina Community College; Zelma L. Frank, Southern

University at New Orleans; Martha S. French, Fairmont State College; Jacqueline A. Hanselinan, Hillsborough Community College; Martha V. Hartung, Chaminade University of Honolulu; Louise S. Haugh, Pima Community College; Jennifer Hurd, Harding University; Ronald A. Huslin, Rider College; Geneva Johnson, University of Southwestern Louisiana; Sherri Kaplan, Rider College; Elise M. Komitzsky, Marian College; James L. Lambrinos, El Paso Community College; Doreen Lechner, North Iowa Area Community College; Virda K. Lester, Tuskegee University; Allan R. Maar, Lansing Community College; Joan Mauldin, San Jacinto College; Nancy McKinley, Laramie County Community College; Barbara L. Miller, Wesley College; Linda Muth, Iowa Central Community College; Shirley Napler, Waiters State Community College; Mary Palumbo, Community College of Finger Lakes; Michael W. Radis, Pennsylvania State University; Margaret Rauch, St. Cloud State University; Keflyn Reed, Bishop State Junior College; Rebecca S. Richter, Enterprise State Junior College; Martha H. Roberts, Chatanooga State Technical Community College; Diane H. Robertson, Columbia State Community College; Martha Rose, Fairmont State College; Kenneth C. Schmidt, Arkansas Technical College; Geraldine Schwartz, North Iowa Area Community College; Celeste Burns Sexauer, Mansfield University; Mary A. I. Sidoti, Kent State University; Jacqueline Simon, Rider College; Pamela Smith, Duval County Public School, Jacksonville, Florida; Milton G. Spann, Appalachian State University; Martha Summers, Louisiana Technical University; Pat Summers, Indiana Vocational Technical College; Anita Ward, Salem College; Gerri Wisdom, Arkansas State University–Beebe; Anne E. Willekens, Antelope Valley College; Paul Wolford, Waiters State Community College; Donna Wood, State Technical Institute at Memphis.

Rhonda Holt Atkinson
Debbie Guice Longman

You, the Reader: Building Your Own Future

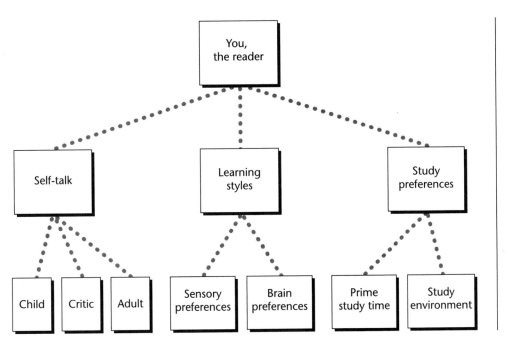

Objectives

After you finish this chapter, you will be able to do the following:

1. Identify and compare different kinds of self-talk.

2. Identify your learning styles.

3. Identify your study preferences.

Chapter Outline

I. Self-talk
   A. Child
   B. Critic
   C. Adult
II. Learning styles
   A. Sensory preferences
   B. Brain preferences
III. Study preferences
   A. Prime study time
   B. Study environment

Dress for Success

Long ago, in ancient Greece, formal education was only for the very rich or very determined. A group of rich people approached a wise old teacher. "Our sons have finished their studies. It is time for them to come home. Tomorrow, we will have a great banquet in their honor. We expect them to be dressed in their finest garments." The old teacher smiled and said, "They will be there," and he added, "appropriately dressed."

The next day, the banquet hall filled with the rich parents and their friends. They wore fine clothes and dazzling jewels. At last, the students and their teacher arrived. Cries of dismay and anger arose from the crowd. The students were dressed, not in fine clothes, but in plain robes. Each student carried a mortarboard, the mark of the common workman.

"Let me explain," said the teacher as he raised his hands for silence. "Your sons are dressed in the clothing of the mason, for their destiny is to build. Some will build cities. Some will build lives. Perhaps one of them may even build an empire. But all will be builders on the solid foundation of knowledge."

And thus, through the years, the mortarboard cap and plain gown have become a traditional part of education and graduation. They symbolize the fact that you, the reader, are a builder—of your own future and the future of the world.

What are you taking this semester? Math? History? Science? English? Foreign language? If so, college might seem like some kind of grade thirteen with many of the same subjects you had in high school. Perhaps you're taking some courses that apply to your specific major—something like computer science, agriculture, or accounting. If so, college might seem like a way to get the credentials you need for your future career. In truth, research indicates that no matter which courses you take, you'll probably forget much of what you learn. And, much of what you think will apply to your career might be outdated by the time you graduate. If that's true, what is the point? Why pursue a college education?

A college education provides you with the tools of thinking. With these tools, you can build almost anything. The content of your classes are simply raw materials with which you work. As you learn, you'll find that you can apply the tools to ideas other than those you address in class.

The first thinking tool you need is the ability to think about your own thinking. This is called **metacognition.** When you listen to what you say to yourself, you are thinking about your thinking. You use metacognition when you learn more about yourself and the ways in which you think, learn, and work. You'll acquire more tools as you work through this text, but this tool—metacognitive thinking—helps you use them more effectively.

This chapter focuses on you, the reader. By the end of this text, you will possess the tools you need to read a variety of postsecondary materials. Your future, and your ability to build the one you want, begins here and now.

Self-Talk

If you're like most people, you talk to yourself all the time. This mental conversation—your thoughts—directs and shapes your behavior. It becomes part of what you believe about yourself. It affects everything you say and do. You are, to a great extent, what you believe about yourself. You can be your greatest supporter or your worst enemy. Sometimes people simply provide information to themselves (e.g., *2 + 2 = 4, Washington, D.C. is the capitol of the United States.*). Other comments— **child comments, critic comments,** and **adult comments**— *READ Exercise 1.1* concern behavior. What kinds of comments do you make? *Exercise 1.1 helps you identify the comments you make most often.*

Child

Everyone has a side that represents a child's point of view. This aspect was the first to develop and stays with you for life. This part of you likes to have fun—and have it *now!* It enjoys life and avoids work. The child in you doesn't like to do anything boring, dull, or distasteful. It is sometimes manipulative. It doesn't think about future results. The child in you wants instant satisfaction no matter what happens later. The child's primary activity is lack of activity. It prefers to party, talk to friends, watch TV, or do anything that keeps you from getting to the business at hand.

Luckily, the child in you often responds to logic and rewards. Unlike a real child who wants only to eat cookies, the child in you knows that a diet of cookies is not good for you. Thus, it is satisfied with a cookie or two after a regular meal. When you have work to do, you tell your child how that work leads to future goals. You let your child know that rewards come after work. For instance, perhaps you have a less-than-exciting lecture to attend or homework to do. If the child in you sees these as steps toward a greater goal—a higher test score, a better course grade, graduation, a good job, and so on, then your child tends to be more likely to work. Even if you are working for future rewards, you also need to give your inner child immediate feedback and rewards. A break from study, time with friends, or your favorite snack often satisfies the child in you and motivates you to get back to work. Table 1.1 provides additional ways to motivate and discipline yourself.

Table 1.1   Motivating and Disciplining Yourself

1. **Take the Lead.** Short leading activities can provide the warm-up you need. Leading activities include reviewing class or text notes, previewing a new chapter, creating a list of terms to learn or objectives to accomplish, organizing your study site, and so on. Such activities set the stage for more intense mental effort.

2. Use a **10-Minute Workout.** You can do almost anything for 10 minutes. If you are avoiding a project, try choosing to work on a project for only that amount of time. At the end of the time, you might find that the task was not as bad as you thought and decide to continue.

3. Find a **Study Group.** If you have a study group that expects you to prepare and meet, you are more inclined to honor that commitment.

4. **Reward Yourself.** Most people get paid in some way. Devise a way to pay yourself (if not in money, then in activities you want to do) for the work you do.

5. **Get Busy.** Varying your tasks and active study prevents the child in you from getting bored and losing interest.

6. **Check It Out.** Play the concentration game with your child. Select a short time period (for example, 20 minutes) and make a check mark each time you become distracted. The goal of the game is to decrease the number of checks you make within the specified time (and thus, increase your attention span).

Critic

Critic comments form a second type of self-talk. Often, you first heard critical comments from others. These comments cause you to doubt your abilities, goals, and self. Your critic says that a task is too hard for you.

Worry is the critic's chief activity. For instance, you might find yourself worrying about a test more than studying for it. As a result, the critic reminds you that you are unprepared for the exam and destined for failure. The critic also encourages perfectionism and overcommitment. These traits seem admirable, but—because you probably can't do it all—often result in work that is of a lesser quality and burnout. This leads to lower grades and fuels your critic. A cycle begins. The more you take on, the less you do, the more the critic worries.

You control critic comments less easily than you do child comments. Because critic comments often become what you believe about yourself, the logical approach and reward system you used to control

> **Whether you think you can or think you can't—you are right.**
>
> —Henry Ford
> *Twentieth century industrialist*

the child often fail to control the critic. You can't out-talk the critic. But, you can replace critic comments with more appropriate ones. For instance, you change, *I'm not good at math* to *I've learned some new things about math that make me a different kind of thinker.* Or, you re-place *I'm going to get nervous and fail the test* with *I've studied differently and I'm confident I'll do better.* Controlling the voice of the critic takes time. The critic comments you've rehearsed for so long cannot be erased overnight. You need a minimum of several weeks of consis-tently replacing comments to create a new belief.

Adult

The adult voice in you is the sound of reason and logic. This part of you knows that some things are no fun but must be completed any-way. It recognizes that you're not perfect, but that you are a person of value. The adult looks for solutions. It learns from past mistakes and enthusiastically supports future efforts.

Problem-solving and decision-making are the adult's strengths. The adult thinks about what it takes to get a job done. It acts accordingly. The adult in you can choose to study or not, but it knows why it is mak-ing the decisions it makes. The adult has a plan and follows it. The adult allows you to recognize mistakes and make changes for the future.

Learning Styles

Everybody is different. But, in most classes, it seems like everyone is expected to learn the same things in much the same way. Everyone has the same assignments. Everyone attends the same lectures. Every-one takes the same tests. But, not everyone gets the same thing out of the course. Not everyone makes the same grade.

What you learn depends, in part, on how you learn. The way you learn is called your **learning style.** Although you can't control how you are taught, you can control how you learn. Knowing your learn-ing style helps you tailor your study to your needs. This allows you to process information in ways that are more effective and efficient.

You possess many different styles of learning. Each forms a kind of lens with which you view yourself. Sensory and brain preferences are two of the styles that affect learning most.

Sensory Preferences

Sensory preferences concern the way or ways in which you like to ac-quire information—by reading and writing, by hearing (auditory), by seeing (visual), or through touch or physical experiences (tactile/kinesthetic). *Exercise 1.2 helps you identify your sensory style and provides you with ways to use your style to maximize your learning.*

READ Exercise 1.2

If you discover that you learn best by reading and writing, you need to read all assignments, focusing on headings and subheadings. This helps you find the author's organization of information. You might find it useful to reread and summarize or rewrite words and notes and use flashcards, lists, and charts to study.

If you are an auditory learner, you prefer to learn by listening. You might think that you should tape your lectures, but that won't help you separate and organize important lecture ideas. Instead, try converting written lecture notes to audiotapes. To do so, first review and edit your notes to identify the main ideas and important details. Then read your notes aloud into a tape recorder. As you speak, leave brief amounts of time between main ideas and questions. This gives you time to think and study. Audiotapes are particularly useful if you commute. Participation in study groups and class discussions also provide ways to learn from what you hear.

If you are a visual learner, you learn best by seeing. You prefer flash charts, visual outlines or maps, and graphics. Adding meaningful symbols, colors, and graphics to notes also provide visual cues. Create mental images of what you need to learn. Try to visualize how information appears on a page. In study groups or discussions, focus on how people look when they speak.

If you learn by touch or physical movement, you learn best from direct experience. The more you do, the more you learn. Highlighting, underlining, labeling information, and writing add movement to learning. Mapping, charting, or creating other graphics also are ways to learn by doing. In addition, role-plays, models, and experiments help you learn actively. Participation in study groups or tutoring others provides additional ways to become an active learner.

You might find that you don't have a single **dominant** style. You might have a combination of styles. If so, you are a **multisensory** (involving many senses) learner. This might mean that you can learn just as easily through one sense as another. Or, it might mean that you learn best through a combination of senses.

Brain Preferences

If you watch TV, you've seen lots of car ads. If you think about it, you'll realize that there are two basic types. One type sells the kind of cars it makes sense to own. Here, advertisers point out low prices, good repair records, and safety features. These are good cars. Logically, they are the ones to buy.

Being busy does not always mean real work. The object of all work is production or accomplishment and to either of these ends there must be forethought, system, planning, intelligence, and honest purpose, as well as perspiration. Seeming to do is not doing.

—Thomas Alva Edison
Nineteenth-century American inventor

Another kind of ad gives few verbal details about the cars. Instead, you see images. Attractive people drive on the beach, in the mountains, and on scenic roads. They look like they are having fun. The cars are brightly colored and seem exciting. You learn nothing about price, gas mileage, or safety. In fact, these are more expensive cars. They probably don't get good gas mileage. Don't even ask about the cost of repairs! But, as you watch the ads, you don't care. You can *see* yourself in the pictures. That could be you driving the car. You want it to be you. It might not make sense, but this is the car you want.

Advertisers know that people think differently. **Analytical** thinkers evaluate, act, and then feel. They evaluate details logically and objectively. They prefer order and organization. Analytical thinking focuses most on words, numbers, and symbols. Thus, if you prefer to think analytically, you will be convinced by the first kind of car ad. The detail and logic of the situation sways your decision.

Global thinkers, on the other hand, don't consider what makes sense. They decide based on what "feels" right. Thus, they feel, act, then think. Their thinking is subjective. They focus on visual images, nonverbal communication, sensory experiences, and intuitive feelings. The second kind of ad appeals to global thinkers because they can "see" themselves in the car even if owning it isn't the logical choice.

READ Exercise 1.3   In learning, you think both globally and analytically. But, you might prefer one way of thinking over the other. *Exercise 1.3 helps you identify your brain preferences.* The greater your score on your preferred side, the greater its role in your learning. If your scores are about the same, you can probably learn just as well with either analytical or global strategies. However, you will maximize your learning by using strategies that use both global and analytical thinking.

Table 1.2 shows aspects of thinking and learning applications for analytical and global thinking. Each chapter in this text opens with both an outline (analytical) and chapter map (global). As you progress through the chapters, these become exercises. In these, details will be left out so that you can develop outlining and mapping skills. The more you know about how your brain learns, the more you can customize your study techniques.

Write to Learn

Respond to the following on a separate sheet of paper or in your notebook: Consider the format of a traditional college course in which the professor delivers information through lectures. Do you think global or analytical learners perform better in this format? Why?

Table 1.2   Brain Preferences and Learning Applications

Analytical Thinking	Application to Learning
Orderly step-by-step sequencing	Ability to order and learn detailed information
Symbolism	Ability to use formulas, acronyms, and acrostics; preference for algebraic and abstract math computation
Logic and realism	Preference for factual information and practical applications
Verbal or written information	Preference for notes, outlines, lectures, textbooks, or auditory review
Emphasis on time, planning, and control	Ability to structure time, ideas, or resources
Focused thinking	Ability to concentrate on one task or idea
Objectivity	Preference for multiple-choice or true-or-false matching formats

Global Thinking	Application to Learning
Holistic thinking	Preference for overviews of information; mapping
Concrete information	Preference for geometry and math facts rather than for algebra and abstract math
Intuition and creativity	Preferences for fictional and interpretive writing; interpreting literature and figurative language; drawing conclusions; use of metaphors and analogies; humor
Kinesthetic learning	Preference for experimentation, hands-on learning, role playing
Visual and spatial learning	Preference for geometry and other visual subjects over algebra and abstract concepts, mapping, charting
Divergent thinking	Ability to multitask and focus on multiple projects or views; unstructured use of time, ideas, or resources
Subjectivity	Preference for essay or short-answer exams; ability to empathize easily with others

Study Preferences

Your study preferences concern the time and place in which you study most effectively and efficiently. You find your study preferences by observing three factors. These are when and where you get the most accomplished, when and where your studying results in higher grades, and when and where you feel most able to concentrate.

Prime Study Time

Prime study time is the time of the day when you are at your best. This time varies from person to person. You might be at your best early in the morning. Or you might be able to recall more if you study in the afternoon or at night.

Your best time of the day should be spent either in your hardest classes or on your most important assignments. Working on the hardest or most urgent task first means you work on that problem when you are fresh.

Threats to prime study time include any physical or mental distractions. For example, sometimes when you study you may find yourself thinking of other tasks you need to do. If so, keep a pad and pencil nearby just for this purpose and make a "worry list" of your concerns. By doing so, you literally put your problems aside until later. Being too hungry or too full also affects concentration. If this occurs, try changing your study or eating schedule.

Some threats to prime study time are harder to control. It can be difficult to rid yourself of friends who are concerned about your social life. Invitations to go out with the gang often come at prime study times. The solution, although simple, is a hard one to enact: saying no in a clear, but tactful way. Sometimes it's easier to just be unavailable. Unplugging your phone or closing the door to your room prevents interruptions. Another way to solve this problem is to put up a "Do Not Disturb" sign. You can get one from a motel (usually free of charge), purchase one at a card store, or make your own. Remember, even though you will probably never rid yourself of all distractions during prime study time, you can minimize them.

At times, study during prime study time can be impossible to achieve. Family responsibilities, work commitments, or your class schedule might override your prime study time. Such situations can be handled in a variety of ways. Compromises might be your first option. Perhaps you can rearrange a work schedule. You might ask another family member or friend to help you. Second, you might be able to devote concentrated study during prime times on weekends. Finally, you might have to simply adjust to the reality of the situation. If this is the case, pay particular attention to setting the stage for study. A few minutes spent in mentally preparing yourself for learning (for example, reviewing your learning goals or organizing your work area) can help make any time prime study time.

Study Environment

Where you study—your study environment—is just as important as when you study. Do you like to study at a desk or seated on the floor? Do you learn more when you study with others or when you study alone? Lighting levels, structure, sound, and temperature either contribute to your concentration or distract you from what you need to do. *Exercise 1.4 helps you identify your optimum study environment.* **External distractions** are things outside of you that affect concentration.

READ Exercise 1.4

> **Write to Learn**
>
> Respond to the following on a separate sheet of paper or in your note-book: Describe the time and place you usually study. Does the environment you described reflect your best study time and location? Describe the steps you can take to accommodate your best time of day and improve your study site.

Although they are physically outside of you, they remain within your control. You decide whether to put yourself into a distracting situation or to set yourself up for reading success. For example, you can choose to study in another location. Or, if you must study in a specific place, you can change the surroundings to make them less distracting. For instance, if the place you study is too noisy, try using ear plugs or a head-phone. If the place you study is too bright, wear tinted glasses.

Chapter Summary

This chapter discusses how you, the reader, can use thinking tools to build your future. Metacognition—your ability to think about your thinking—is the first tool you need. With this, you can think about and control your mental dialogue. You can think about the ways you learn: sensory and brain preferences. You can determine when and where you study best.

Chapter Review

Answer the following questions briefly but completely on a separate sheet of paper or in your notebook:

1. What is metacognition? How does it help you become a better learner?
2. What is self-talk? Identify the three kinds of comments involved in self-talk. Give an example of each.
3. Describe how sensory preferences affect the quantity and quality of what you learn.
4. Compare global and analytical thinking.
5. What factors contribute to an effective study site? How can you control the factors to maximize learning?

> **Terms**
>
> Terms appear in the order in which they occur in the chapter.
>
> **metacognition**
> **child comments**
> **critic comments**
> **adult comments**
> **learning style**
> **dominant**
> **multisensory**
> **analytical**
> **global**
> **prime study time**
> **external distractions**

Exercises

Exercise 1.1   Circle the answer that sounds most like you.

1. One of your instructors nominates you for membership in a campus club. The club involves your career interests. None of your friends are members. In fact, you don't know anyone in the club. You decide

   a. not to join. After all, if none of your friends are in it, it must not be any fun.

   b. not to join. You are worried that no one will talk to you and you won't fit in.

   c. to join. You do want to be in the club. Athough you know you won't know anyone at first, you decide that your common interests will help you make friends.

2. You have a big test tomorrow in your hardest course. You've planned to spend the evening reviewing at the library with a study group. A friend asks you to go out partying for the evening. There's no way to contact the study group to let them know you won't be there. You decide to

   a. party. You decide the study group will never miss you. You'll probably have enough time to study when you get home. Or, you'll get up early and study.

   b. party. Although you go, you feel guilty about letting the study group down. You don't have very much fun because you keep thinking that you should be studying for the test.

   c. study. But, you plan to meet your friend later that evening at the party.

3. Your English composition instructor returns a paper. Your instructor gave you a C– and wrote numerous comments on your paper. You think,

   a. "Who cares? In my major, writing is unimportant."

   b. "I've never been able to write. My instructor must think I'm stupid. I'll never learn how to do this."

   c. "I should read these comments carefully and make an appointment to get some help in writing."

4. You took the first quiz in history and you currently have an A. Your professor assigns a research paper. You

   a. decide not to write the research paper. Who wants to spend all that time in the library anyway?

   b. go to the library and start working; however, none of the topics you consider are quite "good enough" for you so you spend endless hours in the library without really accomplishing much.

   c. go to the library, choose a topic, and start to work.

5. You didn't hear your alarm clock and overslept. You

   a. roll over and go back to sleep. You might as well. You've already missed the first class—which is OK, because you think it's really boring.

   b. think, "I can't believe I did that! I'm always messing up. What is the matter with me? Now I've missed my first class and I'll probably fail the course as the result of it."

   c. think, "I missed the first class of the day, but I'll call some people in my class and get the notes from them. If needed, I'll make an appointment to see the instructor to discuss the work I missed."

6. You go shopping and find a great (shirt, CD, whatever) that is exactly what you wanted; however, it costs twice as much as you planned to spend. You decide to charge it, thinking,

   a. "That's OK. I won't get the bill for a while."

   b. "I shouldn't be doing this. If I do, I might need some money later and I might be over the limit. What if I get my purchase home and decide I don't like it? I always make the wrong choice.

   c. "I'm buying this because it is exactly what I want. Even though it costs more, I can cut expenses somewhere else or work a few extra hours to compensate for the extra cost. I usually like what I buy, so this is a good choice."

7. You go the student center to get something for lunch. You

   a. order French fries and coffee. They're your favorite foods.

   b. have a soft drink and a candy bar. After eating them, you think, "I don't know why I did that. I should have gotten soup because it's a much more healthy choice. That was really stupid."

   c. get the plate lunch special of the day (entrée and two vegetables) because you won't have time to eat again until later in the evening.

8. It's noon. You're sitting in your most difficult class listening to a lecture. You are probably thinking,

   a. "I'm starving. This boring class is never going to end. I am so tired of sitting here. I wonder what I'll get for lunch."

   b. "I am so worried. Everyone else looks like they understand what's going on, but I just don't get this stuff. I know I'm going to fail this class and flunk out just like everyone thought I would. Maybe I shouldn't be in college after all."

   c. "This is really hard, but I've learned difficult things before. Other people have learned this, and I can too. Everyone else looks like they know what's going on, but they're probably just as confused as I am. It makes me nervous to talk in class but I think I'll ask a question."

9. You have joined a campus organization. You have been asked to serve as the treasurer next year. You were planning to take a full load—18 hours of credit next term. You also work 30 hours each week. You think,

    a. "I'm going to refuse. I don't want to be treasurer. It would be so boring to keep up with everyone's money. What fun would that be?"

    b. "I'm going to accept. I really should be the treasurer. The group needs someone to do that job. I ought to be able to handle a job, school, and more responsibility. Still, I really feel overwhelmed."

    c. "I'm going to refuse. This job involves a lot of responsibility and I've already made commitments for next year. I'll tell them that I could serve in another, less demanding, role."

10. Your instructor has assigned a major project in a course that you have enjoyed up to this point. You have never tackled anything like this before and you're not sure what to do. You

    a. decide to drop the course. You think, "The project is going to take too long. Besides I'm never going to need to know this in the future."

    b. spend so many hours trying to get the project going that you don't have time to complete it. You think, "What is the matter with me? I'm in college. I ought to be able to do something like this. I should have worked harder and longer. If the professor knew I didn't know how to do this, he'd fail me for sure."

    c. make an appointment to see the professor and talk to other students about their projects.

Scoring:

Total *A* responses_____

Total *B* responses_____

Total *C* responses_____

Results:

The more *A* responses you have, the more you are likely to listen to your "child" comments. Create a reward system for yourself to balance your child's wants with your goals and objectives.

The more *B* responses you have, the more you are likely to listen to your "critic" comments. Determine what comments you want to make and make plans to change what you're telling yourself.

The more *C* responses you have, the more you are likely to listen to your "adult" comments. Congratulations! You balance work and play rationally. You make the best choices you can at the time and you are satisfied with the results.

Exercise 1.2   Complete the following assessment of sensory style.

1. If you could choose any way to learn, you would choose

_____ a.   reading information for yourself.

_____ b.   listening to a lecture.

_____ c.   participating in an experiment or lab activity.

_____ d.   watching a film or looking at diagrams.

2. When giving directions for how to get someplace, do you

_____ a.   write the directions in sentence form?

_____ b.   describe the directions aloud?

_____ c.   show someone the way by taking them or having them follow you?

_____ d.   draw a map?

3. Are you more likely to recall

_____ a.   what was written in words?

_____ b.   what was said in conversations or lectures?

_____ c.   what you did?

_____ d.   what you saw?

4. Do you prefer an instructor who

_____ a.   assigns readings and other text materials?

_____ b.   facilitates class discussion?

_____ c.   lets you discover ideas through experience?

_____ d.   uses flow charts, diagrams, charts, slides?

5. You are planning to buy a car. What would most influence your choice?

_____ a.   reading promotional materials about cars

_____ b.   talking to friends about their cars

_____ c.   test-driving different cars

_____ d.   advertisements about different cars

6. Are you more likely to recall

_____ a.   the way a person's name is spelled?

_____ b.   the sound of a person's name?

_____ c.   your interactions with a person?

_____ d.   the person's face?

7. Which would you prefer to do?

_____ a. write a story

_____ b. listen to music

_____ c. make something

_____ d. watch a movie

8. Which sentences are most like something you would say or prefer?

_____ a. The handwriting is on the wall. You just have to read between the lines.

_____ b. I hear what you're saying. Listen to me.

_____ c. That feels right. Can you get a handle on this?

_____ d. I see what you mean. Look at it this way.

9. When you recall your dreams, which details are most memorable?

_____ a. specific words describing the dream

_____ b. sounds you heard in the dream

_____ c. actions you did in the dream

_____ d. images within the dream

Scoring:

Total *A* responses _____

Total *B* responses _____

Total *C* responses _____

Total *D* responses _____

Results:

   The more *A* answers you chose, the more likely you learn best through reading or writing.

   The more *B* answers you chose, the more likely you learn best from auditory information.

   The more *C* answers you chose, the more likely you learn by direct experience.

   The more *D* answers you chose, the more likely you learn visually.

Exercise 1.3 Respond to the following questions.

1. How do you prefer making decisions?
   a. intuitively
   b. logically

2. Which do you remember more easily?
   a. names
   b. faces

3. Do you prefer
   a. planning your activities in advance?
   b. doing things spontaneously?

4. In social situations, do you prefer being the
   a. listener?
   b. speaker?

5. When listening to a speaker, do you pay more attention to
   a. what the speaker is saying?
   b. the speaker's body language?

6. Do you consider yourself to be a goal-oriented person?
   a. yes
   b. no

7. Is your main study area
   a. messy?
   b. neat and well organized?

8. Are you usually aware of what time it is and how much time has passed?
   a. yes
   b. no

9. When you write papers, do you
   a. let ideas flow freely?
   b. plan the sequence of ideas in advance?

10. After you have heard music, are you more likely to remember the
    a. words?
    b. tunes?

11. Do you frequently move your furniture around in your home or home?

    a. yes

    b. no

12. Are you a good memorizer?

    a. yes

    b. no

13. When you doodle, do you create

    a. shapes?

    b. words?

14. Clasp your hands together. Which thumb is on top?

    a. left

    b. right

15. Which math subject do you prefer?

    a. algebra

    b. geometry

16. In planning your day, do you

    a. make a list of what you need to accomplish?

    b. just let things happen?

17. Are you good at expressing your feelings?

    a. yes

    b. no

18. How do you organize papers?

    a. filed by subject

    b. stacked in piles

19. Which is true of you?

    a. I throw out things that I don't need.

    b. I save things in case I need them later.

Transfer your responses to the following answer key. Total the number of items you circled in each column. Then add your totals for each column.

Answer Key for Exercise 1.3

Question	Analytical	Global	Question	Analytical	Global
1	B	A	11	B	A
2	A	B	12	B	A
3	B	A	13	A	B
4	B	A	14	B	A
5	A	B	15	A	B
6	A	B	16	A	B
7	B	A	17	A	B
8	A	B	18	B	A
9	B	A	19	B	A
10	A	B	**Total**	____	____
Total	____	____			

Total Analytical ____

Total Global ____

Exercise 1.4   Check ONE statement in each set.

Light

_____ **1.** Low light makes me sleepy, so I often turn on extra lamps for reading. When possible, I prefer to sit by windows or directly under an overhead light when I study. I prefer well-lighted study environments.

_____ **2.** People sometimes tell me I'm reading in the dark. I find I often shade my eyes when reading or writing. I prefer dimly lit study environments.

Structure

_____ **1.** I don't like to sit still for long periods. I have to get up and move around often.

_____ **2.** I would rather study seated on the floor of my room with books and papers around me.

_____ **3.** I would rather work on a computer than read from a text or write on paper.

_____ **4.** I like to sit at a desk with my materials organized in front of me.

_____ **5.** Although I don't like to study with other people, I like to be in a place like the library with people around me.

Interpersonal

_____ **1.** I prefer to study alone.

_____ **2.** I like to study with another person or in a small group.

Temperature

_____ **1.**   I prefer to study in a room that is cool.

_____ **2.**   I prefer to study in a room that is warm.

Sound

_____ **1.**   I like things to be perfectly quiet when I study.

_____ **2.**   I need background noises—conversation, soft music, TV—when I study.

Analysis

Each item you checked contributes to the kind of study environment you prefer. Use the items you selected as your personal checklist for evaluating your current study location.

Web Exercise

A variety of information related to you, the reader, is available on the World Wide Web. For this exercise, search using the phrase *learning style tests.* Complete one of the tests you find and answer the following questions on a separate sheet of paper.

1.   What is the name and URL of the site?

2.   What test did you take?

3.   Why did you choose that test?

4.   Describe how the test compared with the tests in this chapter.

5.   Summarize your results.

6.   What do your results tell you about yourself?

7.   How can you apply the results to maximize your learning?

READ: Keys

Vocabulary and Comprehension

Do you own keys? Have you ever lost them? Keys unlock doors. They provide access. The same is true of reading. The keys of reading are vocabulary and comprehension. These keys unlock meaning and provide access to understanding.

Vocabulary concerns words. That's no big surprise. What might amaze you, however, is the vast number of words in the world. Equally astonishing is the large amount of relationships these words convey. When you use a word, you communicate with others. To use words effectively, you must first become aware of what words mean to you. Rating your understanding of words gives you a way to gauge and monitor your vocabulary development. Based on a theory by Edgar Dale (1958), word knowledge exists in progressive stages. Word knowledge ranges from no knowledge of a word to the ability to use it, to let it live. The stages help you decide what you know about a word. They also tell you what more you need to learn about it.

And, when you know many words and the relationships they convey, you truly understand what you read. Doing so helps you use the second key to reading, comprehension. In fact, without comprehension, real reading does not take place. If you've ever "read" a chapter in a textbook, only to realize you've been "reading" the words while your mind was elsewhere, you know that comprehension, or making connections among words, is necessary for meaningful reading.

Continuum of Vocabulary Development

3   You know you've seen or heard a word and can use it in speaking or writing.

2   You know you've seen or heard a word and can make general associations about its meaning.

1   You know you've seen or heard a word before, but you are unsure about its meaning or associations with it.

0   You see or hear a word you've never seen or heard before, and you know it's a new word.

Relationships Among Words

Many connections exist between and among words. You might think of these connections as being like those in a telephone network. Calls may be made to any person, family, business, or organization. A single phone call could connect you to a single person or to thousands of people who work for a business. You might even get the wrong number. Countless relationships exist between the caller and the person being called. You don't see the connections that link you to others, but they exist.

A similar network exists among information. Your link with a word can give you a single meaning. This link could also connect you with many related meanings. Some relationships might be similar. Others might be opposite in meaning. Still others might be like a wrong number—similar-sounding words but different meanings. As in a phone network, you don't see the connections, but they exist. Just as local phone networks connect with larger networks to form global connections, the connections you possess provide you with more comprehensive understanding.

Your connections, then, constitute all you know about a word and its links. Three common connections exist among words. Words that mean the same but look different are called **synonyms.** Synonyms (for example, *pretty* and *cute*) improve your writing and speech by adding variety and flavor. They relieve monotony and make it easier for you to express yourself. **Antonyms** are words that have opposite meanings (for example, *pretty* and *ugly*). Antonyms are the opposite of synonyms. **Homonyms** are words that sound alike but have different meanings (for example, *there* and *their*). Because homonyms are words that sound alike, you must consider their definitions or contexts in choosing the correct one to use. Because these three terms are often confused, here is an easy way to keep them straight:

Heard alike	**S**ame meaning	**A**n opposite
O	Y	N
M	N	T
O	O	O
N	N	N
Y	Y	Y
M	M	M

As shown in the following table, many other kinds of word relationships are possible. Some come from general information and your knowledge of various subjects. Others focus on your understanding of word structure, grammar, and function. Relationships can also reflect order, such as cause and effect or sequence. Additional word associations are based on specific features. These include whole and parts, composition, degree, classification, and characterization.

When looking at relationships, the order of the words matters. Changing the order changes the relationship. In word relationships, a colon (:) means "is to." For example, instead of writing "good is to bad," you can write "good : bad." Like all abbreviations, this one saves space and time. Thinking of relationships among words in this way also helps you prepare yourself for the study of analogies, a high-level thought process.

Word Relationships and Examples

Relationship	Definition	Examples
Synonym	Same or similar in meaning	ancestors : forefathers domain : home monarchy : kingdom
Antonym	Opposite in meaning	reality : fantasy positive : negative active : passive
Homonyms	Alike in sound	stationary : stationery serf : surf tract : tracked
Words and word structure	Words relate according to structure, grammar, or function	I : we fight : fought quick : quickly
Part to whole	Piece or portion relates to the total object or concept	jury : trial id : personality planet : solar system
Whole to part	Total relates to one of its components	atom : proton cell : chromosome solar system : planets
Degree (age, time, rank, or size)	Concept relates to a younger/older, larger/smaller, earlier/later, or lesser/greater concept	Stone Age : Atomic Age president : vice-president hill : mountain
Person to event, location, or item	Relates a person and his or her corresponding place, time, or deed	Marie Curie : radium Betsy Ross : American flag Charles Darwin : evolution

Using Analogies to Understand Complex Relationships

The philosophers of ancient Greece debated the structure of language. Some thought language developed randomly with no rhyme or reason. This philosophy was called *anomalia,* meaning disorder. If you dislike English class, you may still think this. Others thought language represented regularity of relationships. They termed this philosophy *analogia,* meaning order. This division of thought grew wider after the fall of Alexander the Great's empire in 4 B.C. The Alexandrians in Egypt favored a regular approach. Their enemy, Pergamon in Asia Minor, favored the more random philosophy. When the Alexandrians defeated Pergamon, the result was early Greek grammar, which stressed regularity (McArthur, 1992).

We continue to use analogies today. They define relationships within an unfamiliar or complex concept by comparing them with more familiar or easily understood ideas. According to *The Oxford Companion to the English Language* (McArthur, 1992), an **analogy** helps describe or explain the nature of things in terms we understand. For example, time is often compared to a river. Time flows from past to present to future. A river flows from its beginnings (past) to a designated point (present) and out to sea (future). Once you understand the points of comparison, you understand concepts like "the flow of time" or "the currents of history." Analogies depend on the concept of *as if*. For example, when a storm is described as "assaulting a town," it is *as if* it had a human form. As a result, analogies often take the form of metaphors and similes with inferred points of comparison (see Chapter 6).

An analogy, then, is an implied (unstated) comparison between two pairs of objects. You can learn new words by analyzing the relationships in an analogy. To do so, you decide what type of relationship exists between each pair of words (for example, synonyms, antonyms, homonyms, part to whole, time, place, age, and so on). Indeed, the relationship can be any type of association.

Intelligence tests often contain questions written in analogy form. Thus, analogies seem like complex and difficult concepts. But you probably use them every day. Suppose you are trying to decide where to eat lunch. You say, "I could go to Burgerland for hamburgers, or I could go to Pizza City for pizza." You would be stating the relationship between places and the kind of food served. When transformed into analogy form, this statement would be written "Burgerland is to hamburgers as Pizza City is to pizza." You also use analogies when you decide what to wear. "If it's cold outside, I'll wear a coat. If it's hot, I'll wear shorts." The analogy form would be "cold is to coat as hot is to shorts." Because analogies require you to identify similar relationships between dissimilar objects, understanding analogies is one of the highest levels of thinking.

Analogies also can be written more concisely by using a standard format. Consider again the example of clothing and weather. That analogy could be written as follows: Cold : coat :: hot : shorts. The colon (:) between "cold" and "coat" means "is to." The pair of colons (::) means "as." Most analogies ask you to infer points of comparison.

Finally, the best way to develop vocabulary and comprehension skills is to read, read, read. For this reason, this text contains chapters that focus on individual reading strategies and many excerpts, articles, chapters, stories, and so forth for practice. In addition, each chapter also contains a special section on using the keys to reading success—vocabulary and comprehension—by examining words and their relationships.

READ: Keys Activity Pretest

Rate each of the following words according to your knowledge of them.

Word	Stage 0 *I don't know this word.*	Stage 1 *I've seen this word but I know nothing of its meaning.*	Stage 2 *I've seen this word and can make associations with it.*	Stage 3 *I know this word.*
1. installment				
2. limit				
3. minimum				
4. assessing				
5. federation				
6. advances				
7. fine				
8. adjust				
9. caps				
10. incurring				

READ: Keys Activity 1.1

Read the following textbook excerpt and keep track of your reading time.

Credit Management

Not surprisingly, credit is the area of personal finance that gets the most people into trouble, including many college students. Credit allows a person to receive money, goods, or services by agreeing to repay the lender in the form of a loan for a specified period of time with a specified rate of interest. Credit is available from many sources today, but rates vary, so it pays to shop around. For instance, there are several thousand issuers of Visa and Master-Card credit cards. Some suggestions for picking the right credit card are listed in the "Advice and Tips" section on the next page.

There are two broad types of consumer credit: revolving (or open-end) credit and *installment* credit. Revolving credit is a type of credit arrangement that enables consumers to make a number of different purchases up to a credit *limit,* specified by the lender. The consumer has the option of repaying some or all of the outstanding balance each month. If the consumer carries a balance from month to month, finance charges (interest) are levied. An example of revolving credit is a credit card, such as Visa or MasterCard. An installment loan is a credit arrangement in which the borrower takes out a loan for a specified amount, agreeing to repay the loan in regular installments over a specified period of time. The installments include the finance charge. Student loans, auto loans, and home mortgage loans are examples of installment loans.

There are good reasons for borrowing money, including purchasing large, important goods and services (cars, homes, or a college education); dealing with financial emergencies; taking advantage of opportunities; needing convenience; and establishing or improving your credit rating. All of these reasons are appropriate uses of credit *if* you can repay the loans in a timely manner.

However, a wrong reason for borrowing money is using credit to live beyond your means. For instance, you want to go to Cancun for vacation but really cannot afford to, so you charge the trip. Using credit to live beyond your means often leads to credit problems. Watch for these warning signs:

- meet basic living expenses.
- make impulse purchases.
- advance on one credit card to pay another; your unpaid balance increases month after month.

Consumers who think of credit purchases as a series of small, monthly payments are fooling themselves. The average credit balance carried by college students today is around $2,700. The annual interest rate on credit cards carried by college students averages about 18 percent. How long would it take someone with the average balance to become debt-free, assuming he or she made only the *minimum* payment (typically $25 or 2.5 percent of the outstanding balance, which ever is greater) each month? The answer is 13 years and 5 months, during which time the student would end up paying over $3,000 in interest. The scary details are shown in Table 1. What's more, the preceding example assumes that the person does not charge anything else while paying off the balance.

The simple quiz in Figure 1 is one way of ***assessing*** whether you may have a credit problem. If you feel as though you have a problem with credit, or may be developing one, you should seek help as soon as possible. Your college or university may offer credit counseling services. If not, contact a local not-for-profit credit counseling service or the National ***Federation*** for Credit Counseling (800-388-2227).

According to the experts, one of the keys to the wise use of credit is education. Learning about the pros and cons of borrowing money, as well as learning about responsible spending, can help people avoid future problems with credit.

Advice and Tips: Choosing the Right Credit Card

There are thousands of places where you can get a credit card. When it comes to selecting a credit card, there are four factors to consider:

- **Annual fee.** Not all credit cards charge an annual fee. If you shop around, you can probably find a no-fee credit card.
- **Annual percentage rate.** The annual percentage rate (APR) is the interest rate charged on cash ***advances*** and unpaid balances. If you faithfully pay off your balance each month and avoid taking cash advances, the APR is really not a consideration in choosing a card. If you carry a balance, find the card offering the lowest fixed APR. The average APR on Visas and MasterCards issued to college students is around 18 percent, but some cards offer much lower APRs. You can compare APRs at www.bankrate.com. Also, read the ***fine*** print. Some card issuers will ***adjust*** rates up and down depending on your spending and payment pattern.
- **Credit limit.** The credit limit essentially ***caps*** your spending. Choose a credit limit wisely. Of course, you can always request a *lower* credit limit.
- **Grace period.** The grace period is the amount of time you have to pay for new purchases without ***incurring*** any finance charges. Grace periods average between 25 and 90 days, but some credit cards have no grace period, meaning you pay interest from the date you make the purchase to the date you pay your balance. Furthermore, many cards give you no grace period on new purchases if you carry a balance. Some credit card issuers have reduced the length of the grade period in recent years. Make sure to read any notices you receive from the issuer carefully.

Adapted from D. Hearth, L. E. Boone, and D. L. Kurtz (2002). *A Guide to Your Personal Finances to Accompany Contemporary Business,* 10th ed., pp. 13–14 including Advice and Tips Box, Table 1 and Figure 5. Fort Worth, TX: Harcourt.

897 words / _____ minutes = _____ words per minute.

Calculate your reading time by dividing the number of words in the article by the amount of time it took to read it. Then mark your reading time on the chart located on page 338.

Table 1 How Long It Takes to Pay a Credit Card Balance

Amount owed: $2,700
Annual percentage rate (APR): 18%
Interest owed: .015 x beginning balance
Payment: 2.5% of outstanding balance or $25 (whichever is greater)
Principal repaid: Payment minus interest
Ending balance: Beginning balance minus principal repaid

Payment Number	Beginning Balance	Interest Owed	Payment	Principal Repaid	Ending Balance	Cumulative Interest	Cumulative Principal
1	$2,700	$41	$68	$27	$2,673	$41	$27
2	$2,673	$40	$67	$27	$2,646	$81	$54
3	$2,646	$40	$66	$26	$2,620	$120	$80
4	$2,620	$39	$65	$26	$2,594	$160	$106
5	$2,594	$39	$65	$26	$2,568	$198	$132
6	$2,568	$39	$64	$26	$2,542	$237	$158
7	$2,542	$38	$64	$25	$2,517	$275	$183
8	$2,517	$38	$63	$25	$2,491	$313	$209
9	$2,491	$37	$62	$25	$2,466	$350	$234
10	$2,466	$37	$62	$25	$2,442	$387	$258
11	$2,442	$37	$61	$24	$2,417	$424	$283
12	$2,417	$36	$60	$24	$2,393	$460	$307
60	$1,492	$22	$37	$15	$1,477	$1,834	$1,223
120	$76	$11	$25	$14	$753	$2,832	$1,947
161	$9	$0	$9	$9	$0	$3,089	$2,700

Figure 1 Do You Have a Credit Problem?

T/F 1. You spend money in the expectation that your income will rise.
T/F 2. You take cash advances on one credit card to pay off another.
T/F 3. You spend more than 20 percent of your income on credit card bills.
T/F 4. You fail to keep adequate records of your purchases.
T/F 5. You regularly pay for groceries with a credit card because you don't have enough money in your checking account.
T/F 6. You have applied for more than five new cards in the past year.
T/F 7. You often hide your credit card purchases from your family.
T/F 8. Having several credit cards makes you feel richer.
T/F 9. You pay off your monthly credit card bills but let other bills slide.

T/F 10. You almost always make only the minimum payment on credit cards.

T/F 11. You like to collect cash from friends in restaurants and then charge the entire tab on your credit card.

T/F 12. You have trouble imagining your life without credit.

Scoring (number of "true" responses):

Less than five: Green light—you are probably okay.

5 to 8: Yellow light—pay off your bills and examine your spending habits.

More than 8: Red light—you have or are developing a credit problem.

READ: Keys Activity 1.2

On a separate sheet of paper or in your notebook, answer the following questions about the excerpt you just read:

1. _____ and _____ are the two basic types of consumer credit.

   a. revolving, installment

   b. open-end, revolving

   c. credit cards, open-end

   d. consumer, lender

2. Which of the following is an example of an installment loan?

   a. revolving credit

   b. MasterCard

   c. home mortgage

   d. open-end credit

3. Which of the following is NOT a good reason for using credit?

   a. financial emergency

   b. improvement of credit rating

   c. to meet basic living expenses

   d. taking advantage of opportunities

4. According to this text, the average credit balance carried by college students today is _____.

   a. $3,000

b. about $2,700

c. less than $1800

d. unknown

5. The minimum payment for most credit cards is typically _____.

   a. 18% of the total

   b. 2.5% of the balance or $25, whichever is less

   c. $25 or 2.5% of the balance, whichever is more

6. The annual interest rate on credit cards used by most college students averages _____.

   a. 2.5%

   b. 25%

   c. 18%

   d. 13%

7. Which of the following would NOT be true if you had a credit card balance of $2,700 and made only minimum monthly payments?

   a. The total amount you would pay would be almost $6000.

   b. You would not be eligible to get any additional credit cards.

   c. It would take you almost 14 years to pay off the $2,700.

   d. The interest you paid would be more than the original balance.

8. According to experts, one factor in using credit wisely is _____.

   a. having only one credit card at a time.

   b. only paying cash for what you buy.

   c. using revolving, but not open-ended, credit.

   d. education.

9. Which of the following is true of credit cards?

   a. There is no such thing as a no-fee credit card.

   b. APR should be a prime consideration in choosing a credit card.

   c. The grace period caps your spending each month.

   d. Some credit cards have no grace period for new purchases.

10. If you want to compare APRs, you should_____.

    a. read the fine print on your credit cards.

    b. go to www.bankrate.com

    c. call the National Federation for Credit Counseling

    d. ask your friends about the cards they use

READ: Keys Activity 1.3

Examine each of the numbered phrases or sentences and complete the following on a separate sheet of paper or in your notebook.

(a) Write the boldfaced, italicized word. Identify one or two words that you can put in the place of the boldfaced, italicized word without changing the meaning of the phrase or sentence and write this synonym or synonymous phrase (words that have the same meaning) beside the word. (b) Identify the part of speech of this word as used in the sentence. (c) Look up the boldfaced, italicized word in a dictionary and write the dictionary definition. How does this compare with the definition from context? (d) List the parts of speech this word can sometimes be. (e) Write a complete sentence with each word.

1. There are two broad types of consumer credit: revolving (or open-end) credit and ***installment*** credit.

2. Revolving credit is a type of credit arrangement that enables consumers to make a number of different purchases up to a credit ***limit,*** specified by the lender.

3. How long would it take someone with the average balance to become debt-free, assuming he or she made only the ***minimum*** payment . . .

4. The simple quiz in Figure 1 is one way of ***assessing*** whether you may have a credit problem.

5. If not, contact a local not-for-profit credit counseling service or the National ***Federation*** for Credit Counseling . . .

6. The annual percentage rate (APR) is the interest rate charged on cash ***advances*** and unpaid balances.

7. You can compare APRs at www.bankrate.com. Also, read the ***fine*** print.

8. Some card issuers will ***adjust*** rates up and down depending on your spending and payment pattern.

9. The credit limit essentially *caps* your spending.

10. The grace period is the amount of time you have to pay for new purchases without *incurring* any finance charges.

READ: Keys Activity 1.4

In Part A, use the following list of words to fill in the blanks. In Part B, use the information from Part A to complete the analogies.

Part A

blocks	large	individual	maximum
alliance	maintain	boundary	infinity
continues	payment	disbursing	repaid
acquiring	withholding	tiny	least
levying	change	losing	expansion

Synonym	Word	Antonym
_____	1. installment	_____
_____	2. limit	_____
_____	3. minimum	_____
_____	4. assessing	_____
_____	5. federation	_____
_____	6. advances	_____
_____	7. fine	_____
_____	8. adjust	_____
_____	9. caps	_____
_____	10. incurring	_____

Part B

1. installment : _____ :: fine : large

2. _____ : caps :: levying : assessing

3. maximum : minimum :: _____ : limit

4. federation : alliance :: adjust : _____

5. minimum : _____ :: caps : continues

6. assessing : _____ :: federation : individual

7. installment : loan :: _____ : least

8. fine : _____ :: maintain : adjust

9. large : _____ :: maximum : least

10. disbursing : _____ :: blocks : caps

READ: Keys Activity Posttest

Rate each of the following words according to your knowledge of them.

Word	Stage 0 *I don't know this word.*	Stage 1 *I've seen this word but I know nothing of its meaning.*	Stage 2 *I've seen this word and can make associations with it.*	Stage 3 *I know this word.*
1. installment				
2. limit				
3. minimum				
4. assessing				
5. federation				
6. advances				
7. fine				
8. adjust				
9. caps				
10. incurring				

Previewing

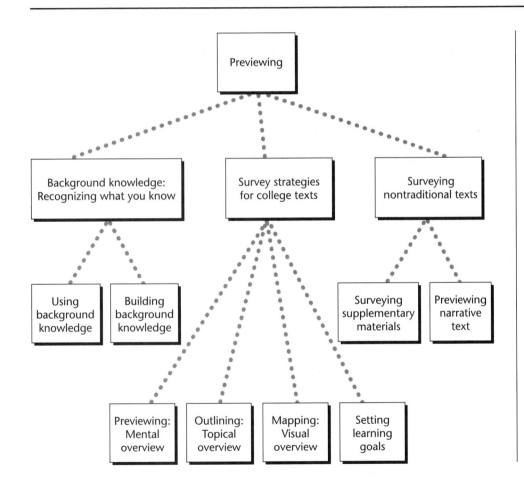

Chapter Outline

I. Background knowledge: Recognizing what you know
   A. Using background knowledge
   B. Building background knowledge
II. Survey strategies for college texts
   A. Previewing: Mental overview
   B. Outlining: Topical overview
   C. Mapping: Visual overview
   D. Setting learning goals
III. Surveying nontraditional texts
   A. Surveying supplementary materials
   B. Previewing narrative text

Consider almost any syllabus for a college course. It probably includes reading assignments . . . lots of reading assignments. Why? According to Noel, Levitz, Saluri, and Associates (1987), you complete 45 to 60 courses before you graduate. To pass those courses, you take 100 to 200 tests. Good test grades depend on your ability to read, understand, and recall about 24,000 to 40,000 pages of information. Good grades also result when you can connect what you already know to what you need to learn. Thus, course readings form the heart of the learning process. Your success in reading and understanding text materials determines, in part, your success as a postsecondary student. Understanding your texts depends on your reading skills and your ability to use what you already know about a subject. This chapter shows you how to use your background knowledge and text clues to maximize your understanding.

> **Reading a book is like rewriting it for yourself . . . You bring to anything you read all your experiences of the world.**
>
> —Angela Carter
> *Twentieth century*
> *British author*

Background Knowledge: Recognizing What You Know

As a student, it's important to think about what you know. But, it's just as important to think about what you don't know. This self-knowledge helps you decide where you stand in your understanding. What you already know is called **background knowledge.**

Your memories form the basis of your background knowledge. Some information is stored as specific memories. This includes such data as the name of your first-grade teacher, your phone number, and what your family looks like. Other information is stored more generally as **stereotypes** (typical information). For instance, when you see a bird (for example, a sparrow), the memory of that exact bird is generalized. Unless the bird's behavior is atypical (for example, diving at you), you will store this memory with others you have about birds (for example, they fly, they live in nests, they eat bugs and worms, and they lay eggs).

You possess background knowledge for movies, stories, objects, characters, events, and ideas. In fact, you have background knowledge for everything. It consists of anything and everything you know about any subject. Each person's background knowledge for a topic differs because each person's experiences and use of that knowledge differs. Some aspects of the information will, however, be the same. For example, the background knowledge for tests could consist of the information found in Table 2.1. These can be organized into smaller segments to make a network of related ideas such as types of tests, test-taking materials, and so on. Items combine and recombine to form infinite connections.

Table 2.1		Background Knowledge for Tests	
bonus	essay	#2 pencil	standardized
monitor	study	true/false	calculator
A,B,C,D,F	questions	grades	curve
texts	directions	old exams	notes
answers	computer sheet	study group	fear
oral	blue books	pass/fail	stress
final	noncomprehensive	subjective	anxiety
paper	coping strategies	objective	midterm
points	multiple-choice	reading	handouts
pen	instructor	pop quiz	cramming

Using Background Knowledge

Your experiences help you know how to use information. What you know and how you use it help you relate to the world appropriately. For instance, you learned manners in this way. You learned to say, "Excuse me" or "Pardon me" when you accidentally bumped into someone. Your background experiences also help you make decisions and solve problems logically.

READ Exercise 2.1   How does what you know affect your understanding of new information? *Exercise 2.1 shows the value of activating background knowledge before you read. Complete this exercise before reading the rest of this chapter.* Not knowing the passage's topic in Exercise 2.1 probably made the passage hard to understand. But, once you knew the topic, you recalled what you knew about the topic and the meaning became clear. Background knowledge reflected your experiences. It guided your understanding.

Background knowledge aids understanding in other ways. Background knowledge helps you organize, as well as interpret, new information. Thus, instead of dealing with completely new ideas and concepts, you identify and make associations among them. Background knowledge also aids recall. The more connections you have for information, the more ways you have to remember it.

Linking new to old information aids comprehension. Analyzing new pieces of information and relating them to what you already know helps you move from simply recalling facts to synthesizing new concepts. Your ability to retrieve this information helps you to make better predictions when you survey new texts.

Building Background Knowledge

The development of background knowledge begins at birth. Even before you knew the meanings of words, you understood concepts—*hot, cold, hungry, comfortable, uncomfortable, loud, soft.* As a child, you had to experience a concept to have a word for it and remember that word. For instance, you had to feel the heat of a fire, stove, or heater to understand *hot.* As you grew older, the need to experience directly faded.

As an adult, you learn new concepts **vicariously** (indirectly) as well as through direct experience. This indirect experience allows you to learn from the experiences of others. For instance, you might never go to the moon, win an Olympic event, or run for president of the United States. Still, you can learn about these experiences from what you see and hear about them. Thus, reading anything and everything expands your knowledge of topics. Watching television and movies or listening to radio programs increases background knowledge. Listening to lectures, conversations, and other forms of verbal information contributes to what you know as well.

This forms the cycle of learning. Your newly acquired concepts expand your background knowledge. This, in turn, provides the basis for you to make sense of and acquire more concepts.

Survey Strategies for College Texts

Surveying forms the first step in connecting you to the text. Surveying text involves examining important chapter features to help you activate and use background knowledge. This helps you set up your background knowledge for a second, more careful reading during which you gain a deeper understanding of text content. Previewing, outlining, and mapping provide ways to survey information. You use these as you set goals for learning.

How do you know what parts of a chapter to survey? Authors provide clues to important information in **prechapter, intrachapter,** and **postchapter guides** to help you identify what you need to know. Prechapter guides appear at the beginnings of chapters and introduce you to chapter content. Intrachapter guides help you find your way through a chapter. Postchapter guides help you summarize and synthesize text content. Table 2.2 identifies different types of chapter guides and purposes for each. You use these guides to preview, outline, and map chapters. Examples of chapter guides appear in Figures 2.1 and 2.2.

Table 2.2   Chapter Guides and Purposes

Prechapter Guides	Purposes
Title	Identify chapter topic or main idea
	Generate interest
Introduction	Summarize main idea(s)
	Provide overview of details
	Generate interest
Prereading questions	Identify important issues
	Assess understanding
	Establish purposes for reading
Terms	Introduce language important to understanding of chapter content
Outline/Map	Organize content
Objectives	Identify what the reader should know or be able to do by reading the chapter
Intrachapter Guides	
Headings/subheadings	Identify differences in organization of information
Terms in context	Identify usage of language as it applies to the subject
Boxed information	Identify related information
Different typefaces	Highlight important information
Graphics	Summarize ideas visually
Marginal notes	Explain or enhance meanings
Postchapter Guides	
Summary	Review main points
Review questions	Check understanding of content
Terms	Check understanding of vocabulary specific to the chapter
Suggested readings	Provide additional background information

Previewing: Mental Overview

Previewing introduces you to chapter content based on the text features (title, headings, terms, and so on). This process gives you a kind of mental overview of chapter topics—a piece-by-piece, ordered, text-based analysis of content. Your success in previewing depends on your ability to analyze text features quickly and determine relationships among them. It also sets the stage for listening and notetaking in class. As you develop your skills in previewing, the process becomes one that

Figure 2.1   Illustrations of Prechapter, Intrachapter, and Postchapter Guides

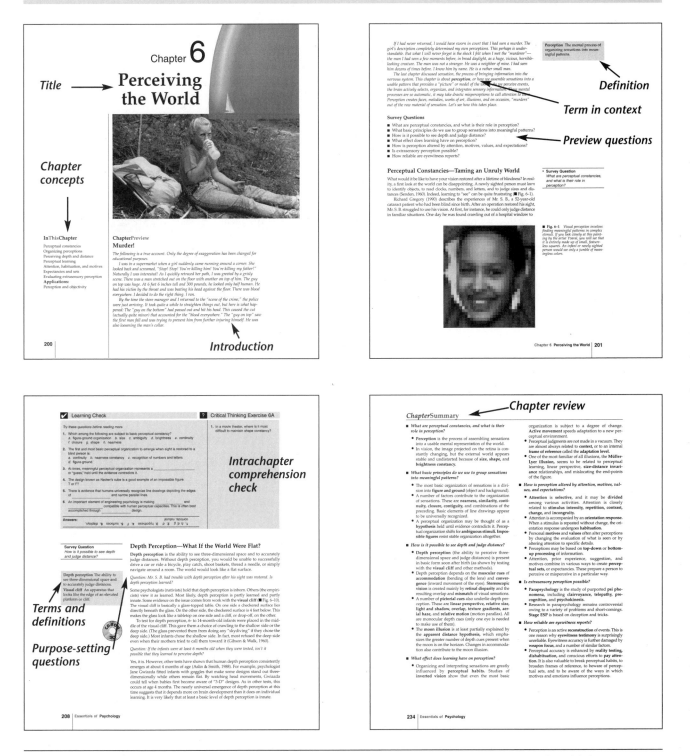

Figure 2.2 Illustrations of Prechapter, Intrachapter, and Postchapter Guides

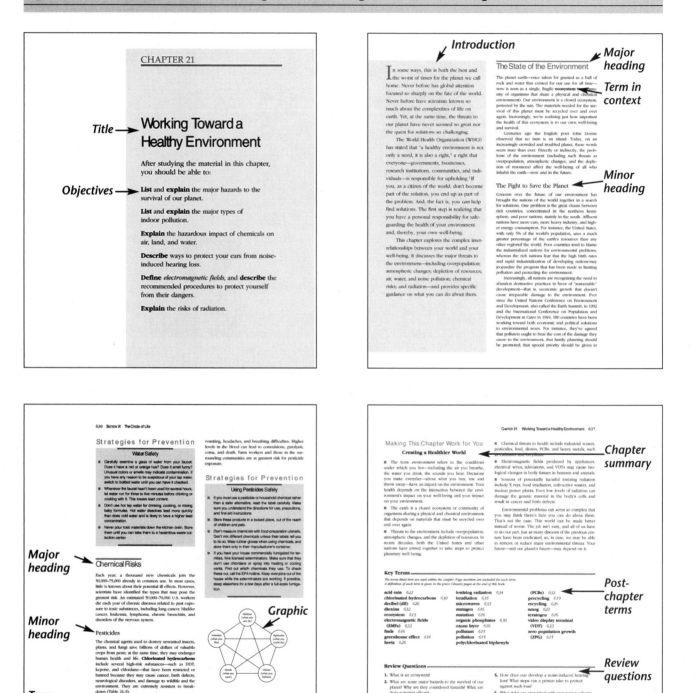

Table 2.3   Steps in Previewing

1. *Read the title.* What is the chapter about? What do you already know about this topic? Write the chapter's title at the top of a separate sheet of paper.

2. *Read the introduction or first paragraph.* This usually provides the main idea. Summarize the main idea in a sentence. Record it beneath the title.

3. *Read the boldface headings throughout the chapter.* These show you structure of the content. Outline or map the headings on your paper.

4. *Read the first paragraph or sentence under each heading.* This provides an overview of each section.

5. *Examine the accompanying graphs, charts, and pictures.* Graphics often stress main points, explain complex processes, or summarize details. In a sentence at the bottom of your page, identify the specific purpose(s) they seem to serve.

6. *Note any typographical aids (boldface, underlining, italics).* In the body of the text, these aids highlight key terms. When in the margins, they can identify important facts or concepts. At the bottom of your page, identify the typographical aid(s) used in the chapter and their use(s).

7. *Read the last paragraph or summary.* This often restates main points or provides conclusions. Compare this information with your introductory main idea. Rewrite or combine the main ideas to reflect any new or more detailed information the summary provides.

8. *Read the objectives at the beginning of the chapter.* Objectives help you set goals and purposes. They help you determine what you should know or be able to do at the end of the chapter. List each one on your page.

9. *Read the terms at the beginning or end of the chapter.* Although you might recognize some of the terms, determine if they have specialized meanings within the context of the chapter's content. List the terms.

---

you can mentally complete. Until then, recording what you find on paper provides a way for you to organize and review what you find. Previewing steps appear in Table 2.3.

Outlining: Topical Overview

An **outline** is a topical collection of ideas ranked according to importance. Every idea is subordinate to or summarized by another idea. Thus, an outline forms a hierarchical overview of information. You determine importance based on how ideas fit together.

When you outline a chapter, the subject of the outline is the same as the subject of your chapter. Each major heading in the chapter is a major heading in your outline. Each subheading becomes a minor heading. Information found under subheadings provides supporting details. You may need to reword these headings and subheadings into phrases, sentences, or questions to aid study. This text gives you opportunities to outline chapters by providing outline exercises at the beginning of Chapters 5 through 10.

Outlines consist of formal or informal formats (see Table 2.4). Formal outlines use Roman numerals (I, II, III, and so on) placed on the left side of the page or margin to note major concepts. You indent ideas that support the major concepts. You indicate these secondary points with capital letters. You show lesser supporting details with indented Arabic numerals (1, 2, 3). Because notes are for your own use, you need not use formal outlines. Informal outlines using indentions or special symbols to visually highlight information are just as effec-

READ Exercise 2.2   tive. *Exercise 2.2 provides practice in outlining and previewing.*

Mapping: Visual Overview

Mapping provides a visual way to determine the plan of a chapter quickly. Maps are pictures that show relationships among concepts. They express patterns of thought. Some students use chapter maps (see Figure 2.3) to survey chapters. You construct a chapter map by using headings and subheadings in a family tree style branching format. The steps in creating a chapter map appear in Table 2.5. This text gives you opportunities to create chapter maps in exercises at the be-

READ Exercise 2.3   ginning of Chapters 5 through 10 in this text. *Exercise 2.3 provides practice in creating chapter maps.*

Table 2.4   Formal and Informal Outline Formats

Formal Outline	Informal Outline with Dashes	Informal Outline with Print Style Differences
I. Personality theorists	Personality theorists	Personality Theorists
A. Psychodynamic	—Psychodynamic	*Psychodynamic*
1. Freud	—Freud	Freud
2. Jung	—Jung	Jung
3. Erickson	—Erickson	Erickson
B. Behavioral	—Behavioral	*Behavioral*
1. Skinner	—Skinner	Skinner
2. Bandera	—Bandera	Bandera

Figure 2.3   Example of Chapter Map

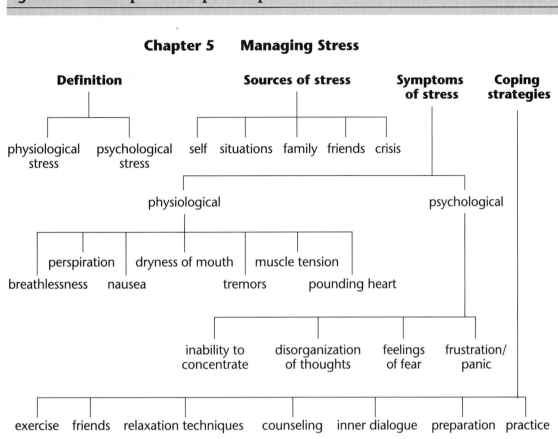

Table 2.5   Steps in Creating a Chapter Map

1. Turn a sheet of paper horizontally.
2. Write the first major heading in the top left corner.
3. Place the next-level headings underneath the major headings with lines showing their relationship to the major heading.
4. Place the next level of heading(s), if any, underneath the second-level heading.
5. Continue the pattern until you come to the next major heading. Write the second major heading to the right of the first major heading.
6. Repeat the process until you reach the end of the chapter.
7. Review your map. How many main topics are covered in the chapter? How are the ideas organized? Which topics are covered in the greatest detail (most levels of headings)? How does your map help you predict the focus of a lecture and future test questions?

> **Write to Learn**
>
> Respond to the following on a separate sheet of paper or in your notebook. Review your responses to Exercises 1.2 and 1.3. Describe how your dominant style affects the type of survey strategy you use.

Setting Learning Goals

Actor Paul Newman once described acting as "a question of absorbing other people's personalities and adding some of your own experience." Setting learning goals makes previewing an active process. Learning goals allow you to define how you will absorb what an author has to say by integrating that information with what you already know— your experience with the subject.

Asking specific questions about a chapter's content helps you set your own learning goals. This focuses your reading and creates a reason for reading other than getting to the end. You read to answer your questions. Thus, your reading becomes an active, thought-provoking process.

How can you ask the right questions before reading? You can change the author's headings and subheadings into questions. What kinds of questions should you ask? Questions that focus on chapter guides help you maximize their use. Few authors use every kind of signal, but most use some sort of prechapter, intrachapter, and postchapter reading guides (see Table 2.2).

Some questioning words help you find main ideas. Others help you locate details. Table 2.6 provides a list of guides with corresponding sample questions for each one. Table 2.7 helps you match the learning goal you set with the question you need to ask.

In setting the learning goals you want to reach, you might have to be a little creative in changing headings or subheadings into questions. Your goals should be to ask the best question about a topic rather than an average or unimportant question. And, your questions should relate to each other as well as to the chapter as a whole. You might even choose to ask more than one question per heading. For instance, suppose you read a chapter on stress management. You find the following three headings: "Your Need for Exercise and Relaxation," "Physiological and Psychological Stress," and "Coping with Stress." Obvious questions would be "What is your need for exercise and relaxation?" "What is physiological and psychological stress?" and "What is coping with stress?" Such questions do set learning goals but not very high ones.

Table 2.6   Chapter Guides and Corresponding Sample Questions

Prechapter Guides	Questions
Title	What do I already know about this topic?
Introduction	What will be the main idea of the chapter? Was the introduction designed to be thought provoking or attention getting?
Prereading questions	What does the author consider to be important questions about the chapter?
Terms	What is the language of this topic? What new words will be introduced in this chapter? What do I already know about their meanings?
Outline/map	How does the author organize ideas?
Objectives	What does the author expect me to know or do by the end of the chapter?
Intrachapter Guides	
Headings/subheadings	How does the author indicate levels of importance among ideas? How do the subheadings relate to the headings?
Terms in context	How are new terms used?
Boxed information	What is the relationship between this information and the rest of the chapter? What is its purpose?
Different typefaces	What kind or kinds of information do different typefaces highlight?
Graphics	Why are these visual aids included? What do they show and mean?
Marginal notes	How do the marginal notes relate to the text? Why were they included?
Postchapter Guides	
Summary	What did the author consider to be the main points of the chapter?
Review questions	What information should I review or reconsider?
Terms	Did I find and understand the vocabulary specific to the chapter?
Suggested readings	Do I need additional background information? If so, which materials would be most useful for my purposes?

Table 2.7   Learning Goals and Corresponding Questions

Question Words for Main Ideas

If you want to know . . .	Then ask . . .
a reason	Why?
a way	How?
a purpose or definition	What?

Question Words for Details

If you want to know . . .	Then ask . . .
a person	Who?
a number or amount	How many? How much?
a choice	Which?
a time	When?
a place	Where?
a fact	What?

Better, more interrelated questions might include, "Why do I need exercise and relaxation and what does that have to do with stress management?" "How do physiological and psychological stress differ? How are they alike?" and "What stress-management activities help me cope with psychological and physiological stresses?" *Exercise 2.4 provides practice asking questions with either outlining or mapping.* As with the previewing process, these questions eventually become an almost unconscious part of your reading and study process. *Exercise 2.5 lets you tailor surveying and questioning strategies to one of your own courses.*

READ Exercise 2.4

READ Exercise 2.5

Surveying Nontraditional Texts

Textbooks are not always one-size-fits-all. Rather, instructors use a textbook as the primary source and provide other materials to tailor it. Such nontraditional texts include **supplementary materials** and **narrative text** (e.g., stories or poetry). Whatever the purpose of the nontraditional reading, you need a specialized strategy for surveying it.

Surveying Supplementary Materials

Course readings often include supplementary materials (articles, parts of other chapters, examples, study guides, or other information). Some are available for purchase. Instructors place others on reserve (limited circulation) in the library or online in electronic formats.

Instructors use supplementary readings to enhance course content. These readings serve three purposes. First, some reinforce information in a text chapter. These might provide extra information about topics briefly discussed in the chapter. Or, they might simplify complex concepts. Others, such as study guides, help you organize and learn text information more easily. Second, such materials often present more current information. This information can provide new or conflicting perspectives on the topic. Finally, supplementary materials can provide general background information. For instance, a psychology chapter about personality generally focuses on major personality theories. Supplementary materials might include biographies of the theorists or case studies. Surveying such materials helps you decide how this information relates to the chapter. Then, you verify your prediction when reading.

The format of some supplemental readings is much like that of a text chapter. That is, they contain headings, subheadings, and summaries. You preview these just as you did text chapters (see Table 2.3). On the other hand, some include no text features to help you locate main points. Here, you use the title and any introductory or summary statements to preview the content. Reading the first sentence of each paragraph also adds to your overview of the material.

Previewing Narrative Text

Previewing narrative text or poetry demands a specialized previewing strategy. When an instructor assigns literary selections, he or she usually outlines the purposes for your reading. Such tasks might include summarizing the reading, analyzing character development or identifying plot. Sometimes, however, instructors make assignments without a specific focus for reading. When this happens, you might not know which goals to set yourself. After all, narrative text contains no special features to guide your reading. Table 2.8 provides some suggestions for examining narrative text before reading.

Write to Learn

Respond to the following on a separate sheet of paper or in your notebook. Review your responses to Exercises 1.3 and 1.4 and Exercises 2.2 and 2.3. Describe how your survey strategies affect or could affect your level of background knowledge for each of those chapters.

Table 2.8 Questions for Previewing Narrative Text

---

1. What kind of literature is this? How is it representative of the period in which it was written? How is it representative of its genre?
2. What can I determine from the title, size of print, illustrations, chapter headings, and opening pages?
3. For what age range is this literary selection appropriate?
4. What interests are reflected in this literary selection?
5. Who is the author of this selection? What do I know about him/her?

Chapter Summary

Survey techniques such as previewing, outlining, and mapping help you link background knowledge with text materials. Questioning allows you to actively interact with texts before reading and set reading goals. Specialized survey strategies are needed for nontraditional texts, such as supplementary materials and narrative text.

Chapter Review

Answer the following questions briefly but completely on a separate sheet of paper or in your notebook:

1. How does background knowledge aid you in reading and remembering information?
2. Describe specifically how surveying each type of chapter guide (prechapter, intrachapter, and postchapter) helps you connect your background knowledge to chapter content.
3. Review the chapter guides identified in Table 2.2. Which prechapter, intrachapter, and postchapter guides do you find to be most helpful to you? Why?
4. Could survey strategies prepare you to listen to class lectures and take notes? How?
5. Which survey strategy—previewing, outlining, or mapping—do you prefer? Create an argument to support your choice.
6. How could outlines and maps help you predict test content?
7. Why might an instructor assign supplementary readings?
8. How does converting chapter guides into questions increase your interactions with text information?
9. How can you use questions to set learning goals?

Terms

Terms appear in the order in which they occur in the chapter.

background knowledge
stereotypes
vicariously
surveying
prechapter guides
intrachapter guides
postchapter guides
previewing
outline
mapping
supplementary materials
narrative text

Exercises

Exercise 2.1

Read the passage below. On a separate sheet of paper or in your notebook, identify its topic. After you have identified the topic, turn to the last page of this chapter for further instructions.

> The procedure is actually quite simple. First, you arrange things into different groups. Of course, one pile may be sufficient depending on how much there is to do. If you have to go somewhere else due to lack of facilities that is the next step. Otherwise, you are pretty well set. It is important not to overdo things. That is, it is better to do too few things at once than too many. In the short run, this may not seem important but complications can easily arise. A mistake can be expensive as well. At first, the whole procedure will seem complicated. Soon, however, it will become just another facet of life. It is difficult to foresee any end to the necessity for this task in the immediate future, but then one can never tell. After the procedure is completed, one arranges the materials into different groups again. Then they can be put into their appropriate places. Eventually they will be used once more and the whole cycle will have to be repeated.

From Bransford, J. D., & Johnson, M. K. "Contextual prerequisites for understanding: Some investigations of comprehension and recall." *Journal of Verbal Learning and Verbal Behavior,* 2: 6, 1972.

Exercise 2.2

Following the directions in Table 2.3, Steps in Previewing, construct a written outline of the Sample Chapter "Opportunities to Work in the Theater" (found at back of this book) on a separate sheet of paper or in your notebook.

Exercise 2.3

On a separate sheet of paper or in your notebook; create a chapter map for the Sample Chapter "Opportunities to Work in the Theater" at the back of this book. Now compare your outline from Exercise 2.2 with your map. Which appeals more to you?

Exercise 2.4

On a separate sheet of paper or in your notebook, create goal-setting questions for each of the headings and subheadings found in the selection for Exercise 2.2. Outline or map these questions.

Exercise 2.5   To complete this exercise, use a textbook from another course in which you are enrolled or any other textbook. Complete the exercise on separate sheets of paper or in your notebook. Choose any chapter from the text.

1. Create a chart that shows the prechapter, intrachapter, and postchapter guides the chapter contains. At the bottom of the chart, write an evaluation of how well the author provided guides to support your understanding.

2. Create an outline or map of the chapter.

3. Create goal-setting questions for each major heading of the chapter.

Web Exercise   A variety of information related to concept mapping is available on the World Wide Web. For this exercise, access one of the following demo versions of mind mapping software and recreate the chapter map you created in Exercise 2.3. Choose from one of the following

Ygnius™

http://www.buzan.com.au/software.htm

Inspiration

http://www.inspiration.com/

Or one of the other concept mapping software applications at the Concept Mapping Resources Web site

http://users.edte.utwente.nl/lanzing/cm_home.htm).

READ: Keys

READ: Keys Activity Pretest

Rate each of the following words according to your knowledge of them.

Word	Stage 0 *I don't know this word.*	Stage 1 *I've seen this word but I know nothing of its meaning.*	Stage 2 *I've seen this word and can make associations with it.*	Stage 3 *I know this word.*
1. whims				
2. configuration				
3. ecliptic				
4 standardized				
5. simplified				
6. variant				
7. exerted				
8. predetermined				
9. affinities				
10. impetus				

READ: Keys Activity 2.1

Read the following textbook excerpt and keep track of your reading time.
Note: Underlined, boldfaced words will be used in Chapter 6, Exercise 6.9. Underlined, italicized words will be used in Chapter 7, Exercise 7.9.

Astrology and Astronomy

Many ancient cultures regarded the planets and stars as representations or symbols of the **gods** or other *supernatural* forces that controlled their lives. For them, the study of the heavens was not an abstract subject, it was directly connected to the life-and-death necessity of understanding the actions of the gods and **currying** favor with them. Before the time of our scientific perspective, everything that happened in nature, from the weather, to diseases and accidents, to **celestial** surprises like eclipses or new comets, was thought to be an expression of the **whims** or *displeasures* of the gods. Any signs that helped people understand what these gods had in mind were considered extremely important.

The movements of the seven objects that had the power to "wander" through the **realms** of the sky—the Sun, Moon, and five planets visible to the *unaided* eye—clearly must have special significance in such a system of thinking. Most ancient cultures associated these seven objects with various supernatural rulers in their *pantheon* and kept track of them for religious reasons. Even in the comparatively sophisticated Greece of **antiquity,** the planets had the names of gods and were credited with having the same powers and influences as the gods whose names they bore. From such ideas was born the ancient system called **astrology,** still practiced by some people today, in which the positions of these bodies among the stars of the zodiac are thought to hold the key to understanding what we can expect from life.

The Beginnings of Astrology

Astrology began in Babylonia about two-and-a-half millennia ago. The Babylonians, believing that the planets and their motions influenced the fortunes of kings and nations, used their knowledge of *astronomy* to guide their rulers. When the Babylonian culture was absorbed by the Greeks, astrology gradually came to influence the entire Western world and eventually spread to the Orient as well.

By the 2nd century B.C., the Greeks democratized astrology by developing the idea that the planets influence every individual. In particular, they believed that the **configuration** of the Sun, Moon, and planets at the moment of birth affected a person's personality and fortune, the doctrine called **natal astrology.** *Natal astrology* reached its zenith with Ptolemy 400 years later. As famous for his astrology as for his astronomy, Ptolemy compiled the *Tetrabiblos,* a **treatise** on astrology that remains the "Bible" of the subject. It is essentially this ancient religion, older than Christianity or Islam, that is still practiced by today's astrologers.

The Horoscope

The key to natal astrology is the **horoscope,** a chart showing the positions of the planets in the sky at the moment of an individual's birth. In charting a horoscope, the planets (including the Sun and Moon, classed as wanderers or planets by the ancients) must first be located in the zodiac. When the system of astrology was set up, the zodiac was divided into 12 sectors called signs, each 30º long. Each sign was named after a _constellation_ in the sky through which the Sun, Moon, and planets were seen to pass—the sign of Virgo after the constellation of Virgo, for example.

When someone today casually asks you your "sign," what they are asking for is your "sun-sign"—which zodiac sign the Sun was in at the moment you were born. But more than 2000 years have passed since the signs received their names from the constellations. Because of precession, the constellations of the zodiac slide westward along the **ecliptic,** going once around the sky in about 26,000 years. Thus today the real stars have slipped around by about 1/12 of the zodiac—the width of one sign.

In most forms of astrology, however, the signs have remained assigned to the dates of the year they had when astrology was first set up. This means that the astrological signs and the real constellations are out of step; the sign of Aries, for example, now occupies the constellation of Pisces. When you look up your sun-sign in a newspaper astrology column, because of precession, the name of the sign associated with your birthday is no longer the name of the constellation in which the Sun was actually located when you were born. To know that constellation, you must look for the sign _before_ the one that includes your birthday.

A complete horoscope shows the location of not only the sun but each planet in the sky by indicating its position in the appropriate sign of the zodiac. However, as the celestial sphere turns (owing to the rotation of the earth), the entire zodiac moves across the sky to the west, completing a circuit of the heavens each day. Thus the position in the sky (or "**house**" in astrology) must also be calculated. There are more-or-less **standardized** rules for the interpretation of the horoscope, most of which (at least in Western schools of astrology) are derived from the _Tetrabiblos_ of Ptolemy. Each sign, each house, and each planet, the last supposedly acting as a center of force, is associated with particular matters.

The detailed interpretation of a horoscope is therefore a very complicated business, and there are many schools of astrological thought on how it should be done. Although some of the rules may be standardized, how each rule is to be weighed and applied is a matter of judgment—and "art." It also means that it is very difficult to tie astrology down to specific _predictions_ or to get the same predictions from different astrologers.

Astrology Today

Astrologers today use the same basic principles laid down by Ptolemy nearly 2000 years ago. They cast **horoscopes** (a process much **simplified** by the development of appropriate computer programs) and suggest interpretations. Sun-sign astrology (which you read in the newspapers and many magazines) is a recent simplified **variant** of natal astrology. Although even professional astrologers do not place much trust in such a limited scheme, which tries to fit everyone into just 12 groups, sun-sign astrology is taken seriously by many people (perhaps because it is so commonly discussed by the media). In a recent poll of teenagers in the United States, more than half said they "believed in astrology."

Today, we know much more about the nature of the planets as physical bodies, as well as about human genetics, than the ancients could. It is hard to imagine that the positions of the Sun, Moon, or planets in the sky at the moment of our birth could have anything to do with our personality or future. There are no known forces, not gravity or anything else, that could cause such effects. (For example, a simple calculation shows that the gravitational pull of the obstetrician delivering a newborn baby is greater than that of Mars.) Astrologers thus have to argue that there are unknown forces **exerted** by the planets that depend on their configurations with respect to one another and they do not vary according to the distance of the planet—forces for which there is no evidence.

Another curious aspect of astrology is its emphasis on planet configurations at *birth*. What about the forces that might influence us at conception? Isn't our genetic makeup more important for determining our personality than the circumstances of our birth. Would we really be a different person if we had been born a few hours earlier or later, as astrology claims? (Back when astrology was first conceived, birth was thought of as a moment of magic significance, but today we understand a lot more about the long process that precedes it.)

Actually, very few thinking people today buy the claim that our entire lives are **predetermined** by astrological influences at birth, but many people apparently believe that astrology has validity as an indicator of **affinities** and personality. A surprising number of Americans make judgments about people—whom they will hire, associate with, and even marry—on the basis of astrological information. To be sure, these are difficult decisions and you might argue that we should use any relevant information that might help us make the right choices. But does astrology actually provide any useful information on human personality? This is the kind of question that can be tested using the scientific method.

The results of hundreds of tests are all the same. There is no evidence that natal astrology has any predictive power, even in a statistical sense. Why then do people often seem to have anecdotes about how well their own astrologer advised them? Effective astrologers today use the language of the zodiac and the horoscope only as the outward trappings of their craft. Mostly they work as amateur therapists, offering simple truths that clients like or need to hear. (Recent studies have shown that just about any sort of short-term therapy makes people feel a little better. This is because the very act of talking about our problems is in itself beneficial.)

The scheme of astrology has no basis in scientific fact, however. It is an interesting historical system, left over from prescientific days and best remembered for the **impetus** it gave people to learn the cycles and patterns of the sky. From it grew the science of astronomy, which is our main subject for discussion.

From A. Franknoi, D. Morrison, & S. Wolff (2000). *Voyages to the Planets,* 2nd ed., Saunders/Harcourt, Section 1.3, pp 27–29.

1533 words / _____ minutes = _____ words per minute.

Calculate your reading time by dividing the number of words in the article by the amount of time it took to read it. Then mark your reading time on the chart located on page 338 of this text.

READ: Keys Activity 2.2

On a separate sheet of paper or in your notebook, answer the following questions about the excerpt you just read:

1. Where did astrology begin?

    a. Greece

    b. United States

    c. Babylonia

    d. Rome

2. Which of the following is NOT true of Ptolemy?

    a. He was a famous astronomer.

    b. He was a famous astrologer.

    c. He wrote a book called the *Tetrabiblos.*

    d. He wrote the Bible.

3. Why is the zodiac divided into 12 30º sectors?

    a. When combined, they form a 360º circle.

    b. There are 12 months in the calendar year.

    c. No one knows why the zodiac is divided into 12 30º sectors.

    d. Ancient people could only see 12 celestial bodies.

4. When did astrology begin?

    a. 2nd century B.C.

    b. About 2500 years ago

    c. 400 years ago

    d. almost 2000 years ago

5. What is true of constellations?

    a. They move eastward.

    b. They rotate around the sun in approximately 365 days (1 calendar year).

    c. They have moved approximately $30°$ since sun-signs were first identified.

    d. They are stationary.

6. What is the major flaw in using the sun sign associated with a person's birth date to determine aspects of personality?

    a. The sign associated with a person's birth date no longer matches the sign in which the person was actually born.

    b. Few individuals are trained in the "art" of interpreting horoscopes.

    c. The date of conception is more accurate than the date of birth.

    d. Gravitational pull is a better predictor.

7. The results of scientific tests concerning natal astrology indicate that it

    a. has predictive value for some people.

    b. is never predictive.

    c. is most appropriate when cast by professional astrologers.

    d. is more accurate when signs, houses, and planets are used to make predictions.

8. What is true of sun-sign astrology?

    a. It is often used in popular media.

    b. It is less popular because it is more difficult to use and interpret.

    c. It takes constellation changes into account when casting horoscopes.

    d. It is the most scientific form of astrology in Western schools.

9. What appears to be the primary personal benefit of astrologers to the individuals they advise?

    a. professional casting of horoscopes

    b. amateur short-term therapy

   c. astrological information that assists individuals in choosing friends and spouses.

   d. computerized interpretations of astrological charts

10. What appears to be the primary scientific benefit of astrology?

   a. It has no value.

   b. It provided an important topic for scientific investigation.

   c. It fostered the development of the language of the zodiac and horoscope.

   d. It led to the scientific field of astronomy.

READ: Keys Activity 2.3

Examine each of the numbered phrases or sentences and complete the following on a separate sheet of paper or in your notebook.

(a) Write the boldfaced, italicized word. Identify one or two words that you can put in the place of the boldfaced, italicized word without changing the meaning of the phrase or sentence and write this synonym or synonymous phrase (words that have the same meaning) beside the word. (b) Identify the part of speech of this word as used in the sentence. (c) Look up the boldfaced, italicized word in a dictionary and write the dictionary definition. How does this compare with the definition from context? (d) List the parts of speech this word can sometimes be. (e) Write a complete sentence with each word.

1. Before the time of our scientific perspective, everything that happened in nature, from the weather, to diseases and accidents, to celestial surprises like eclipses or new comets, was thought to be an expression of the ***whims*** or displeasures of the gods.

2. In particular, they believed that the ***configuration*** of the Sun, Moon, and planets at the moment of birth affected a person's personality and fortune, . . .

3. Because of precession, the constellations of the zodiac slide westward along the ***ecliptic,*** going once around the sky in about 26,000 years.

4. There are more-or-less ***standardized*** rules for the interpretation of the horoscope . . .

5. They cast horoscopes (a process much ***simplified*** by the development of appropriate computer programs) and suggest interpretations.

6. Sun-sign astrology (which you read in the newspapers and many magazines) is a recent simplified *variant* of natal astrology.

7. Astrologers thus have to argue that there are unknown forces *exerted* by the planets that depend on their configurations with respect to one another . . .

8. Actually, very few thinking people today buy the claim that our entire lives are *predetermined* by astrological influences at birth . . .

9. . . . many people apparently believe that astrology has validity as an indicator of *affinities* and personality.

10. It is an interesting historical system, left over from prescientific days and best remembered for the *impetus* it gave people to learn the cycles and patterns of the sky.

READ: Keys Activity 2.4

In Part A, use the following list of words to fill in the blanks. In Part B, use the information from Part A to complete the analogies.

Part A

repulsions	arrangement	desires	irregular
harder	disorder	momentum	easier
oval	version	applied	undetermined
similarity	set	dislikes	attractions
unforced	inaction	patterned	square

Synonym	Word	Antonym
_____	**1.** whims	_____
_____	**2.** configuration	_____
_____	**3.** ecliptic	_____
_____	**4.** standardized	_____
_____	**5.** simplified	_____
_____	**6.** variant	_____

_____ **7.** exerted   _____

_____ **8.** predetermined   _____

_____ **9.** affinities   _____

_____ **10.** impetus   _____

Part B

1. whims : _____ :: impetus : momentum

2. predetermined : set :: affinities : _____

3. standardized : patterned :: simplified : _____

4. _____ : applied :: eclipitic : oval

5. configuration : _____ :: variant : version

6. simplified : _____ :: exerted : unforced

7. ecliptic : _____ :: predetermined : changed

8. affinities : _____ :: impetus : inaction

9. standardized : _____ :: variant : similarity

10. configuration : _____ :: simplified : harder

READ: Keys Activity Posttest

Rate each of the following words according to your knowledge of them.

Word	Stage 0 *I don't know this word.*	Stage 1 *I've seen this word but I know nothing of its meaning.*	Stage 2 *I've seen this word and can make associations with it.*	Stage 3 *I know this word.*
1. whims				
2. configuration				
3. ecliptic				
4 standardized				
5. simplified				
6. variant				
7. exerted				
8. predetermined				
9. affinities				
10. impetus				

Exercise 2.1 Key

The topic of the passage is *washing clothes*. Now reread the passage in Exercise 2.1. How has your understanding of the passage changed?

Reading

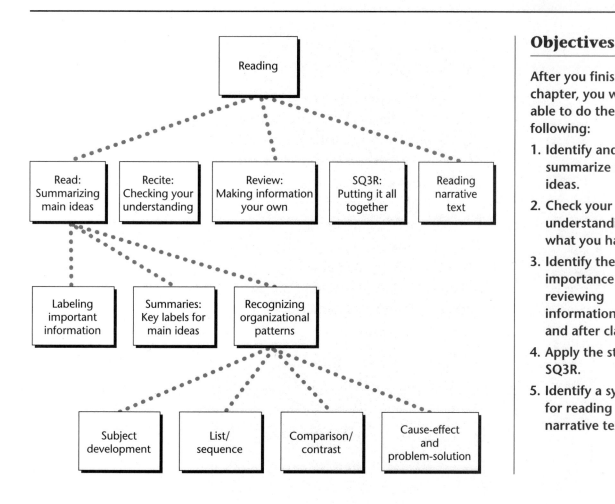

Objectives

After you finish this chapter, you will be able to do the following:

1. Identify and summarize main ideas.

2. Check your understanding of what you have read.

3. Identify the importance of reviewing information before and after class.

4. Apply the steps in SQ3R.

5. Identify a system for reading narrative text.

Chapter Outline

Reading is more than just sitting and staring at a text. Reading involves doing and understanding. It is an active process. You ask questions and look for their answers. You look for patterns, or connections, among information. You summarize main ideas. You draw conclusions. In short, reading requires work. Taking this action leads to understanding.

> In learning, it is said, "we hear and we forget; we see and we remember; we do and we understand."
>
> *Anonymous*

Read: Summarizing Main Ideas

At first, college looks pretty simple. You're only in class a few hours a week. There's time to learn the campus, meet others, and have fun. Then come exams. Suddenly, you realize that college is no joke. You've got to hit the books to make the grades. But, how?

Labeling Important Information

To hit the books successfully, you need to see college texts as tools for learning. To maximize your texts, you use them to make reading active. One way to do so is by taking notes in the outside margins of the books you read.

Your goal in taking notes from your textbook, also called **text labels,** is to identify important information and respond to it. How do you know what is important? You recognize the value of information in several ways. First, your chapter preview (see Chapter 2) provides clues about what information is of worth. Second, your instructor's lectures are also reliable sources. If lecture information is repeated in the text, this information is probably vital to your understanding. However, the text might use phrases that differ from those given in lecture. Having two versions of the same information increases your understanding and recall. Perhaps one of the sources explains the information more clearly than the other does. Perhaps one gives additional details. Whatever the case, when you find information that you think is important, you highlight or underline it. Then you label what you marked in the text's margins.

Why is labeling necessary? Consider the marked text in Example 3.1. It appears to be appropriately marked. However, the answer to the question, "How do you organize course content to set reading goals?" ranges across much of the section. Reviewing for a test several weeks later, you might forget how the information relates. You would need to reread most of what you marked to identify your thoughts.

In addition to forming an index for future study, text labels help you know if you understood what you read. If you can't pinpoint the main idea or identify relationships within the information, you didn't

> You've really got to start hitting the books because it's no joke out here.
>
> —Spike Lee
> *Twentieth century American filmmaker*

Example 3.1   Text Marking

Organizing Course Content to Set Reading Goals

Think again about how you best learn information (see Chapter 1). Outlines and maps help you predict and organize information while surveying. This is particularly true if you rephrase headings and subheadings into questions or connect chapter titles with headings and subheadings to questions. Questions require you to look for answers and, thus, make reading more active. You read to answer *what, how, when, who, which, where,* and *why* (see Table 2.3). When previewing, you will normally be looking for main ideas. Thus, *why, how,* and *what* questions will form the basis of your previewing outline. Question outlines and maps make previewing less covert and more concrete. They help set goals for reading.

Table 3.1   Shorthand Symbols for Text Labels

Symbol	Meaning	Symbol	Meaning
Ex	example or experiment	circled word	summarizes process
FOR	formula	?	disagree or unclear
Conc	conclusion	TERM	important term
MI	main idea	SUM	summary
! or *	important information	{	indicates certain pieces of information relate
→	results, leads to, steps in a sequence	OPIN	author's opinion, rather than fact
(1), (2), (3)	numbered points—then label what the points are		

---

understand it. This means that you need to reread, ask your instructor, or consult another source. Because your notes are for your use, using abbreviations and symbols (see Table 3.1) increases your efficiency. Example 3.2 shows a text with labels. You use text labels to identify key concepts, summarize main ideas, note relationships, or comment on information in other ways (see Table 3.2).

What if you rented or borrowed a text and cannot take notes in it? The key to learning is not where the notes are, but what information is contained within them. Record your text labels in a separate notebook or as a supplement to your lecture notes. To do so, draw a line down the middle of your notebook page. On one half of the page, write your

---

Example 3.2   Marked and Labeled Text

Organizing Course Content to Set Reading Goals

Think again about how you best learn information (see Chapter 1). Outlines and maps help you predict and organize information while surveying. This is particularly true if you rephrase headings and subheadings into questions or connect chapter titles with headings and subheadings to questions. Questions require you to look for answers and, thus, make reading more active. You read to answer *what, how, when, who, which, where,* and *why* (see Table 2.3). When previewing, you will normally be looking for main ideas. Thus, *why, how,* and *what* questions will form the basis of your previewing outline. Question outlines and maps make previewing less covert and more concrete. They help set goals for reading.

Stated Information:
  Outlines / Maps = ways to organize info

Translation:
  Main Ideas = why, how, what

Application:
  maps / outlines also used for test preparation??

Table 3.2   Types, Purposes, and Examples of Text Labels

Purpose	Type
directly stated information	list or sequence
	quotation
	date
	person
	place
	accomplishment/event
restated information	restate problem
	explanation
	description
comment	agree/disagree
	unclear
	possible test question
	bias/propaganda
conclusion or generalization	group or classify information
	generalize details to main idea
	summarize
application	other uses, situations, and so on based on background knowledge
analysis	relationships (for example, cause/effect)
	comparisons/contrasts
synthesis	combine or condense information

text notes, taking care to identify the textbook page number from which the notes come. Then you can use the other side of the pages to take class notes. No matter which set of notes you take first, organize your notebook by arranging the second set of notes to mirror the first. In this way, you actively work with the information and begin your synthesis for future study.

Summaries: Key Labels for Main Ideas

Main ideas tell you what's critical about a topic. Thus, it's important to label them. But, how do you find the main ideas? Consider the **topic** *hamburger.* What exactly makes a hamburger different from any other sandwich? The meat patty and bread are all that's needed for a hamburger to exist. They are the **main idea** of the sandwich. The trimmings, or **details,** make each hamburger unique.

Similarly, a paragraph consists of a topic, main idea, and details. Its topic concerns a broad general subject. Its main idea is the essential elements that define the topic. The main idea expresses the key concept. Details limit or describe the main idea. Pictures, conversations, movies, commercials, reading selections, and paragraphs all contain topics, main ideas, and details. For instance, consider the television show, "America's Most Wanted." The topic—elusive criminals—remains constant. The main idea (the crime) and the details (the victims, the setting, and so forth) change each week.

Details support the main idea by telling *how, when, how much, how many, why,* or *what kind.* Because details give information about one topic, they relate to each other in some way. Locating the topic, main idea, and details helps you understand the writer's point(s). Finding them increases your understanding. Figure 3.1 shows the relationship of topic, main idea, and details. Table 3.3 shows the process for finding main ideas in paragraphs. Once you find the main idea, how do you label it? Consider the following example:

> The jobs that U.S. presidents held before office are varied. Some held more than one job. Over half were lawyers. Many were governors of states before becoming president. At least one-fourth were farmers, ranchers, or planters. Six were soldiers. Six were educators. Two worked with newspapers. One was an engineer. Another had been a tailor. One was even a movie star.

What is this paragraph about? It tells the work presidents did before their elections. The specific jobs are important details. A text label for this paragraph might look Figure 3.2.

Figure 3.1   Relationships Among Topic, Main Idea, Details, and Organization

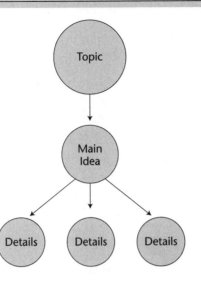

Table 3.3   Steps for Finding Main Ideas in Paragraphs

1. Read the paragraph.
2. Ask yourself what one thing the paragraph covers. This is the topic.
3. Look for details that point to or support the idea the paragraph covers.
4. Look for or create a sentence that says this key concept, or main idea. This sentence, in abbreviated form, forms a summary text label.

Figure 3.2   Text Labeling

The jobs that U.S. presidents held before office are varied. Some held more than one job. Over half were lawyers. Many were governors of states before becoming president. At least one-fourth were farmers, ranchers, or planters. Six were soldiers. Six were educators. Two worked with newspapers. One was an engineer. Another had been a tailor. One was even a movie star.

Jobs before becoming prez
  Law
  Farmers
  Soldiers
  Govs of states
  Educ
  Journalists

Table 3.4 Steps for Finding Main Ideas in Passages

1. Read each paragraph in the passage.

2. Find the main idea for each paragraph.

3. Identify the topic that all or most of the paragraphs have in common.

4. Locate or create a sentence that says what the paragraphs have in common. A similar sentence might be found in the introduction or summary of the passage. This sentence should answer your goal-setting question for the section (see Chapter 2).

5. Write it in abbreviated form as your text summary. This text label is the main idea of the passage.

Getting the main idea of paragraphs is crucial to reading. Often a paragraph contains a **topic sentence** that states the main idea. Although the topic sentence is often first, as in this paragraph, it could also appear anywhere in the paragraph. Sometimes you have to write the topic sentence yourself. Your topic sentence should effectively summarize the main idea and details.

Finding the main idea of a passage is often like finding the main idea of a paragraph (see Table 3.4 and Example 3.3). But, working with a whole passage is sometimes more difficult. That's because the whole is often equal to more than the sum of its parts. For example, in playing cards, the deck (the whole) is more than just individual cards (the parts). Single cards are not as useful as a deck is. It's hard to play a card game when some cards are missing. To find the main idea of a passage, look at each part. Then use the parts to summarize the whole (the main idea). *Practice finding main ideas of paragraphs and passages in*
READ Exercise 3.1 *Exercise 3.1.*

Recognizing Organizational Patterns

Finding links among the ideas within a paragraph or passage helps you organize them into a complete whole. This grouping of details helps you understand main ideas. Consider the next paragraph:

> The lipids you eat come in the form of water-insoluble triglycerides, cholesterol, and phospholipids, with the triglycerides in the majority (composing about 95 percent of dietary fat). Both of the body's systems of transportation—lymph and blood—are watery fluids. Clearly, if the lipids were thrown "as is" in the bloodstream, they would bunch together and form chunks of fat that would then block the arteries.

Example 3.3   Summary Text Labels in a Passage

Children of Alcoholics

terms
COA
7 mil
ACOA
2.1 mil

Alcohol affects not only the parents in an alcoholic family; it also affects the children, both while they are living at home and for years afterwards. Approximately 7 million children younger than eighteen are children of alcoholics (COA) who are living at home. Twenty-one million are the adult children of alcoholics (ACOA) (Lord et al., 1987). Because of family denial, many children of alcoholics may not be aware of the existence of alcoholism in their families.

Children Living in Alcoholic Families

general-ization

Alcoholic families tend to have rigid rules that affect everyone in the family (Wegscheider, 1981). The impact can be especially devastating on the children. The arguments and tensions filling alcoholic homes are often more upsetting than the actual drinking. Children often fear for their own safety, as alcoholism is often a part of child abuse and incest. Children of alcoholics learn three important rules:

3 rules

"Don't talk. Don't trust. Don't feel."

children's roles

In order to survive family chaos, children take on certain roles. According to Sharon Wegscheider (1981), the four roles are hero, scapegoat, mascot, and lost child. The hero, who is usually the oldest child, becomes the family caretaker, the parent surrogate who runs the family. He or she is often a high achiever in school and sports. The scapegoat is the problem child whose problems and troubles draws attention away from the alcoholism. The mascot is carefree and minimizes the alcoholism by clowning and joking around. The lost child withdraws in order to isolate himself or herself from the family turmoil. These roles, however, only superficially resolve the children's emotional problems in dealing with their family's alcoholism. Sooner or later, as adults, they may have to confront the painful consequences.

cause
effect

In attempting to cope, children may develop obsessive or rigid personalities; they frequently have poor self images. They often feel guilty for not being able to "save"

Mommy or Daddy from drinking. A twenty-one-year-old daughter recalled (Desmond, 1987): "When we were kids and our parents were drunk, it was our problem. Somehow it seemed that we should be super people and make our family healthy."

Adult Children of Alcoholics

conse-quences

The consequences of family alcoholism may follow children long after they leave their families. One out of four children of alcoholics become alcoholics themselves in contrast to one out of ten adults in the general population. According to Janet Woititz (1983), adult children of alcoholics may display some or all of the following traits to varying degrees. They:

test question

- Must guess what normal behavior is
- Find it difficult to complete a project
- Lie even when it would be easy to tell the truth

effects

- Judge themselves harshly
- Have difficulty having fun
- Take themselves very seriously
- Have difficulty in intimate relationships
- Overreact to changes beyond their control
- Seek affirmation and approval constantly
- Feel different from others
- Act excessively responsibly or irresponsibly
- Are extremely loyal, even if the loyalty is undeserved
- Lock themselves into courses of actions without considering the consequences

conclu-sion

Because COAs grew up in dysfunctional families, they did not have healthy adult role models. As a consequence, they are likely to repeat many of the same patterns as their parents. Since they were used to caring for their parents, they choose partners who also need their care. They are willing to marry alcoholics or other troubled individuals because they have learned to tolerate unacceptable behavior. Unacceptable behavior may indeed seem quite normal.

From Strong, B. & DeVault, C. (1989). St. Paul: West. *Marriage & Family Experience* 4/e, p. 415.

Although the last sentence of this paragraph indicates that this procedure is a "clear" one, the process is still hard to follow. The next example shows comparing a difficult concept to a common event to clarify the process:

> The lipids you eat come in the form of water-insoluble triglycerides, cholesterol, and phospholipids, with the triglycerides in the majority (composing about 95 percent of dietary fat). Both of the body's systems of transportation—lymph and blood—are watery fluids. Clearly, if the lipids were thrown "as is" in the bloodstream, they would bunch together and form chunks of fat that would then block the arteries.
>
> This is the same thing that happens when you put greasy foods down a kitchen sink: The drain becomes clogged. Luckily, the body is smarter with lipids than you may be with your kitchen grease. While arteries occasionally clog, it is not because pure grease travels through them.

Although the main ideas of both paragraphs are the same, the second one is easier to understand and recall. Two reasons account for this. First, the association between the common event and the more complex process makes it easier to understand. Second, because you can visualize the process, it is easier to recall.

Similarly, **organizational patterns** provide the structure for relating details to the main idea. They vary according to content, topic, and author's purpose. Identifying this pattern often helps you find the main idea and supporting details. Knowing the pattern also helps you relate your background knowledge to the text more easily. And, instead of recalling many separate details, you recall large blocks of information.

Four patterns appear most often in textbooks. However, these patterns are seldom pure. This means features of various patterns often appear together. Still, you can often identify a major pattern.

You determine the pattern based on the content of the information or by the **signal words** within it. They show direction and organization of ideas. They also help you draw conclusions and find the main idea. Table 3.5 lists the four patterns, a short description of each, and corresponding signal words. *Exercise 3.2 asks you to consider reading goals as you find main ideas, mark and label text, summarize main ideas, and identify organizational patterns.*

READ Exercise 3.2

Subject Development. The **subject-development pattern** names the topic. This forms the basis for the collection of details. The details describe and define the topic in various ways. They relate to the topic but might not relate to each other. A biography is an example of subject development. The details (name, age, birthplace, honors) relate to the person they describe. Without the topic, the details support but do not relate to each other. In other words, there's no relationship between

Table 3.5   Organizational Patterns, Descriptions, and Corresponding Signal Words

Pattern	Description	Signal Words
Subject-development	Names topic and gives numerous facts.	(Identified by heading and/or combination of heading and initial sentences.)
List/sequence	Lists main points, orders a list of main points, or presents a problem and steps for its solution.	*First, second, third, and so on; next, then, finally*
Comparison/contrast	Describes how concepts are alike or different.	Comparison—*similarly, both, as well as, like-wise;* contrast—*however, on the other hand, on the contrary, but, instead of, although, yet*
Cause-effect	Shows the result(s) of action(s).	*Therefore, thus, as a result, because*

Example 3.4   Subject Development Organization

References to geology abound in *The German Legends of the Brothers Grimm,* and Jules Verne's *Journey to the Center of the Earth* describes an expedition into the Earth's interior. On one level, the poem "Ozymandias" by Percy B. Shelley deals with the fact that nothing lasts forever and even solid rock eventually disintegrates under the ravages of time and weathering. References to geology can even be found in comics, two of the best known being *B.C.* by Johnny Hart and *The Far Side* by Gary Larson.

From Wicander, R. and Monroe, J. S. (1995). *Essentials of Geology.* Minneapolis: West.

---

a person's age and birthplace. In some cases, you identify this pattern by the kinds of details included in the content. In a text chapter, headings and initial sentences often signal this pattern. To use this pattern, you identify (1) the topic and (2) the relationships between the supporting details and the topic.

In Example 3.4, the topic of the paragraph is *literary references to geology.* The author provides four details to develop the subject. Sentence 1 identifies two stories that refer to geology. Sentence 2 identifies a poem that discusses geology.

List/Sequence. The **list/sequence pattern** notes major points in one of two ways. First, in a list, items appear in a somewhat random order. Thus, all items share equal importance or rank. Grocery lists and New Year's resolutions are common examples of this pattern. Second, if points occur in a specific order, the list is sequenced. Such a step-by-step progression of ideas could show order through alphabetical placement, rank, direction, size, or time. This structure describes solutions to problems, answers to questions, or proofs of thesis statements. Directions for recipes and descriptions of a route are common sequence patterns.

Signal words often show how points or steps progress. You might or might not be told initially how many points in the list will be discussed. The total number of steps or ranks in the sequence might or might not be given.

To use this pattern, you identify (1) the topic, concept, procedure, or problem; (2) the number of points to be discussed or steps in the sequence; and (3) the signal words that indicate the numerical or sequential order of the points or steps. It is a good idea to count and write numbers beside each point or step. This ensures that the number of points or steps you find matches the number said to be in the text. Example 3.5 provides examples of list and sequence patterns.

In the *list* paragraph of Example 3.5, the first sentence identifies the topic as the value of gold. The next two sentences describe what gold is not used for. The following sentence provides a list of uses for gold. The last sentence identifies reasons gold is desired. The items in these lists can be arranged in any order.

In the *sequence* paragraph of Example 3.5, the dates show a time-line, or sequence, of events. They cannot be arranged in any other order. The topic of the paragraph is important dates in the discovery of gold in the United States. Sentence 1 identifies the time and place in which gold was first profitably mined. Sentence 1 also shows, in order, the next two major gold finds. The second sentence tells more about the third gold discovery. The last sentence describes the most profitable time period during the American gold rush.

Comparison/Contrast. The **comparison/contrast pattern** shows connections between objects or concepts. Comparisons show how objects or concepts are alike. Contrasts show how they differ. Thus, comparison/contrast patterns discuss likenesses and differences.

These patterns compare details of an object or concept in one of two ways. First, they compare or contrast one detail of an object or concept with a corresponding detail of another object or concept. Or, second, they list all details about one object or concept and compare or contrast that list to a complete listing of corresponding details about another object or concept.

Example 3.5   List/Sequence Organization

List

Why is gold so highly prized? Certainly not for use in tools or weapons, for it is too soft and pliable to hold a cutting edge. Furthermore, it is too heavy to be practical for most utilitarian purposes (it weighs about twice as much as lead). During most of historic time, gold has been used for jewelry, ornaments, and ritual objects and has served as a symbol of wealth and as a monetary standard. Gold is desired for several reasons: (1) its pleasing appearance, (2) the ease with which it can be worked, (3) its durability, and (4) its scarcity (it is much rarer than silver).

Sequence

In the United States, gold was first profitably mined in North Carolina in 1801 and in Georgia in 1829, but the truly spectacular finds occurred in California in 1848. This latter discovery culminated in the great gold rush of 1849 when tens of thousands of people flocked to California to find riches. Unfortunately, only a few found what they sought. Nevertheless, during the five years from 1848 to 1853, which constituted the gold rush proper, more than $200 million in gold was recovered.

From Wicander, R. and Monroe, J. S. (1995). *Essentials of Geology.* Minneapolis: West.

Example 3.6   Comparison/Contrast Organization

The term theory has various meanings. In colloquial usage, it means a speculative or conjectural view of something—hence the widespread belief that scientific theories are little more than unsubstantiated wild guesses. In scientific usage, however, a theory is a coherent explanation for one or several related natural phenomena that is supported by a large body of objective evidence. From a theory are derived predictive statements that can be tested by observation and/or experiment so that their validity can be assessed. The law of universal gravitation is an example of a theory describing the attraction between masses (an apple and the Earth in the popularized account of Newton and his discovery).

From Wicander, R. and Monroe, J. S. (1995). *Essentials of Geology.* Minneapolis: West.

Some paragraphs contain both comparisons and contrasts; however, the structure often consists of only comparisons or only contrasts. Signal words show whether likenesses or differences are being identified.

To use this pattern, you identify (1) the items that are related and (2) the signal words that show comparisons and contrasts. Example 3.6 provides an example of the comparison/contrast pattern.

Example 3.6 compares and contrasts meanings for the term theory (sentence 1). It compares colloquial usage (sentence 2) with scientific usage (sentence 3). The next sentence describes the kind of information derived from theorists. The last sentence provides an example of a theory.

> ┌───┐
> **Example 3.7**   Cause-Effect/Problem-Solution Organization
>
> Geology has also played an important role in history. Wars have been fought for the control of such natural resources as oil, gas, gold, silver, diamonds, and other valuable minerals. Empires throughout history have risen and fallen on the distribution and exploitation of natural resources. The configuration of the Earth's surface, or its topography, which is shaped by geologic agents, plays a critical role in military tactics. Natural barriers such as mountain ranges and rivers have frequently served as political boundaries.
>
> From Wicander, R. and Monroe, J. S. (1995). *Essentials of Geology.* Minneapolis: West.
> └───┘

Cause-Effect and Problem-Solution. The **cause-effect pattern** shows that an action or response had a preceding basis or reason (cause). It describes what happened (effect) and why it happened. Example 3.7 provides an example of the cause-effect pattern. The **problem-solution pattern** identifies a problem and a remedy or remedies for it. To use this pattern, you identify (1) the effect or problem and (2) the cause(s) of the effect or solutions to the problem.

The paragraph in Example 3.7 describes geology's role in history (sentence 1). The world's natural resources (cause) have resulted in many effects. Sentence 2 identifies war as the way one country controlled important natural resources. The third sentence describes how the desire for natural resources resulted in the rise and fall of empires. The fourth sentence tells how topography affects military tactics. The final sentence explains how natural barriers serve as political boundaries.

Recite: Checking Your Understanding

The best way to check your understanding of the text involves use of the preview outline or map you made before reading (see Chapter 2). As you read, you should try to answer the questions you created as part of your initial survey of the chapter. If you can recite correct answers to these questions, continue reading.

What if you cannot completely answer your questions? One of two things has happened. Either you asked the wrong questions, or you have not understood what you read.

You decide where the problem lies by looking at your questions in light of the content of the passage. Could the content answer your questions? If not, you asked the wrong ones. Your skill in developing purpose-setting questions improves with practice.

Recitation becomes easier and more active when you study with someone. This helps you see how others think of questions and find answers. Another way to practice involves writing your questions on index cards. Again, after reading, determine if your questions were appropriate. Then, write your answers on the back of the card.

If your questions seem inappropriate, create new questions and reread. If your questions appear to be correct but you can't answer them, reread each paragraph carefully. Look for the main idea in each one. Make sure you understand the words as used in the text. Perhaps noting organizational words will help you see relationships that were unclear in the first reading.

Reciting allows you to assess your text marking. If you marked too much, you might not be able to separate important from unimportant information. If you overmark often, use a pencil while marking. This allows you the freedom to rethink your notations. If you overmark only on occasion, you can remark text with a contrasting ink or highlighter. If you marked too little, you might not have enough information to comprehend fully. Thus, you need to reexamine the text and make more specific notations. Be sure you have labeled and summarized all text markings. If you have done so, you can see at a glance where important information lies. If your labels or summaries are unclear, then reread and resummarize your text. These labels should concisely, yet completely, summarize what you've marked. *Exercise 3.3 asks you to evaluate your understanding of the information you summarized in Exercise 3.1.*

READ Exercise 3.3

Write to Learn

Student 1: "I don't see why I should read, mark, and summarize my books at all. I can buy a copy of the notes for this class, and that's all I need."

Student 2: "An old Chinese proverb states, 'Give a man a fish and you feed him for a day. Teach a man to fish and you feed him for a lifetime.'"

On a separate sheet of paper or in your notebook, respond to the following: Does Student 2 agree with Student 1? Explain what Student 2 means.

Review: Making Information Your Own

Reviewing takes many forms. Studying for an exam is the review you probably know best (see Chapter 4 for more information). Other types of review, though less often practiced by many students, are equally—if not more—effective.

One kind of review occurs immediately after class. This brief review (five to ten minutes) involves an active inspection of your class notes. As you review the notes, mentally replay the lecture. If you write only on the front sides of your pages, you can even lay out the notes so that you can see everything at once. Now you can see the outline and scope of the information. This might not have been clear at the start of the class. As you review, you see relationships among the information. You insert missing information. You mark unclear statements so you can seek other sources of information or ask questions about them before the next class.

Another five-to-ten minute review should occur just before your next class. This review allows you to refresh your recall and mentally regain your place in the course content. To make this review more active, focus on lecture method as well as on course content. If your class features a lecture format, your review summarizes what has occurred thus far. Based on your text previews and readings, you predict which topics might be covered next. Review for a discussion class differs because you must take an especially active role. Your review focuses on questions you develop through reading or thinking about course content and the direction of comments in the discussion. Lab courses help you apply or practice what you learn. Here, you review results of experiments or practice sessions and analyze your performance to determine if you need to alter your efforts.

Frequent short reviews boost your memory more than a single lengthy review does. The more often you hear or read something, the easier it is to recall. The "Ebbinghaus curve," or curve of forgetting (see Figure 3.3), shows the relationship between time and recall. The graph compares amount recalled with length of time since the material was presented. Note that after one exposure, most information is lost within the first 24 hours. This curve explains why you are sometimes confused by notes or text labels that seemed clear when you wrote them. Reviewing information within 24 hours of the first time you first see or hear it helps you remember more efficiently.

Postlecture reading is another way to review. By the time a lecture ends, you should have seen lecture information at least twice. First,

Figure 3.3   The Curve of Forgetting

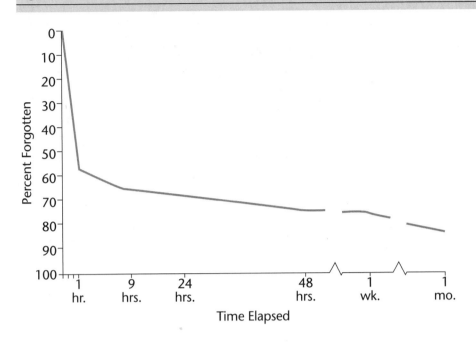

you either read or previewed the chapter. Your second exposure was during the lecture. Postlecture reading helps you focus on information stressed in the lecture. If you completely read the chapter before the lecture, review the areas that confused you or that were stressed in class. If you previewed the text, this final reading provides information to support the main ideas of the lecture. Postlecture reading fills the gaps in your knowledge.

SQ3R: Putting It All Together

Until now, you, like many students, might have approached a reading assignment by simply opening the text and getting started. Now you know that reading involves more than just looking at words on a page—a lot more. It requires your having the motivation and a method for surveying text, strategies for understanding what you read, and a technique for making that information your own. You also need a way to check your progress so that you always know where you are and what you need to do to finish your reading task. The entire process seems almost overwhelming, doesn't it? How will you ever complete it and know that you've done so?

Example 3.8   Notetaking System Applied to Characters
in *After the First Death*

Code Directory Inside Front Cover

I – innocence

B – bravery

L – love

P – physical

I – intellectual

E – emotional

S – social

Code Directory Inside Back Cover

I   129, 144, 183
B   146, 211,
L   145,

Kate
P – 68, 144
I – 68, 69
E – 68, 69, 99, 105, 123,
S – 69, 129–130

Page 68 Coded

P   . . . She was blond, fair skinned, slender, no
weight problems, had managed to avoid
adolescent acne. A healthy body with one
P   exception: the weak bladder. . . . cheer-
leader, prom queen, captain of the girls'
P   swimming team, budding actress in the
Drama Club. . . . But there were other Kate
Forresters, and she wondered about them
sometimes. The Kate Forrester who awoke
E   suddenly at four in the morning and for no
reason at all couldn't fall back to sleep. The
Kate Forrester who couldn't stand the sight
of blood. . . .

Page 69 Coded

She wanted to find somebody to love, to love
forever . . . That question brought up another   **E**
Kate Forrester disguise. Kate the manipulator
. . . Getting straight A's from Mr. Kelliher in   **E**
math and barely lifting a finger to do so but
knowing how to smile at him, feign interest
. . . She'd always been an excellent student in   **I**
math. She didn't know why she'd gone out of
her way to charm Mr. Kelliher. Just as she didn't
know why she used the same charm to win
the role of Emily in the Drama Club's presenta-
tion of *Our Town*. She knew she could play the
part, she was certain of her talent. . . . Gene
Sherman. Kate had been enthralled by him . . .   **S**
until they sat together during a lunch break . . .

From Tomlinson, L.M. (1997). A coding system for notemarking in literature: Preparation for journal writing, class participation, and essay tests. *Journal of Adolescent & Adult Literacy*, 40 (6), 468–476.

SQ3R, a reading plan developed by Francis Robinson, helps you check and control your reading. Better yet, SQ3R is a process you now know. Chapter 2 focused on the first two steps of the plan: **s**urveying and **q**uestioning and this chapter addressed the three Rs of the plan: **r**eading, **r**eciting, and **r**eviewing.

Reading Narrative Text

The use of SQ3R depends on the kinds of headings and subheadings found in subject-area texts. You need another way to read short stories, literature, and other forms of **narrative text** that have no headings or subheadings. Tomlinson (1997) created a six-step process for taking notes from literature. It lets you progress from simple recall of details to a deeper understanding. Step 1 suggests that you give a code letter to each theme, character, and concept you need to trace throughout the text. In Step 2, you create a directory of your codes either in the front of your book or in your notebook. Consistent use of a code for a particular concept simplifies the process. In Step 3, list the code letters in your notebook, leaving space between the letters. In step 4, you read your text and place the appropriate code letter beside relevant information. List the page number next to the code number you have already written in your notebook in Step 5. Step 6, the last one, suggests you keep a notebook page for each major theme, character, or concept and write a brief summary or make notes about key details. You should also note text page numbers for future reference. Example 3.8 contains an example of this notetaking system. *Exercise 3.4 asks you to use this system to take notes from narrative text.*

Chapter Summary Exercise

On a separate sheet of paper or in your notebooks, complete the chapter summary by filling in the blanks with the following words:

recite	subject-development
overmark	passage
mark	list/sequence
main ideas	signal words
label	comparison/contrast
organizational patterns	cause-effect
topic	checking your understanding
undermark	paragraph
details	problem-solution

Recognizing main ideas is an essential part of reading. To understand and recall _____ more easily, you also need to _____ and _____ them. Finding the _____ and

_____ of a paragraph or passage helps you identify the main idea. When marking, you need to decide how much is too much. Often students either _____ or _____. Either one leads to less-than-useful notes. Labeling main ideas in each _____ in a passage is the first step in labeling the main idea of the _____ itself. Finding _____ also helps you recognize what to mark and label. _____ help you identify patterns of organization. There are four types of organization: _____, _____, _____, and _____. Text marking and labeling also aids you in _____ of the text. When you read (mark and label) and _____ main ideas, you are ready for the final step of the SQ3R process—review.

Terms

Terms appear in the order in which they occur in the chapter.

text labels
topic
main idea
details
topic sentence
organizational patterns
signal words
subject-development pattern
list/sequence pattern
comparison/contrast pattern
cause-effect pattern
problem-solution pattern
SQ3R
narrative text

Chapter Review

Answer the following questions briefly but completely on a separate sheet of paper or in your notebook:

1. What is the relationship between text marking and text labels?
2. How are text labels similar to and different from lecture notes? How are they similar to and different from topic sentences?
3. List and define the types of organizational patterns. Find examples of each in any textbook you currently use.
4. How does summarizing paragraphs help you summarize passages?
5. What do you do first when your comprehension fails? What other strategies might you try?
6. The Curve of Forgetting shows that review right before or after taking notes improves recall, so why do most students wait until right before an exam to review notes?
7. Identify three times during a typical class day when you have at least five minutes to read over notes you have recently taken. Be specific.
8. List the steps in SQ3R and identify the purpose of each.
9. How does taking notes from narrative text differ from taking notes from subject-area text?

Exercises

Exercise 3.1   On a separate sheet of paper or in your notebook, create a goal-setting question for each title, heading, or subheading in the passage below. Identify the main idea and important details of each paragraph by marking key words. Next, write a text label that summarizes each paragraph. Then, write a summary for each section and a summary for the entire passage.

How Advertisements Work

The word *advertise* originally meant to take note or to consider. By the 1700s, that meaning had changed. To advertise meant to persuade. "If we consider democracy not just as a political system," says Daniel J. Boorstin, "but as a set of institutions which do aim to make everything available to everybody, it would not be an overstatement to describe advertising as the characteristic rhetoric of democracy."

Common Characteristics

Boorstin says that advertising in America shares three characteristics: repetition, style, and ubiquity.

Repetition. When Robert Bonner bought the *New York Ledger* in 1851, he wanted to advertise his newspaper in the competing *New York Herald,* owned by James Gordon Bennett. Bennett limited all of his advertisers to the same size typeface, so Bonner paid for an entire page of the *Herald,* across which he repeated the message "Bring home the *New York Ledger* tonight." This is an early example of the widespread practice of repeating a simple message for effect.

An Advertising Style. At first, advertising adopted a plain, direct style. Advertising pioneer Claude Hopkins, says Boorstin, claimed, "Brilliant writing has no place in advertising. A unique style takes attention from the subject . . . One should be natural and simple . . . in fishing for buyers, as in fishing for bass, one should not reveal the hook."

The plain-talk tradition is a foundation of what advertisers call modern advertising. But advertising today often adopts a style of hyperbole, making large claims for products. Boorstin calls this "tall talk."

The tall-talk ad is in the P. T. Barnum tradition of advertising. Barnum was a carnival barker and later impresario who lured customers to his circus acts with fantastic claims. You may recognize this approach in some of the furniture and car ads on television, as an announcer screams at you that you have only a few days left until all the chairs or all of the cars will be gone.

Both plain talk and tall talk combine, Boorstin says, to create advertising's new myth:

> *This is the world of neither true nor false—of the statement that 60 percent of the physicians who expressed a choice said that our brand of aspirin would be more effective in curing a simple headache than any other brand . . . It is not untrue, and yet, in its connotation it is not exactly true.*

Ubiquity. In America, advertising can be and is everywhere. Advertisers are always looking for new places to catch consumers' attention. Ads appear on shopping carts, on video screens at sports stadiums, atop parking meters.

> *The ubiquity of advertising is, of course, just another effect of our uninhibited efforts to use all the media to get all sorts of information to everybody everywhere. Since the places to be filled are everywhere, the amount of advertising is not determined by the needs of advertising, but by the opportunities for advertising, which become unlimited.*

In some cases this ubiquity works to advertising's disadvantage. Many advertisers shy away from radio and TV because the ads are grouped so closely together. In 1986, in an attempt to attract more advertisers, TV began selling the "split–30" ad, which fits two 15-second ads into a 30-second spot. Even 10-second ads are available. Wherever these shorter commercials are sold, the station runs twice as many ads for different products, crowding the commercial time even more.

Grabbing Attention

To sell the products, advertisers must catch your eye or your ear or your heart (preferably all three). A study by the Harvard Graduate School of Business Administration reported that the average American is exposed to 500 ads a day. With so many ads competing for your attention, the advertiser must first get you to read, listen to, or watch one ad instead of another. "The immediate goal of advertising [is to] tug at our psychological shirt sleeves and slow us down long enough for a word or two about whatever is being sold."

The Psychology of Ads

You make your buying decisions based on several other sources of information besides advertising: friends, family, and your own experience, for example. To influence your choices, the advertising message must appeal to you for some reason, as you sift through the ads to make judgments and choose products. Humanities and human sciences professor Jib Fowles in his book *Mass Advertising as Social Forecast* enumerated 15 appeals, which he calls an "inventory of human motives" that advertisers commonly use in their commercials:

1. *Need for sex.* Surprisingly, Fowles found that only 2 percent of the television ads he surveyed used this appeal. It may be too blatant, he concluded, and often detracts from the product.
2. *Need for affiliation.* The largest number of ads use this approach: You are looking for friendship. Advertisers can also use this negatively, to make you worry that you'll lose friends if you don't use a certain product.
3. *Need to nurture.* Every time you see a puppy or a kitten or a child, the appeal is to your maternal or paternal instincts.
4. *Need for guidance.* A father or mother figure can appeal to your desire for someone to care for you, so you won't have to worry. Betty Crocker is a good example.
5. *Need to aggress.* We all have had a desire to get even, and some ads give you this satisfaction.
6. *Need to achieve.* The ability to accomplish something difficult and succeed identifies the product with winning. Sports figures as spokespersons project this image.
7. *Need to dominate.* The power we lack is what we can look for in a commercial: "Master the possibilities."

8. *Need for prominence.* We want to be admired and respected, to have high social status. Tasteful china and classic diamonds offer this potential.

9. *Need for attention.* We want people to notice us; we want to be looked at. Cosmetics are a natural for this approach.

10. *Need for autonomy.* Within a crowded environment, we want to be singled out, to be "a breed apart." This can also be used negatively: You may be left out if you don't use a particular product.

11. *Need to escape.* Flight is very appealing; you can imagine adventures you cannot have. The idea of escape is pleasurable.

12. *Need to feel safe.* To be free from threats, to be secure is the appeal of many insurance and bank ads.

13. *Need for aesthetic sensations.* Beauty attracts us, and classic art or dance makes us feel creative, enhanced.

14. *Need to satisfy curiosity.* Facts support our belief that information is quantifiable and numbers and diagrams make our choices seem scientific.

15. *Physiological needs.* Fowles defines sex (item no. 1) as a biological need, and so he classifies our need to sleep, eat, and drink in this category. Advertisements for juicy pizza are especially appealing late at night.

From Biagi, S. (1996). *Media. Impact: An Invitation to Mass Media.* Belmont, CA: Wadsworth, pp. 219–222.

Exercise 3.2   On a separate sheet of paper or in your notebook, use the Sample Chapter "Opportunities to Work in the Theater" (found at the end of the text), to complete the following:

1. Reexamine the questions you asked for reading the chapter in Exercise 2.4.

2. Mark the important information within each paragraph.

3. Create text labels that identify and organize important information.

4. Summarize the main idea of each paragraph.

5. Identify four paragraphs (one for each type) that show organizational patterns discussed in this chapter.

Exercise 3.3   On a separate sheet of paper or in your notebook, list the questions you formed during your preview of the information in Exercise 3.1. Compare your text summaries with the questions you formed during preview to check your understanding. If your notes answer your question, write the answer below the question. If not, use the strategies discussed in this chapter to perfect your understanding until you can correctly answer each question.

Exercise 3.4   On a separate sheet of paper or in your notebook, following the six steps in Tomlinson's notetaking system for narrative text to read and take notes on the short story from Chapter 5's READ Keys.

Web Exercise

A variety of information related to reading college texts is available on the World Wide Web. For this exercise, access one of the following Web sites or find a site of your own about reading textbooks:

Six Reading Myths from Dartmouth University Learning Enhancement Services:
http://www.dartmouth.edu/admin/acskills/success/reading.html (download from this site).

Efficient Reading at the University of Melbourne, Australia (Learning Skills Unit):
http://www.services.unimelb.edu.au/lsu/resources/flyers/efficientreading.pdf

How Can I Organize my Textbook Reading? Or Unraveling the Textbook Maze at Purdue University Center for the School of Liberal Arts:
http://www.sla.purdue.edu/studentserv/learningcenter/handouts/txtvid94.htm

Study Guides and Strategies (click on Reading Skills section) ISS—Learning Center at the University of St. Thomas, Minnesota:
http://www.iss.stthomas.edu/studyguides/

On a separate sheet of paper or in your notebook, create a chart that compares the information in this chapter with the information at the Web site you accessed. Then, below the chart, create a list of suggestions or steps for reading texts.

READ: Keys

READ: Keys Activity Pretest

Rate each of the following words according to your knowledge of them.

Word	Stage 0 *I don't know this word.*	Stage 1 *I've seen this word but I know nothing of its meaning.*	Stage 2 *I've seen this word and can make associations with it.*	Stage 3 *I know this word.*
1. muses				
2. enigmatic				
3. aura				
4. mythology				
5. simultaneously				
6. insatiable				
7. equivalency				
8. amiable				
9. exorcism				
10. unfathomable				

READ: Keys Activity 3.1

Read the following essay and keep track of your reading time.
Note: Italicized and underlined words will be used in Exercise 5.8.

The Most Precious Gift

Sometimes I do wonder where I came from, **_muses_** Robert Howard Allen of West Tennessee, who had never seen the inside of a classroom until, in 1981, at age 32, he entered college. No, he was not a late-blooming genius; but last May, after just a decade of school, he graduated from Vanderbilt University in Nashville with a master's degree and a Ph.D. in English. A gentle, unworldly spirit who plays the _banjo_ and loves to make puns, he adds with an **_enigmatic_** _grin,_ "Maybe I just fell out of the sky."

When Allen first appeared on the campus of Bethel College, a small Presbyterian school in McKenzie, 15 miles from his backwoods home, administrators were even more baffled. Here was a grown man who had never been to grammar school or high school, yet he had "blown the lid off" his college placement tests. He stood 6 feet tall, with unkempt red hair, and his tattered sweater was held together with safety pins. There were holes in his shoes and his front teeth were gone. He had rarely set foot outside Carroll _County,_ 120 miles west of Nashville, where he was born. He lived in a _ramshackle_ farmhouse—one of three homes in the tiny _hamlet_ of Rosser—without indoor plumbing. He had never ridden a bicycle or been inside a _movie_ theater or out on a date.

With an **_aura_** of innocence, however, Allen's blue eyes sparkled from behind his steel-rimmed glasses as if he had a secret. And it turned out that he did—a secret that amounts to a triumph of faith.

From the age of 7, Robert Allen read books. Not just several books or even a few hundred, but thousands of every description—from Donald Duck comics to the Bible, from Homer to James Joyce—to the point where his head was filled with history and classical literature. The scope of his learning was far greater than that of any professor at Bethel, where he was invited to skip most of his freshman courses and enter as a sophomore. Yet, having spent his whole life in virtual isolation with elderly relatives, Allen himself had no idea how special he was.

He turned up at Bethel on a _whim_. "I'd started my own upholstery business in back of the house," he recalls, "but when the 1980 recession came on, there was no more work. So I thought I'd give education a whirl. I didn't think I could succeed at it, though. I just assumed that people in college knew more than I did."

In three years, he graduated _summa cum laude_.

Without realizing it, Robert Allen had proved the power of reading to transform an individual life. In circumstances that otherwise would have been unbearable, he had read as an unconscious act of sheer survival. "Books were my great comfort," he says simply. "They were my pastime and my playmates." Reading whatever he could get his hands on, he traveled freely across time and space, meeting the world's greatest philosophers and poets down through the ages.

"He's at home in mythological Babylon and in eighth-century Judea," says Dr. William Ramsay, one of his Bethel advisers. "He became a citizen of the world without ever leaving Tennessee."

"Robert retains everything," says Professor Vereen Bell, who teaches English at Vanderbilt, "so his head is just full of all this historical and mythological stuff that he has accumulated. In a sense, he missed the 20th century. He's in a kind of time warp, and I think he forever will be."

Allen's triumph had its seeds in suffering. His parents were divorced a few months before he was born. He yearned for his father but, to this day, had never seen him. His mother, Hazel, worked as a waitress and all but ignored him. "She was in the generation between the farmers and me," he says, "so I think she felt caught in that condition." When Robert was 6, his mother abandoned him, running off with a traveling shoe salesman. She left him to be raised by elderly relatives—his grandfather and three great-aunts and a great-uncle—living in the same household.

Even today, Allen can express his youthful pain only through his poetry, as when he writes that the mother "had no love for her stray mistake of a child" and that his grandmother, "died just one spring later, too soon to fill my childhood with any love." It was his Uncle Eddie Jones, his guardian, who decreed that school was "a waste of time" and blocked authorities from enrolling him.

"I never entirely understood it," Allen says, adding that he was also told that his father might return, "to kidnap me, even though there was no evidence that he even knew I existed." In any event, he adds, "They kept me home. I really was pretty much isolated."

The county sent teachers for the homebound twice weekly for a year, but from age 7, the boy's formal education was over. In a house where at least one of his relatives was always sick or dying, growing up without friends, Allen listened to endless family stories, and Aunt Bevie Jones, Uncle Eddie's wife, began reading to him. "She had gone up to the eighth grade," he says, "but that was the only education in our family." Aunt Bevie taught him to read; his grandfather taught him to write; and the boy, in turn, read the King James Bible to his blind Aunt Ida, going through it twice from cover to cover.

Allen's male ancestors had been farmers, but since the '30s the men had become carpenters and house painters. The boy was destined to pick up these trades; but at age 12, while he was helping care for sick relatives at home, he began reading an old set of Shakespeare's works. "I opened it up and just about read it through at a sitting," he says, and today he'll quote long passages from *King Lear* and *The Tempest*—to name just two of his favorites—at a moment's notice.

Hungry for more, he began picking up books at yard sales for pennies apiece—words of **mythology,** history, poetry, and anything else he could find. By his early 20s, Robert had some 2000 volumes and a goal: "I followed a vague, overall plan, which I more or less fulfilled," he recalls, "to study literature in the context of history from the earliest times to the present."

When he saw the Carroll County Library in nearby Huntingdon, it was like discovering gold. "Sometimes his Grandfather Jim and Aunt Bevie came with him," recalls Claudine Halpers, the staffer who eventually encouraged him to try for college. "They showed up every week or two, regular as clockwork. They were poor but not ashamed. Robert was his own person—unassuming, but very bright with a keen sense of humor."

On the shelves, Allen found the complete set of Will and Ariel Durant's *The Story of Civilization* and spent the next two years wading through its 10 massive volumes, ***simultaneously*** reading histories and classics for each time period. Out of pure enjoyment, he worked his way through the entire library, also teaching himself to read Greek and French to better absorb original versions. The words of Milton, Burns, Keats, Whitman, Wordsworth, and other poets continued to feed his ***insatiable*** appetite for knowledge and what he now calls "language used to its highest potential."

At age 30, Robert Allen took a high school ***equivalency*** test and easily earned his diploma. Two years later, when Bethel College officials saw his placement scores, they eased his way with a work-study grant combining scholarship funds and a campus job.

By 1984, after three years as an ***amiable,*** older and unquestionably "different" figure on the Bethel campus, he topped his senior class with straight A's in all but typing. He scored a 3.92 out of a possible 4.0 grade-point average. As graduate presents, the faculty bought him his first suit—which he accepted reluctantly, saying they should give it to "someone who really needs it"—and a set of new front teeth. Aunt Bevie, by now 77, attended the ceremonies where he received his diploma. The newspaper ran a story about him.

Accepting a fellowship from Vanderbilt, with an eye toward ultimately teaching, Robert Allen packed up his belongings that fall and moved with Aunt Bevie to Nashville. It was his first venture beyond the green hills of West Tennessee and his entrance into the modern world of a "big city" where he took his first elevator ride.

During the first half of 1991, aside from attending graduation ceremonies at Vanderbilt, Robert Allen taught a semester of English at Bethel College. During the summer, he continued to live alone in McKenzie. There, he set aside a copy of *War and Peace* one afternoon to talk about the future. "I'd like to continue teaching and writing poetry," he told me. "In the past year I've been turning family history into a long series of poems, loosely linked together." What does the Ph.D. mean to him? "Well," he shrugged, "it means I can get a job." Any thoughts of eventually getting married? "No," he said with a smile—as if that were a possibility too far down the road to see.

"Robert is struggling with great courage to make himself more a part of the contemporary world," says Professor Bell, "so his story is going to go on and on."

At the doorway of his small, rented home, Robert Allen, age 42, stands with his Tolstoy edition in one hand, waving with the other. He smiles his enigmatic smile before turning and disappearing, at least for a while, into a distant time and place. Reading is what saved him; writing poetry about his family is both an ***exorcism*** of painful experiences and a bold journey of personal evolution. His secret seems to lie at some ***unfathomable*** depth, as if he were not only destined but determined, to finally solve the mystery for himself—to keep on falling out of the sky.

From Whittemore, H. (1991). The Most Precious Gift, *Parade Magazine,* Dec 22, 1991, page 4–6.

1695 words / _____ minutes = _____ words per minute.

Calculate your reading time by dividing the number of words in the article by the amount of time it took to read it. Then mark your reading time on the chart located on page 338.

READ: Keys Activity 3.2

On a separate sheet of paper or in your notebook, answer the following questions about the essay you just read:

1. When was Robert Howard Allen born?

    a. 1949

    b. 1953

    c. 1960

    d. 1981

2. How many total years of schooling did Allen have?

    a. 5

    b. 10

    c. 15

    d. 20

3. According to the article, which of Allen's relatives had the most extensive education?

    a. Uncle Eddie

    b. Aunt Bevie

    c. Grandfather Jim

    d. Aunt Ida

4. Who wrote *King Lear* and *The Tempest?*

    a. Keats

    b. Burns

    c. Wordsworth

    d. Shakespeare

5. Who were Will and Ariel Durant?

   a. historians

   b. faculty at Bethel College

   c. poets

   d. Allen's relatives

6. Who wrote *War and Peace?*

   a. Whitman

   b. Shakespeare

   c. Professor Bell

   d. Tolstoy

7. According to the article, what was Allen's secret?

   a. He had never been to school.

   b. He had never been out of the state of Tennessee.

   c. He did not have indoor plumbing.

   d. He read books.

8. When did Allen graduate from Vanderbilt?

   a. at age 30

   b. in 1984

   c. in 1991

   d. in 1981

9. Based on the article, which of the following does NOT describe Allen?

   a. He is a musician.

   b. He is a poet.

   c. He grew up as an only child.

   d. He is a painter.

10. Based on the article, which of the following does NOT describe Allen's family?

   a. His mother abandoned him.

   b. His father was a kidnapper.

   c. His grandfather knew how to write.

   d. His Aunt Ida had a physical disability.

READ: Keys Activity 3.3

Examine each of the numbered phrases or sentences and complete the following on a separate sheet of paper or in your notebook.

(a) Write the boldfaced, italicized word. Identify one or two words that you can put in the place of the boldfaced, italicized word without changing the meaning of the phrase or sentence and write this synonym or synonymous phrase (words that have the same meaning) beside the word. (b) Identify the part of speech of this word as used in the sentence. (c) Look up the boldfaced, italicized word in a dictionary and write the dictionary definition. How does this compare with the definition from context? (d) List the parts of speech this word can sometimes be. (e) Write a complete sentence with each word.

1. Sometimes I do wonder where I came from, ***muses*** Robert Howard Allen of West Tennessee, who had never seen the inside of a classroom until, in 1981, at age 32, he entered college.

2. A gentle, unworldly spirit who plays the banjo and loves to make puns, he adds with an ***enigmatic*** grin, "Maybe I just fell out of the sky."

3. With an ***aura*** of innocence, however, Allen's blue eyes sparkled from behind his steel-rimmed glasses as if he had a secret.

4. Hungry for more, he began picking up books at yard sales for pennies apiece—words of ***mythology,*** history, poetry and anything else he could find.

5. On the shelves, Allen found the complete set of Will and Ariel Durant's *The Story of Civilization* and spent the next two years wading through its 10 massive volumes, ***simultaneously*** reading histories and classics for each time period.

6. The words of Milton, Burns, Keats, Whitman, Wordsworth, and other poets continued to feed his ***insatiable*** appetite for knowledge and what he now calls "language used to its highest potential."

7. At age 30, Robert Allen took a high school ***equivalency*** test and easily earned his diploma.

8. By 1984, after three years as an ***amiable,*** older and unquestionably "different" figure on the Bethel campus, he topped his senior class with straight A's in all but typing.

9. Reading is what saved him; writing poetry about his family is both an ***exorcism*** of painful experiences and a bold journey of personal evolution.

10. His secret seems to lie at some ***unfathomable*** depth, as if he were not only destined but determined, to finally solve the mystery for himself—to keep on falling out of the sky.

READ: Keys Activity 3.4

In Part A, use the following list of words to fill in the blanks. In Part B, use the information from Part A to complete the analogies.

Part A

superficial	mysterious	deep	guesses
considers	addition	ordinary	elimination
impression	friendly	certainty	restrained
unlikable	legend	equal	correspondingly
greedy	truth	different	separately

Synonym	Word	Antonym
_____	**1.** muses	_____
_____	**2.** enigmatic	_____
_____	**3.** aura	_____
_____	**4.** mythology	_____
_____	**5.** simultaneously	_____
_____	**6.** insatiable	_____
_____	**7.** equivalency	_____
_____	**8.** amiable	_____
_____	**9.** exorcism	_____
_____	**10.** unfathomable	_____

Part B

1. _____ : greedy :: equal : different

2. deep : _____ :: exorcism : elimination

3. mysterious : enigmatic : _____ : mythology

4. aura : certainty :: muses : _____

5. correspondingly : separately :: insatiable : _____

6. equivalency : _____ :: amiable : friendly

7. ordinary : mysterious :: legend : _____

8. unlikable : amiable :: exorcism : _____

9. superficial : unfathomable :: _____ : simultaneously

10. think : _____ :: insatiable : greedy

READ: Keys Activity Posttest

Rate each of the following words according to your knowledge of them.

Word	Stage 0 *I don't know this word.*	Stage 1 *I've seen this word but I know nothing of its meaning.*	Stage 2 *I've seen this word and can make associations with it.*	Stage 3 *I know this word.*
1. muses				
2. enigmatic				
3. aura				
4. mythology				
5. simultaneously				
6. insatiable				
7. equivalency				
8. amiable				
9. exorcism				
10. unfathomable				

Memory and Test-Taking

Objectives

After you finish this chapter, you will be able to do the following:

1. Identify strategies for coping with test anxiety.
2. Identify the importance of synthesizing information for review.
3. Identify how rehearsal and memory techniques increase depth and permanence of learning.
4. Apply strategies for reading objective tests, subjective tests, and final exams.
5. Demonstrate how to read and review a returned exam.

Chapter Outline

I. Coping with test anxiety
   A. Taking care of your health
   B. Making test anxiety work *for* you

II. Reviewing for exams
   A. The importance of synthesis
   B. Constructing charts

III. Maximizing learning
   A. Rehearsal formats
      1. Spaced study
      2. Cramming
      3. Study groups or partners
      4. Overlearning
   B. Memory techniques
      1. Acronyms and acrostics
      2. Location
      3. Word games
      4. Mental and physical imagery

IV. Strategies for reading and taking exams
   A. Objective tests
   B. Subjective tests
   C. Final exams

V. Reading and reviewing returned tests

Sailing into Uncertain Territory

In the Middle Ages, sailors used a chart called a *portolano* to navigate the Mediterranean Sea. These maps showed the outlines of coasts and harbors. As sailors traveled, they recorded where they'd gone. Mapmakers gradually added this information to maps. Thus, *portolanos* showed all the areas known to sailors of that day. To show that there was more to the world than had been explored, mapmakers sketched ferocious-looking dragons on the edges of maps.

The dragons served as threats to the sailors who took them literally—they thought that dragons really awaited them in unexplored regions. These sailors let their fears immobilize them. They never went beyond what they knew to be safe. For them, the old saying "Nothing ventured, nothing gained" was all too true.

For other sailors, the dragons symbolized challenge. These sailors saw the dragons as almost a dare. They wanted to be the first "to go where no man has gone before." The dragons spurred them to greater adventures and new insights.

> **Backward,
> Turn backward,
> O Time,
> In your flight
> And tell me
> Just one thing
> I studied last night.**
>
> —Hobart Brown

In many ways, students and tests resemble the sailors and dragons of long ago. Many students see tests as horrible fates. They feel exams are always lurking around the corner, waiting for the right time to strike. Other students see tests as opportunities to prove their worth. They seek the chance to slay the dragon and win the day.

Fortunately, there exists a safety net for those students who fear the words "Close your books and take out a sheet of paper." Freedom from danger rests in coping with test anxiety and preparing for exams. This chapter helps you sail smoothly through any exam you face. It provides tips for coping with test anxiety, exam preparation techniques, strategies for reading and taking exams, and a method for reading and reviewing returned tests.

Coping with Test Anxiety

Taking tests bothers everyone, from new freshmen to graduate students. Feeling insecure or fearful before, during, or after an exam is called **test anxiety.** It is a common experience. Test anxiety, when unchecked, impairs your ability to read and judge information accurately.

The *Test Anxiety Scale* (TAS) identifies students whose anxiety hurts their performance on tests. How anxious are you? Take the TAS and find out. *It appears in Exercise 4.1.*

READ Exercise 4.1

When you experience anxiety, everything worries you. You need an oasis where you can withdraw from **stress,** your physical and emotional response to demands made on you. However, there seldom exists the chance to leave school and travel to a deserted isle during test time. Because you can't run from stress, you need to learn to cope. Coping results in peace of mind.

Taking Care of Your Health

Staying mentally and physically fit helps you cope with test anxiety, or stress. You're more likely to feel stress if your mind or body is tired. You'll also feel less in control and more reluctant to face the exam. Thus, you need to get a full night's sleep before an exam. Rest helps you think more clearly and confidently.

In the same way, you need to eat something before taking an exam. Even if you have an early-morning test, don't skip breakfast. Your body needs the energy food supplies. However, don't overeat. When you do, most of your blood rushes to your digestive tract, and less is left for mental processing. As a result, you'll feel sluggish rather than energetic. Anxiety is an enemy of physical and mental well-being.

Making Test Anxiety Work *for* You

Most people only think of the negative form of stress—distress. But positive stress—**eustress**—is stress that challenges you to do your best. Actors and athletes use it to improve their performances. For instance, Juergen Klinsmann, a striker on the German national soccer team, uses the time just before a game to ignite his competitive fires (Gower, 1991). As a result, Klinsmann's team has been a World Cup champion.

Likewise, when you direct and control stress, you think more clearly and quickly. This motivating anxiety carries you through the situation. You turn distress into eustress by using coping strategies (see Table 4.1) and by being prepared.

Write to Learn

On a separate sheet of paper or in your notebook, describe your biggest fear in test taking and how you can best cope with this anxiety.

Table 4.1   Coping Techniques

If You Feel Anxious Before or After a Test:

1. *Try exercise.* You don't have to be a professional athlete to use exercise for handling stress. Any physical activity, from strenuous sports to simply walking around the block, helps. Exercise releases tension and increases stamina.

2. *Take a class.* Many schools offer courses in relaxation techniques, time management, study skills, and test taking. Even if your college offers no such courses, your campus library should have books or tapes on all these topics. You can also find information about these topics on the Internet.

3. *Talk to others.* Discussing your feelings and fears with others can control stress. Counselors, teachers, and fellow students can react to your comments and offer suggestions and advice.

4. *Avoid cramming.* Last-minute study sessions tend to increase test anxiety and stress. Use distributed practice over an extended period. This helps you feel prepared, rather than panicked.

5. *Visualize success.* Picture yourself calmly walking into class and sitting down. Imagine yourself listening carefully to verbal instructions. See yourself preview the exam. Watch yourself take the test, cool and confident. See yourself thinking about information and recalling it accurately. Watch yourself complete the test and turn it in. Picture yourself leaving the room, satisfied with your performance.

6. *Relax.* Sit or lie in a comfortable position with your eyes closed. Picture yourself in a place where you felt relaxed in the past. Breathe deeply, hold for one count, and exhale. Flex and relax your toes, feet, ankles, legs, and so forth. Let your thoughts drift. Allow them to come and go freely. Remain calm and quiet. If possible, stay this way for at least 20 minutes. Open your eyes and savor the feeling of relaxation.

7. *Use self-talk.* Self-talk (see Chapter 1) is one time when talking to yourself makes sense. It involves stopping negative thoughts and repeating positive statements to yourself. Prepare for an exam question with talk like this: "I know this information. Worry won't help me, so I'm stopping it now." After the exam, reinforce your coping with talk like this: "It worked! I tried every question. It wasn't as bad as I feared. Me and my imagination! When I control it, I control my fear."

If You Feel Anxious During a Test:

1. *Pause and breathe deeply.* Brief breaks ease tension. Turn your test over. Close your eyes. As you slowly inhale, say, "calm." As you slowly exhale, say "down." Repeat. Once you feel calm, return to the test.

2. *Answer a question you know.* This gives you confidence in your knowledge. Such confidence reduces stress.

3. *Ask for information.* Questions that confuse you increase stress. The problem might not reside with you. Perhaps the question is ambiguous. What's unclear to you might be unclear to others, so asking your instructor for additional information is a good idea.

4. *Use self-talk.* Face each question by saying, "I can meet this challenge. One question at a time, I can complete this test. I won't think about fear—I'll just do what I have to do." Avoid feeling panicked by repeating, "Stay focused. What does the question ask of me? This exam won't last forever—life goes on." Chapter 1 provides more information about self-talk.

Reviewing for Exams

Reviewing is more than looking over notes or memorizing facts for a test. **Review** is the active process that converts text and lecture information into personal understanding. Reviewing, then, is the way that you think about and learn information. Where and when you review contributes to the effectiveness of your review. What information you review and how you organize it helps you synthesize for greater understanding.

Reviewing for exams involves three tasks. First, judge yourself and the information. What are your strengths and weaknesses? What are the content and logic of the information? Next, analyze and synthesize. Focus on relationships between information. What does the text emphasize? Why? What does the instructor emphasize? Why? How does the text compare and contrast with lecture notes? To adequately organize the information, create a **synthesis** of text information and lecture notes.

The Importance of Synthesis

Synthesis is a way to combine information from various sources. When you synthesize for review, you determine how lecture and text information fit together. Perhaps the lecture summarizes text information. Maybe the text provides background knowledge for concepts in the lecture. The text might provide opposing viewpoints, or it might support the lecture completely. Whatever the relationship, you no longer have text information and lecture notes. You have a body of knowledge that incorporates both.

Constructing Charts

To construct a chart as a synthesis review, you create a column for each information source. For example, you might have three sources: notes, text information, and a supplementary reading. Starting with what you think is the most complete source—usually the text or class notes—list the points you feel are most important. This analysis usually includes terms, key concepts, and major details. Using your next source, look for information that matches what you already identified. For information not found in your primary source, decide if it provides new and important ideas and add these to your chart. Repeat this process until all sources are used. Figure 4.1 shows a synthesis chart created from notes and text. *Practice creating synthesis charts in* *READ Exercise 4.2* *Exercise 4.2.*

Figure 4.1   Examples of Synthesis Charts

Charts for Terms in Any Subject

Term	Definition	Connotation	Personal Example/Association

Chart for Artists, Authors, and Musicians in Humanities Classes

Title	Artist	Theme	Setting	Description of Action	Main Characters

Chart for Discoveries in Applied and Social Sciences

Who?	From where?	What?	When?	How?

Maximizing Learning

What you do during a review session is as important as how long you review. Most review techniques help transfer information into memory through **maintenance** or **elaboration.** No matter which you choose, you need to attend to—or focus on—the information at hand.

Maintenance activities usually involve simple repetition of information. Repeating a phone number over and over until you call the number is an example of maintenance review. Such activities are simply used to store information.

In elaboration activities, you think about the meaning of information and connect it to what you already know. For instance, think about your hometown. Unless you live in a very small town, you probably couldn't name all the streets in it. But, you probably can trace mentally routes for getting to specific places. Your memory for streets in your hometown isn't a simple memorized list. It is a connected network of meaningful locations.

One way to elaborate on information is to think about it at different levels. Bloom (1956) suggested that thinking and learning occur at six levels. Each level involves different requirements, and skills (see

Table 4.2). Each level also results in different kinds of questions. Your ability to identify the kinds of questions your instructors ask helps you identify the kinds of thinking they require.

Once you know what you need to learn, you need to practice and focus on specific details. These involve different rehearsal formats and memory techniques.

Rehearsal Formats

In addition to processing information more deeply, you need to practice information more often. Some people live by the old adage, "Practice makes perfect." In truth, "Practice makes permanent," because whatever you practice—right or wrong—becomes a habit. To build learning habits, you need a variety of rehearsal formats.

Spaced Study. Spaced study (distributed practice) consists of alternating short study sessions with breaks. To do so, you set study goals through time (for example, 15 minutes) or task limits (such as three pages). After reaching these goals, you allow yourself some free time. For instance, you could take a walk, have a soft drink, or call a friend.

Spaced study works for many reasons. First, spaced study rewards hard work. The breaks in spaced study serve as your reward for completing a set amount or length of study. Second, knowing you have a certain amount of time or work to study motivates you. Third, because memory has limited capacity, breaks provide time for you to absorb information. Fourth, when you're studying complex, related information, study breaks keep you from confusing details. Spaced study gives you the familiarity you need for in-depth learning. It strengthens learning and recall and forms the basis of critical understanding.

Cramming. Cramming involves frantic, last-minute (and sometimes all-night) memorization. When you cram, you rent, rather than own information. Thus, short-term benefits rarely translate into long-term results. You fail to learn the information, so you must memorize it repeatedly. Cramming, then, is one of the least effective means of study.

But, what if it *is* the night before the exam and you really do have twelve chapters left to read? Your best bet is to use parts of the SQ3R process (see Chapters 2 and 3) to maximize your efforts. Begin by reading all chapter introductions and summaries. These provide you with the most basic condensation of information. Then construct chapter maps or outlines. These show you connections among ideas. Finally, examine the terms to see how they support chapter concepts.

These measures will not ensure a good grade. They only represent a more informed means of cramming.

Table 4.2   Bloom's Levels of Learning and Associated Skills and Words

Level of Learning	What Is Required of You	Skill(s) Required of You	Possible Testing Words
Knowledge	Recognize facts	Memorizing	Define Name/list Who, What, When, Where Questions Enumerate
Comprehension	Organize information	Paraphrasing	Describe Restate Explain/Discuss Compare/Contrast Outline/Trace/Rank Summarize/Compile Match
Application	Solve problems	Employing rules or processes to find answers; providing examples	Classify Choose Determine/Use/Apply Demonstrate/Show
Analysis	Break into components parts	Identifying cause and effect; drawing conclusions; generalizations	Analyze Support Why Infer Examine Criticize/Judge Associate/Relate
Synthesis	Think creatively	Combine pieces in new ways; originating	Predict Produce Design Develop Construct Devise
Evaluation	Judge value, accuracy, or merit	Determining worth based on background knowledge and given facts	Assess Justify Decide Evaluate Argue Document

Study Groups or Partners. The old saying "Two heads are better than one" describes using **study groups** or partners in review sessions. Their purpose is discussion of information. Therefore, learning becomes a more active process. As group members explain and listen to each other, auditory, visual, and physical senses are engaged. Combining these sensory impressions adds to the active learning. It extends the depth of understanding and makes learning more permanent. Finally, group discussions motivate members. This happens because members make deliberate decisions to prepare for and come to study sessions.

Group members must make two commitments. First, they need to arrive on time for all meetings. Second, they need to be prepared to discuss the topic at hand. The group functions best when each member contributes to the overall learning of the group, and no member uses the group to replace personal learning.

One benefit of study groups is that they simulate the kinds of learning that occur in business and other nonacademic settings. In this respect, they prepare you for the work world. For example, consider how a committee or other group works at a business location. These groups identify problems and seek solutions. Members of business groups must think about the problem collectively as they consider options and reach conclusions. Now, consider how a study group performs. First, the study group identifies a problem. As members examine and discuss options for solving the problem, they contribute and learn from each other. The overall result benefits all. Study group participation encourages you to practice the kinds of cooperative efforts and individual development fostered in nonacademic settings. Thus, study groups prepare you for success in your career.

Two notes of caution concern how groups practice. One, because most groups discuss information aloud, members sometimes neglect practicing their writing. If you have difficulty composing written responses to test items, you also need to practice putting information on paper. Another factor to consider concerns the composition of the study group. Group members need to be friendly and responsible. Arguing and bad feelings often prevent members from making the most of their study time. A member's lack of preparedness can interrupt the flow of study.

Overlearning. Overlearning (Tenney, 1986) consists of overlapping review. For instance, suppose you need to learn a list of 40 terms in history. You can overlearn the list in one of two ways (see Table 4.3). Overlearning reinforces information following initial learning. *Practice working with memory strategies in Exercise 4.3.*

READ Exercise 4.3

Table 4.3   Methods of Overlearning

Method I	Method II
1. List each item separately on note cards.	**1.** Divide the list into manageable units (3 to 5 items per unit, depending on the difficulty of the material).
2. Learn the first three cards.	**2.** Learn one set.
3. Add one card.	**3.** Add another set.
4. Practice all four cards.	**4.** Practice all sets.
5. Add one card.	**5.** Repeat steps 3 and 4 until you know all items.
6. Practice all five cards.	
7. Delete the card from the original set that you know the best and add one card.	
8. Practice with all five cards.	
9. Repeat steps 7 and 8 until you know all items.	

Memory Techniques

Memory needs training and exercise. **Mnemonics** consist of techniques for improving your memory skills. Combining methods strengthens memory because you have more ways to recall information. **Acronyms** and **acrostics, location, word games, mental imagery,** and **physical imagery,** are mnemonics that link information. Table 4.4 lists questions that can help you choose the best technique.

Acronyms and Acrostics. Many courses require you to learn lists of information. Forming acronyms or acrostics helps you recall these. When you make a word from the first letter or first few letters of the items on the list, you form an acronym. *FACE,* a commonly used acronym, helps you recall spaces on a treble clef in music. *HOMES,* another common acronym, cues your memory for the names of the Great Lakes (*Huron, Ontario, Michigan, Erie,* and *Superior*). Another acronym to aid your recall of the Great Lakes might be *sho me.* Acronyms, then, need not be real words. Like other mnemonics, the best ones are those you create for yourself.

Table 4.4   Questions for Developing Mnemonics

1. Can you rearrange any letters to form a word? If so, try *acronyms.*
2. Can you make a sentence using the first letter of each word in a list? If so, try *acrostics.*
3. Does the item sound like or rhyme with a familiar word? If so, try *word games.*
4. Can you associate the item with a familiar route or place? If so, try *location.*
5. Can you add meaningful doodles to make the information more visually memorable? If so, try *location* or *physical imagery.*
6. Do you know any gimmicks to associate with the term or item? If so, try *word games.*
7. Does the item remind you of something? If so, try *mental* or *physical imagery.*
8. Can you visualize something when you think of this item? If so, try *mental* or *physical imagery.*
9. Can you draw a picture to associate with the item? If so, use *physical imagery.*

Acrostics consist of phrases or sentences made from the first letter or first few letters of the items on a list. For example, "*Every good boy does fine*" helps you recall the lines in a treble clef. Acrostics need not be grammatically correct. They need only make sense to you.

Location. This technique dates back to a gruesome event in ancient Greece. According to Cicero (Bower, 1970), Simonides—a Greek poet—had just recited a poem when someone asked him to step outside. As he left, the roof fell. Everyone inside was killed. The bodies were crushed beyond recognition. Simonides figured out who was who by recalling where each person sat. Likewise, location memory occurs when you link a concept with a place. You might think of when you heard the concept, how it looked in your notes, which graphics were on the page with it, and so forth.

You can also make an abstract memory map. To do this, you think of a familiar place. You link what you need to know with features of that place. Then, you imagine walking around and looking at each feature. As you go, you recall the topic you've linked with it. For instance, suppose you want to learn the bones in the body. You choose a familiar route, like the route from the college bookstore to your math class. As you pass each building, you assign it a bone. Later, in class, you picture your route. As you pass each place, you think of the bone it represents.

Word Games. Playing games with information also aids memory. This occurs in two ways. First, you think about the information to create the game. Second, you create clues that entertain you and stimulate your recall.

Advertisers realize the value of rhymes and jingles in making their products memorable. The same principles that help you think of General Electric when you hear "We bring good things to life." work just as well in helping you recall academic information. A common academic rhyme is "*I* before *E* except after *C* or when sounded like *A* as in neighbor or weigh."

You create **puns** and **parodies** when you humorously copy common words or poems, stories, and songs. Puns use words or phrases to suggest more than one meaning. Parodies use humor to copy serious works or phrases. Such puns and parodies bring mental benefits. Like other mnemonics, they make learning imaginative and entertaining. For instance, suppose you want to learn the meaning of *numismatist* (a coin collector). You might parody the children's nursery rhyme "Four and Twenty Blackbirds." Instead of the king being in his counting house, counting all his money, you change the rhyme to "The numismatist was in his counting house, counting all his money." Or, you might make a pun to help you recall the definition. This could be something like "two numismatists getting together for old 'dime's' sake."

Mental and Physical Imagery. You experience mental imagery when you see pictures in your mind. Mental imagery is a natural occurrence because you often think in pictures, rather than words. For instance, think of a car. Do you think *c-a-r,* or do you picture how a car looks, smells, feels, and so on. Using other senses aids your recall of both familiar and unfamiliar items. Suggestions for making mental images appear in Table 4.5.

Mental pictures link concrete objects with their images (for example, a picture of a car with the word *car)* or abstract concepts with their symbols (for example, a picture of a dove with the word *peace).* They also link unrelated objects, concepts, and ideas through visualization. For instance, suppose you want to recall the 21st president, Chester Arthur. You can visualize an author writing the number "21" on a wooden chest. This mental picture helps you relate chest, author, and 21. Thus, you recall Chester Arthur was the 21st president.

When you draw your mental image, you use another sense, your **kinesthetic perception.** Such drawings are called **mnemonigraphs.** By making mental images physical ones, you provide yourself with

Table 4.5   Suggestions for Maximizing Mental Images and Examples

Goal: To remember the four basic foods in the food pyramid: milk, meat, fruit and vegetables, and breads and cereals.

Suggestion	Example
1. Use common symbols, such as a heart for *love* or a dove for *peace*.	A cornucopia overflowing with cheese (*milk*), sausages (*meat*), fruits, and breads
2. Use the clearest and closest image.	Your family sitting at your dining table and eating fully-loaded cheeseburgers (bread, meat, cheese, lettuce, tomatoes, onions, and so forth)
3. Think of outrageous or humorous images.	A *milk* cow (*meat*) eating a banana (*fruit*) sandwich (*bread*)
4. Use sexual connotations.	For males, seeing an attractive woman and thinking of the acrostic: "*Momma mi*a, look at that *foxy babe!*" For females, seeing an attractive man and thinking of the acrostic: "That *macho machine* has a *fantastic build.*"
5. Create action-filled images.	See 2, 3, and 4 above

repetition, which strengthens memory. Drawing or diagramming information also helps. Instead of learning lists, you sketch a drawing that includes the items you need to learn. For instance, suppose you need to know the parts of a computer. Drawing and labeling the parts aid recall.

Strategies for Reading and Taking Exams

Most exams are instructor-made, so the instructor is the best source of information about them. Most instructors want you to do well. Thus, they will answer questions about test content and format. No matter the type of exam you take, some test-taking strategies apply (see Table 4.6).

Tests are **objective** or **subjective** or both (see Table 4.7). Objective tests often require you to choose an answer from several choices. You write your own answers on subjective tests. Each type demands different skills of you. Subjective tests require you to recall main ideas and supporting facts. They ask you to describe these in written form. Objective tests ask you to recognize and apply information based on available choices. Because different skills are required for each, you need to study for them in different ways (see Tables 4.8 and 4.9). *Exercises 4.4 and 4.5 provide practice predicting test questions for study.*

READ Exercises 4.4 & 4.5

Table 4.6   General Suggestions for Taking Exams

1. *Arrive on time.* If you're early, talking to others could confuse you. If you're late, you may feel rushed and panicked. Panic causes you to forget what you do know.

2. *Be alert.* Listen carefully to all verbal directions. Read all written instructions. Make sure you understand what to do. Ask questions if you are unsure of anything.

3. *Expect mental blocks.* If you get a mental block on a question, go on. Return to that question later. You'll lose time if you delay too long on any one item. Remember, mental blocks are normal.

4. *Find out if you are penalized for guessing.* If you leave an answer blank, you'll get no points. If you guess at an answer and get it wrong, what have you lost? If it won't hurt your score, never leave blanks. Be a gambler! Take a guess!

5. *Don't spend too much time on any one question.*

Table 4.7   Types of Test Questions

Objective	Subjective
Multiple-choice	Short answer
Matching	Essay
Fill-in-the-blank	Fill-in-the-blank
True or false	

Objective Tests

Objective tests give you a choice of answers. They often require memorizing facts. This includes such information as dates, names, lists, and formulas. They sometimes demand that you know more detailed information than subjective tests do. However, some objective questions might ask you to apply information, draw conclusions, or identify main ideas. Objective tests consist of multiple-choice, true/false, matching, or fill-in-the-blank questions. Table 4.10 shows examples of test questions. Table 4.11 lists steps for reading objective tests. *Exercise 4.6 gives you a chance to practice these test-taking skills.*

READ Exercise 4.6

Table 4.8   PORPE: Study System for Subjective Exams

Three Days Before the Exam:

Predict:

Predict information about the test by answering these questions:

What does the test cover?

Is the test comprehensive or noncomprehensive?

How many questions will the test contain?

How much will this test count in my final course grade?

When and where is the test to be given?

What material(s) will I need to take the test?

Predict essay test questions by answering these questions:

What materials do I need to study: textbook, handouts, lecture notes, supplemental readings, or old exams?

What information is stressed most often in these materials?

What questions appeared in both my text preview and in the chapter's review or study guide?

What terms did the instructor emphasize?

Predict at least three times as many questions as your instructor has indicated will be on the exam.

Two Days Before the Exam:

Organize:

Organize information by answering these questions:

What type of text structure will best fit my predicted questions?

What information is essential for answering these questions?

What information adds relevant details or examples?

What is the best way to organize (chart, cards, map, outline) this information?

Rehearse:

Lock information into your memory by answering these questions:

What mnemonic techniques (for example, acronyms, acrostics, word games) can I use to practice this information?

What study and memory aids should I use?

How much time do I have before the exam?

How much time will I need to study for this test?

How much time each day will I study?

When and where will I study?

How will I distribute my study time?

When and where will my study group and I meet?

What obligations might interfere with study time?

Construct study and memory aids.

Use overlearning to practice mnemonic aids overtly (writing or speaking them).

One Day Before the Exam:

Practice:

Practice writing your answers in essay format.

Evaluate:

Write an objective assessment of the quality of your essay by answering these questions:

Did I answer the question that was asked?

Did I include topic and summary sentences? Was my answer well organized?

Did I include all essential information? Did I use transitions?

Did I check spelling, grammar, and legibility?

If you answered "no" to any of these questions, repeat the final four stages of PORPE until you answer all these with "yes." Retain your final evaluation.

After the exam, compare your instructor's comments with the final evaluation. Look for negative trends to avoid or positive trends to stress when you study for your next exam.

File your PORPE plan, course materials, study aids, and evaluation data for future use.

Table 4.9   POSSE: Study System for Objective Exams

Plan:

Answer these questions:

What does the test cover?

Is the test comprehensive or noncomprehensive?

How many questions will the test contain?

Will I be asked to apply or otherwise use information?

How much will this test count in my final course grade?

When and where is the test to be given?

What material(s) will I need to take the test?

Organize:

Answer these questions:

What materials do I need to study: textbook, handouts, lecture notes, supplemental readings, or old exams?

What information is stressed most often in these materials?

In what form might this information be asked?

What study and memory aids should I use?

Can I find a study group to join?

Gather these materials together.

Construct study and memory aids.

Schedule:

Answer these questions:

How much time do I have before the exam?

How much time will I need to study for this test?

How much time each day will I study?

When and where will I study?

How will I distribute my study time?

When and where will my study group and I meet?

What obligations might interfere with study time?

Construct a time schedule.

Study:

Use overlearning to practice mnemonic aids overtly (writing or speaking them).

At the end of each study session, answer these questions:

Am I studying actively (that is, writing or speaking)?

Am I distributing my study time to avoid memory interference and physical fatigue?

Am I following my schedule? Why or why not?

What adjustments do I need to make in my schedule?

Am I learning efficiently? Why or why not?

How might I study more effectively?

Evaluate:

After the test has been returned, complete an After-Exam Inventory (see Figure 4.2) and answer these questions:

What pattern(s) emerge(s) from the worksheet?

What type of questions did I miss most often?

How can I avoid these trends in the future?

File your POSSE plan, course materials, study aids, exam, worksheet, and evaluation for future reference.

Table 4.10 **Examples of Test Questions**

Type	Example
Multiple-choice	The author of Romeo and Juliet is _____
	a. Oprah Winfrey
	b. John Grisham
	c. William Shakespeare
	d. Martha Stewart

Matching		
	1. *Romeo and Juliet*	a. Mark Twain
	2. *Tom Sawyer*	b. Margaret Mitchell
	3. *Gone with the Wind*	c. William Shakespeare

Fill in the Blank	_____ wrote *Romeo and Juliet*.

Table 4.11 **Steps for Reading Objective Tests**

1. *Survey the test.* Just as surveying a text chapter prepares you for a second, more careful reading, surveying a test prepares you for its contents. It gives you a feel for the test. By glancing through all its parts, you determine what information you need and how much questions are worth. This helps you allot your test time wisely.

2. *Read through the whole exam and answer the questions you know first.* This gives you confidence. Also, you get credit for the ones you know. Check or mark questions that confuse you.

3. *Go back to questions you didn't know.* Reread each one carefully. Try to answer the question in your own words. Then look for a matching response.

4. *If you do not know the answer, try to figure out what the answer is not.*

   Example

   The capital of Belgium is _____.

   a. New York

   b. Texas

   c. London

   d. Brussels

   Explanation: You may not know the capital of Belgium. However, you can eliminate the following:

   a. New York is in the United States.

   b. Texas is a state, not a capital.

   c. London is in England.

   Therefore, *d* must be the correct answer.

5. *Read all choices before answering a multiple-choice question.* Don't choose the first answer that seems correct. Sometimes the choice may be between a good answer and the best answer. Or, the answer might be a combination of responses (all of the above, both a and b, and so forth). Answer by eliminating obviously incorrect answers. Then select the *most correct* answer that remains.

Continues

Table 4.11   *Continued*

6. *If the test contains a true/false section, read each question thoroughly.* Watch for key words, such as *always, never, seldom,* and *frequently.* Statements with *always* or *never* are often false. Statements with *seldom* or *frequently* allow for more exceptions. Make sure a statement is completely true before answering true. True/false tests often contain statements that are almost true but not quite true.

7. *If the test concerns math or science, watch your time closely.* Don't spend so much time on more difficult problems that you cannot finish the test. When you're stumped, move on to the next question.

8. *Watch for double negatives as you read.* What is -2×-2? Answer, $+4$. Negative times negative equals positive. The same rule is true in writing. Two negative terms make the idea positive.

    Example

*not un*loved	2 negatives; means "loved"
*never un*clear	2 negatives; means "clear"
*never in*visible	2 negatives; means "visible"
*not with*out hope	2 negatives; means "has hope"
not sight*less*	2 negatives; means "has sight"

9. *There are also some tricks of the trade for taking math tests.* Estimation and logical thinking help you answer some problems without working them!

    Example

    $12{,}365 \times 112 =$

    a. 1,384,880

    b. 1,236,511

    c. 1,384,886

    d. 5,678,920

    Explanation: You can get the answer without working the problem. Look at the last digit of each number in the problem. They are 5 and 2. The product of those two numbers is 10. That means that the answer will end in zero. Thus, you eliminate answers b and c. Neither one ends in zero. Now round off each number in the problem. You get 12,000 and 100. Multiply those two together. The answer is 1,200,000. The correct answer should be higher than your estimate because you rounded each of the numbers down. Based on your estimated answer of 1,200,000, answer *d* is, then, much too high. The correct answer is *a*.

Subjective Tests

Unlike objective tests, subjective tests provide no options from which to choose. Instead, you consider your knowledge of the subject and create answers of your own. There are three basic kinds of subjective tests: essay, short answer, and fill-in-the-blank (see Table 4.12).

Essay tests require lengthy, written answers. Your goal is to write the maximum amount of point-earning information in the shortest possible time. Points on essay questions are based on what you say and how you say it. Thus, your answer needs to be logical and organized. The words in the question itself can help you organize and write

Table 4.12 Examples of Subjective Test Questions and Typical Responses

Fill-in-the-Blanks

A combination of analog and digital computers is called a _____.

You would answer this question by filling in the blank with the word *hybrid,* as follows:

A combination of analog and digital computers is called a <u>hybrid</u>.

Essay

Contrast the types of computers.

A typical response would be as follows:

> There are two general groups of computers. First, some computers process data. These types consist of analog and digital. An analog computer measures continuous physical processes. The digital type operates by counting. A combination of these two types is called a hybrid. The second kind of computer is grouped by function. A computer of this type is either special purpose or general purpose. A special-purpose computer does a single job. However, a general-purpose computer can do many different tasks.

Short Answer

Briefly identify the kinds of computers that process data.

A typical response would be as follows:

1. Analog—measures continuous physical process
2. Digital—operates by counting
3. Hybrid—combination of analog and digital exams

your response. For them to help you, though, you must know what those words are and what they mean (see Table 4.13).

Short answer questions form a second kind of subjective test format. Like an essay test, you must do more than identify correct answers. Unlike an essay test, you do not have to be concerned with sentence construction and grammar.

A third kind of subjective test, fill-in-the-blank, differs from short answer or essay questions that require somewhat lengthy answers. A fill-in-the-blank test focuses on specific details and short responses. The steps for taking subjective tests appear in Table 4.14.

Table 4.13   Question Types and Suggestions for Completing Essay Exams

If You Are Asked to . . .	Then . . .	By Using Transition Words Like . . .
Compare or match	Identify similarities	Similarly, in addition, also, too, as well as, both, in comparison, comparatively
Contrast or distinguish	Identify differences	However, but, unless, nevertheless, on one hand, on the other hand, on the contrary, in contrast, although, yet, even though
Discuss or describe	Provide details or features	To begin with, then, first, second, third
Enumerate, name, outline, or list	Identify major points	Next, finally, meanwhile, more, another, soon, now, while, later, at last, first, second, third
Sequence, arrange, trace, or rank	List information in order	Furthermore, later, before, after, during, while, first, second, third, then, next, finally, lastly
Outline	List major points	
Demonstrate or show	Provide examples	For example, for instance, in other words
Criticize or analyze	Review features or components	As an illustration, to illustrate, thus, also
Relate or associate	Show associations	As a result, because, this leads to, if . . . then, in order that, unless, since, so that, thus, therefore, accordingly, so, yet, consequently
Restate, paraphrase, summarize or compile	Provide a short synopsis	Any of the previous transition words
Apply	Show use for	Any of the previous transition words
Construct, develop, or devise	Create	Any of the previous transition words
Explain, defend, or document	Give reasons for support	Any of the previous transition words

Final Exams

What do you think of when you hear the word *finals?* Often college finals have a bad reputation. But there's really nothing to fear.

Perhaps you've been doing all the right things to make a good grade in the course. You've gone to class regularly. You've kept up with your assignments. All you have to do now is take the final. To prepare for the final, review the suggestions for taking other kinds of exams. The same rules apply. Use them. What if you haven't been doing all the right things? Use the SQ3R approach and try to cram constructively. Don't waste time berating yourself or wishing things were different. Resolve to change your academic behavior next semester.

Table 4.14   Steps for Reading and Answering Essay Tests

1. *Relax.* Take a minute to become calm. Read all the questions. Estimate the amount of time you want to spend on each. Note the number of points each question is worth.

2. *Read and study the question.* Decide what you think the instructor wants. (See the list of question types in Table 4.13 for more information.) Organize your thoughts before beginning to write. Your ability to express yourself is also being tested. Thus, your answer must be written so the instructor knows you know the subject.

3. *Briefly outline your answers.* This ensures you include important information.

4. *Answer the essay question you know best first.* This helps you relax and gives you confidence. It also gives you a chance to think about the other questions.

5. *Like writing an essay or theme in English class, writing answers to essay questions takes time and patience.* Begin with an introduction to your response. Provide supporting details in the middle to reinforce your answer. End with a summary of the important details. Include a topic and summary sentence. Think of examples as you write. Even if you don't include all of them, they'll help you clarify your thinking.

6. *Save 5 to 10 minutes at the end of the test to read and review what you've written.* Proofread your answers. This means correcting any mistakes made when your thoughts raced faster than your pen. Check for content accuracy and careless omissions. Look carefully for spelling and punctuation mistakes. You often improve your grade by simply correcting an error or adding an omitted detail.

7. *Neatness is also important.* If your answers are difficult to read, the instructor may count them wrong. Let your test's appearance work for you, not against you.

8. *If there is a question on the test you don't know, write down any related information you do know.* Don't pretend to know the answer, but answer as best you can. You might get partial credit, especially if others had problems with the same question.

9. *Take your time on untimed tests.* Don't race to be the first one to leave. Use any extra time to check over your answers. Proofread written responses.

10. *Don't worry if others finish the test before you.* Some students always seem to turn their papers in much sooner than anyone else. However, these students may not have known many answers. They could be on their way to drop the course. Don't panic! Get back to work.

In addition, find out when and where the exam will be. Final exam schedules do not always follow regular class times. You will really panic if you get to your class and nobody is there.

Many finals are more long than hard. They are almost like tests of endurance. They are usually no harder than other tests, just longer. Because they are longer, finals are often fair tests of your knowledge. They cover more information. You have a better chance because they focus on many topics.

Reading and Reviewing Returned Tests

What do you do when a test is returned to you? Do you throw it away? Or do you carefully examine it? A review of your test paper provides information about your skills. It reduces the stress you feel about taking another test in the same course. You use this information to improve your future grades on tests. It helps you decide which of your study and test-taking strategies were successful and which need more emphasis.

Figure 4.2 provides a form for examining your returned tests. To complete it, first list each item you missed in the first column. Then mark an X under the description that best explains why you missed that question. Sometimes you will have to mark more than one reason for each question. Next, you tally the number of Xs under each reason. These numbers indicate the areas of study and test-taking strategies on which you must place more effort in the future.

After you assess your test performance, seek information about how your instructor constructs exams. Look for patterns in the types of questions asked, the stress placed on lecture or text notes, grading patterns, and so forth. This valuable information helps you prepare for the next exam. *Use Exercise 4.7 to help you evaluate your test performance.*   **READ Exercise 4.7**

Figure 4.2 Worksheet for Examining Returned Exams

Test Item Missed	Insufficient Information						Test Anxiety					Lack of Test-Wisdom						Test Skills					Other	
	I did not read the text thoroughly.	The information was not in my notes.	I studied the information but could not remember it.	I knew main ideas but needed details.	I knew the information but could not apply it.		I studied the wrong information.	I experienced mental block.	I spent too much time daydreaming.	I was so tired I could not concentrate.	I was so hungry I could not concentrate.	I panicked.	I carelessly marked a wrong choice.	I did not eliminate grammatically incorrect choices.	I did not choose the *best* choice.	I did not notice limiting words.	I did not notice a double negative.	I changed a correct answer to a wrong one.	I misread the directions.	I misread the questions.	I made poor use of the time provided.	I wrote poorly organized responses.	I wrote incomplete responses.
Number of Items Missed																							

Chapter Summary Exercise

On a separate sheet of paper or in your notebooks, complete the chapter summary by filling in the blanks with the following words:

exams	mnemonics	synthesis	purposes
acronyms	PORPE	cramming	location
spaced study	overlearning	mental images	maps
POSSE	final	study groups and partners	

Different kinds of reviews achieve different _____. The one you

choose depends on your course and the depth of learning you want

to achieve. Charts and _____ help you organize information for

_____ with less interference and better recall. A variety of rehearsal

formats and memory techniques combine to form deeper and more

permanent learning. Rehearsal techniques include _____, _____,

_____, and _____. Memory techniques (_____) include

_____ and acrostics, _____, word games, physical im-

agery, and _____. All students must prepare for and read

tests effectively to succeed in higher education. Your instructor is

your best resource for determining a test's content and format. Once

you know that information, study systems such as _____ and

_____ provide you with plans for preparing for tests. Although

general suggestions for taking tests help you on any exam, specific

strategies for other exams, like _____ exams, may also be neces-

sary. Reading and reviewing returned _____ to identify pat-

terns of questions, subject emphasis, and errors helps you maximize

performance on future tests.

Terms

Terms appear in the order in which they occur in the chapter.

test anxiety
stress
eustress
review
synthesis
maintenance
elaboration
spaced study
cramming
study groups
overlearning
mnemonics
acronyms
acrostics
location
word games
mental imagery
physical imagery
puns
parodies
kinesthetic perception
mnemonigraphs
objective
subjective

Chapter Review

Answer the following questions on a separate sheet of paper or in your notebook.

1. Compare maintenance activities with elaboration activities.

2. Create a chart that identifies three kinds of reviews, when they should occur, and their purposes.

3. Using the memory technique of your choice, create a way to learn Bloom's six levels of thinking (see Table 4.2) in order.

4. Create a chart that identifies coping techniques to use before or after a test, the effect of each technique on stress, and any problems you foresee in applying that technique.

5. Compare/contrast PORPE and POSSE.

6. Review the general suggestions for taking tests in Table 4.6. How can each suggestion help you convert distress into eustress?

7. Using the content of this chapter, create a test question for each of the following types:
   a. multiple-choice
   b. fill-in-the-blank
   c. true/false
   d. matching (at least three sets)
   e. essay

8. Compare/contrast final exams with other exams in terms of difficulty and stress level of students.

9. What can be the benefit of reviewing a test after it is returned to you?

10. How might reviewing a test that's been returned to you increase/decrease test anxiety? Why?

Exercises

Exercise 4.1   Answer the following questions as truthfully as possible. Mark *T* if the statement is generally true for you; *F* if the statement is generally false. A scoring key and explanation of your score appear on the last page of this chapter.

1. _____ While taking an important exam, I perspire a lot.

2. _____ I feel very panicky when I have to take a surprise exam.

3. _____ During tests, I find myself thinking of the consequences of failing.

4. _____ After important tests, I am frequently so tense that my stomach gets upset.

5. _____ While taking an important exam, I find myself thinking of how much brighter the other students are than I am.

6. _____ I freeze up on big tests like finals.

7. _____ If I were about to take a big test, I would worry a lot before taking it.

8. _____ During course exams, I find myself thinking of things unrelated to the course material.

9. _____ During course exams, I frequently get so nervous that I forget facts I really know.

10. _____ If I knew I was going to take a big exam, I would feel confident and relaxed beforehand.

11. _____ I usually get depressed after taking a test.

12. _____ I have an uneasy, upset feeling before taking a test.

13. _____ When taking a test, I find my emotions do not interfere with my performance.

14. _____ Getting a good grade on one test doesn't seem to increase my confidence on the second test.

15. _____ After taking a test, I always feel I have done better than I actually have done.

16. _____ I sometimes feel my heart beating very fast during important examinations.

Exercise 4.2   Following is an excerpt and lecture notes concerning the topic of love. Complete the synthesis chart with information from both sources.

Love—Intimacy, Passion, and Commitment

Love is one of the most intense of all human experiences. At one time or another, most people must ask themselves, "Is this love or lust?" "Is it real or infatuation?" "What am I really feeling?" All of which raises the question: What is love? Think, for instance, about the different ways we love our parents, friends, and spouses or lovers. Of the many feelings that affect personal relationships, love is among the strongest.

Question: How does romantic love differ from friendship?
To get an angle on **romantic love,** psychologist Zick Rubin (1973) chose to think of it as an attitude held by one person toward another. This allowed him to develop "liking" and "love" scales to measure each "attitude." Next, he asked dating couples to complete each scale twice; once with their date in mind and once for a close friend of the same sex.

Question: What were the results?
Scores for love of partner and love of friend differed more than those for liking. In other words, dating couples liked *and* loved their partners, but mostly liked their friends. Women, however, were a little more "loving" of their friends than were men. Does this reflect real differences in the strength of male friendships and female friendships? Maybe not, since it is more acceptable in our culture for women to express love for one another than it is for men. Nevertheless, a recent study confirmed that dating couples feel a mixture of love and friendship for their partners. In fact, 44 percent of a group of dating persons named their romantic partner as their closest friend (Hendrick & Hendrick, 1993).

   Another way in which love and friendship differ is mutual absorption. Romantic love, in contrast to simple liking, usually involves deep **mutual absorption** of the lovers. In other words, lovers (unlike friends) attend almost exclusively to one another. It's not surprising then, that couples scoring high of Ruben's love scale spend more time gazing into each other's eyes than do couples who score low on the scale. As the song says, "Millions of people go by, but they all disappear from view—'cause I only have eyes for you" (Rubin, 1970).

Question: How do various kinds of love differ from one another?
This is the question that led psychologist Robert Sternberg to propose his **triangular theory of love.** Although the theory is still preliminary, it may help you think more clearly about your own loving relationships.

Love Triangles

According to Sternberg (1986, 1987), love is made up of three elements: **intimacy, passion,** and **commitment.** Each factor can be visualized as one side of a triangle. Notice also that the three elements can combine to produce seven different types of love. We will return to these types in a moment, but let's briefly explore love's three "ingredients."

Intimacy A relationship has intimacy, or closeness, if affection, sharing communication, and support are present. Intimacy grows steadily at first, but in time levels off.

After it does, people in long-term relationships may gradually lose sight of the fact that they are still very close and mutually dependent.

Passion Passion refers mainly to **heightened arousal.** This arousal may be sexual if it includes other sources, too. Arousal, no matter what the cause, may be interpreted as passion in a romantic relationship (Bersheid & Walster, 1974b). This is probably why passionate love often occurs against a backdrop of danger, adversity, or frustration—especially in soap operas and romance novels! Passion is a primary source of love's *intensity.* It's not surprising, then, that romance inspires the strongest feelings of love. In contrast, love for siblings is least intense (Sternberg and Grajeck, 1984).

Commitment The third side of the love triangle consists of your decision to love another person and your degree of long-term commitment to them. Commitment starts at zero before you meet a person and it grows steadily as you get acquainted. Like intimacy, commitment tends to level off. However, it may waver up and down with a relationship's good times and bad times. Commitment drops rapidly when a relationship is in serious trouble.

Seven Flavors of Love

The presence or absence of intimacy, passion, and/or commitment produces eight triangles. The first defines non-love, a total absence of all three elements.

In **liking,** you feel close to a person and communicate well with her or him. However, you do not feel any passion or deep commitment to the person. A likable classmate might fall into this category.

Romantic love mixes intimacy (closeness and sharing) with passion (often in the form of physical attraction). Despite its intensity, romantic love does not involve much commitment at first. Think, for example, of a summer romance that ends in a relatively easy parting of ways.

Fatuous love describes commitments made rapidly on the basis of physical attraction (passion), but without much emotional intimacy. Fatuous love is of the boy-meets-girl-and-they-get-married-a-month-later type. Relationships started this way risk failure because lovers make a commitment before they really get to know each other well.

Infatuation is an even more superficial form of love. In this case a person is inflamed with passion, but shares no intimacy or commitment with the beloved. In time, of course, infatuation may lead to more lasting kinds of love.

Companionate love refers to affection and deep attachment that is built on respect, shared interests, and firm friendship. Companionate love is lower key emotionally. However, it is steady and long term and tends to grow in time. Companionate love is the "kind of affection we feel for those with whom our lives are deeply intertwined" (Walster & Walster, 1978).

Couples sometimes reach a point where there is little passion or intimacy left in their relationship. If they stay together merely out of commitment or habit, they experience **empty love.**

Consummate love occurs when two people are passionate, committed to one another, and emotionally close. Complete, balanced love of this kind occurs only in very special relationships.

How Do I Love Thee? The categories described here are certainly not the last word on love. Undoubtedly, other kinds of love also exist. In addition, Sternberg's theory may place too much emphasis on passion. In most relationships, intimacy and commitment are a bigger part of love than passion is (Clark & Reis, 1988).

Our culture also tends to place much emphasis on passion as the main basis for "falling" in love. However, this overlooks the fact that the passionate, breathless stage of love typically lasts only about 6 to 30 months (Walster & Walster, 1978). What happens when this period ends? Quite often, people separate.

There is a degree of danger in expecting to live forever on a romantic cloud. People who are primarily caught up in passionate love may neglect to build a more lasting relationship. Rather than downplaying companionate love, it is helpful to realize that lovers must also be friends. In fact, consummate love is basically a blending of romantic love and companionate love.

You may be tempted to match the love triangles with your own relationships. If you do apply the theory, remember that relationships vary greatly and that few are perfect (Trotter, 1986). In another study, Sternberg and Michael Barnes (1986) found that relationships are generally satisfying if you think the other person feels about you the way you would *like* for her or him to feel about you.

From Dennis Coon, 1997, *Essentials of Psychology*, 7th ed. Pacific Grove, CA: Brooks/Cole Publishing Company.

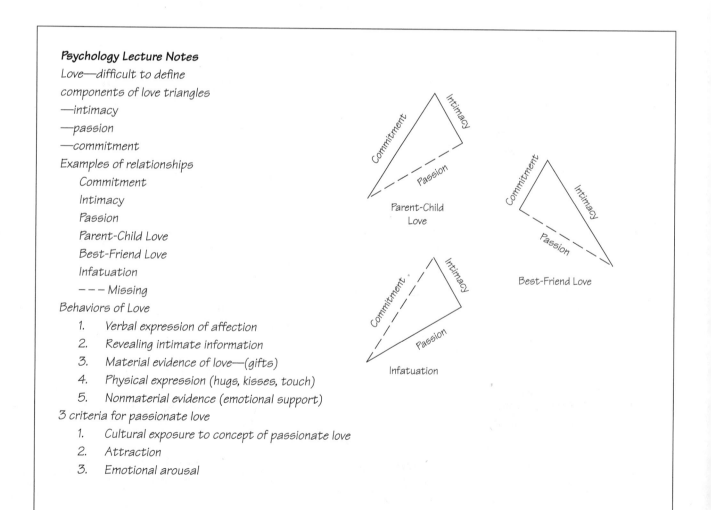

Psychology Lecture Notes

Love—difficult to define

components of love triangles

—intimacy

—passion

—commitment

Examples of relationships

   Commitment

   Intimacy

   Passion

   Parent-Child Love

   Best-Friend Love

   Infatuation

   – – – Missing

Behaviors of Love

   1.   Verbal expression of affection

   2.   Revealing intimate information

   3.   Material evidence of love—(gifts)

   4.   Physical expression (hugs, kisses, touch)

   5.   Nonmaterial evidence (emotional support)

3 criteria for passionate love

   1.   Cultural exposure to concept of passionate love

   2.   Attraction

   3.   Emotional arousal

Triangular Theory of Love	Text Excerpt	Lecture Notes
Definition		
Aspects		
Examples		

Exercise 4.3   Answer the following questions on a separate sheet of paper or in your notebook.

1. Using the suggestions in Table 4.4, create an image other than the one suggested in your text for remembering that Chester Arthur was the 21st president of the United States.

2. Referring to the definition of *metacognition* in Chapter 1, create a mental image to help you remember its meaning.

3. Referring to the four organizational structures of paragraphs and passages discussed in Chapter 3, create and sketch a physical image to help you remember each of them.

4. Referring to the excerpt in Exercise 4.2, develop and describe an acrostic for remembering the behaviors of love.

5. Referring to the excerpt in Exercise 4.2, identify the three components of love triangles and create an acronym for remembering them.

6. Review the seven flavors of love identified in Exercise 4.2. Describe or sketch a familiar route you could use to create a location memory map for them. Identify the places at which you would post each type of love.

7. Referring to the excerpt in Exercise 4.2, choose a mnemonic of your choice and devise a strategy for recalling the types of love.

Exercise 4.4   On a separate sheet of paper or in your notebook, predict an objective question for each level at Bloom's taxonomy (*knowledge, comprehension, application, analysis, synthesis, evaluation*) for Sample Chapter 11, "Opportunities to Work in the Theater." Label each question accordingly.

Exercise 4.5   On a separate sheet of paper or in your notebook, predict a subjective question for each level at Bloom's taxonomy (*knowledge, comprehension, application, analysis, synthesis, evaluation*) for the narrative text found in this chapter's READ Keys. Label each question accordingly.

Exercise 4.6   Complete the following test as quickly as possible. Write your answers on a separate sheet of paper or in your notebook.

1. 236,515 x 113 = _____
   a. 22,726,195
   b. 26,726,195
   c. 16,726,190
   d. 31,723,211

2. 95,683 – 74,864 = _____
   a. 101,329
   b. 20,819
   c. 20,815
   d. 28,051

3. The book was not incomplete. It was _____
   a. only begun.
   b. finished.
   c. half complete.
   d. unfinished.

4. _____ is the capital of Spain.

    a. New York

    b. France

    c. Madrid

    d. England

5. The old man was not sightless. He could _____

    a. see.

    b. be classified as blind.

    c. not see.

    d. none of the above.

6. True or false? All mammals' offspring fully develop in the womb of the mother.

7. True or false? Frequent coughing is a sure sign of lung cancer.

8. The opposite of "not in" is _____

    a. out.

    b. in.

    c. there.

    d. missing.

9. True or false? Presidents of the United States never veto bills that increase taxes.

10. The people who uncovered the structure of DNA were _____

    a. Watson and Crick.

    b. Romeo and Juliet.

    c. Lewis and Clark.

    d. Bush and Quayle.

Exercise 4.7   Photocopy the After-Exam Analysis form in Figure 4.2. Use the form to analyze your performance on the last test you took. Is there a pattern to your test-taking errors? If so, how can you change your test-taking in order to improve your performance on future exams?

Web Exercise

A variety of information related to memory and test taking is available on the World Wide Web. For this exercise, access one of the following Web sites or find a site of your own about memory or test taking:

Memory Techniques and Mnemonics
http://www.demon.co.uk/mindtool/memory.html

Memory Strategies
http://www.ma.psu.edu/~malc/memory.htm

NASA Cognition Lab: Five Games for Cognitive Psychology
http://olias.arc.nasa.gov/cognition/tutorials/index.html

Preparing for and Taking Exams
http://www.yorku.ca/cdc/lsp/ep/exam.htm

How to Avoid Cramming for Tests
http://www.Dartmouth.edu/~acskills/docs/review_principles.doc

Test Anxiety
http://www.counsel.ufl.edu/selfHelp/testAnxiety.asp

On a separate sheet of paper or in your notebook, create a chart that compares the information in this chapter with the information at the Web site you accessed. Then, below the chart, create a list of suggestions or steps for remembering information or for taking tests.

READ: Keys

READ: Keys Activity Pretest

Rate each of the following words according to your knowledge of them.

Word	Stage 0 *I don't know this word.*	Stage 1 *I've seen this word but I know nothing of its meaning.*	Stage 2 *I've seen this word and can make associations with it.*	Stage 3 *I know this word.*
1. conjures				
2. subtle				
3. homogenous				
4. dialect				
5. inadvertently				
6. intermediaries				
7. assimilated				
8. novelty				
9. retrospect				
10. burgeoning				

READ: Keys Activity 4.1

Read the following essay and keep track of your reading time.

A Different Kind of Foreigner
Carrie Chen

Waiguo ren—foreigner

Whenever one thinks of an American, one usually ***conjures*** up an image of a Caucasian speaking flawless English instead of a black-haired, brown-eyed, olive-skinned person of Asian descent.

As I was born in the U.S., I'm automatically a citizen of the United States. By blood, I'm Chinese. For the past 23 years I've pondered whether it was more accurate to be thought of as "Chinese-American" or "American-Chinese" or just "Chinese" in America and "American" in foreign countries (pretty confusing).

Do I identify more with my Chinese heritage over my American upbringing? Or am I something like "Americanized" Chinese food, about as authentic as chicken chow mein?

After a lifetime of trying to sort out the Chinese and American percentages of myself, I finally visited Taiwan this summer. It was probably the first time in my life that I've been considered foremost an "American," as I've always considered myself Chinese first. All of a sudden I was labeled as a foreigner—a "Waiguo ren"—a strange identity I had never worn until then.

I wasn't a pale-faced, yellow-haired foreigner. Instead, the differences were much more ***subtle.*** Only the "native-born" Chinese and Taiwanese had the 3-D glasses that illuminated the waiguo ren among a ***homogenous*** crowd of dark heads. I had a certain "American look" in my eyes such that even complete strangers could tell with a glance.

The trip showed me how little I knew of my Chinese heritage. If I had paid more attention in Chinese school, maybe I wouldn't have felt like such a foreigner in my parents' native land. I might have been able to communicate better with my relatives, and I might have seemed more "Asian" to my overseas family.

To my relatives, according to their standards, I was completely American. The obvious barrier was language. We simply couldn't communicate very well with my limited Mandarin and their speaking a different ***dialect,*** Hakka.

So we spoke with heapings of large portions on my plate during ten course meals and small but generous red packages of money or hung bao. I showed my appreciation and respect by heartily eating whatever was put on my plate and sitting with my relatives even though I didn't understand what they were saying.

Inadvertently, my parents were the ***intermediaries*** in the conversation, spanning the language gap when they spoke in Mandarin. For years they unknowingly trained me to be a good listener whenever they spoke in

Mandarin such that I could pretty much figure out what they were saying, especially when they were talking about me. Sometimes I felt like Peppermint Patty, catching bits and pieces of the lecture her teacher was giving.

I could tell from salespeople, taxi drivers and strangers on the street that I really stuck out. This was always apparent when I went shopping, hailed a taxi or just waited at the corner of the street. Perhaps they zeroed in on my shorts and T-shirt as too casual for Taipei, listened to my English and tagged me as an American.

Listening to their conversations was like listening to my parents. I could see and hear their reactions to me. Whenever I went shopping, I would always receive the curious looks from shop girls. I was always asked, "Where did you originate from?" as I rode in taxicabs.

Once, while I was waiting for a taxi with friends, somehow every black head on a moped or in a car, waiting for the light to change, was drawn by the sight of Americans with Chinese coloring at the street corner. The prolonged stare we received surprised us and struck us as hilariously funny. Did we really stick out even among strangers? Absolutely.

Many students from Taiwan studying in America are always surprised by my "Americanness" despite the way I look. They always say, "Wow, just like an American!"—as if I've successfully **assimilated** into a culture they long to be a part of. Just as I envy their Chinese speaking abilities, they wish they could speak flawless English.

My visit to Taiwan made me realize how much of a foreigner I am and how different I am from the people there. Besides the way I dress, speak and carry myself, I'm different on the inside. As shown by the reactions of my relatives and strangers in Taiwan, there is a much greater American part of me due to my upbringing in the United States.

By blood I'll always be Asian, but without trying to learn more about Taiwan or China, I'll lose the "Asianness" about me. My summer in Taiwan was fascinating not only because of the **novelty**—but rather learning about my culture and, in **retrospect,** learning about myself, made it memorable.

I finally understood what my parents' favorite foods were because I got to try them. I gained an appreciation for Asian history which was never emphasized in history classes.

I also got a glimpse of the future. Taiwan's **burgeoning** economic, social and political aims give the nation a lot of potential in becoming a force in Asia and the world.

Some small part of me will always identify with Taiwan because of tradition and upbringing. Someday I hope to be able to continue my education there after graduate school—not necessarily as a stepping stone in my career, but as an opportunity to live, learn and experience what Taiwan has to offer.

I'll always be something of a foreigner. For those of us raised in America, there are two sides to our personalities: the Asian side and the American side. Living in America, I've kept my Chinese side in the background. But by experiencing Taiwan from a Taiwanese point of view, maybe I can rediscover what my heritage has to offer—and understand it enough to call it mine.

From Carrie Chen, *East Wind.* University of North Carolina, at Chapel Hill.

962 words / _____ minutes = _____ words per minute

Calculate your reading time by dividing the number of words in the article by the amount of time it took to read it. Then mark your reading time on the chart located on page 338.

READ: Keys Activity 4.2

On a separate sheet of paper or in your notebook, answer the following questions about the essay you just read:

1. Where is Carrie visiting?

   a. China

   b. Taiwan

   c. Little China in San Francisco

   d. Little China in New York

   e. Japan

2. What language did Carrie's Chinese family speak fluently?

   a. Mandarin

   b. Hakka

   c. Chinese

   d. English

   e. Taiwanese

3. What does the author think of "Americanized" Chinese food?

   a. It tastes better than authentic Chinese food.

   b. It is easier to prepare than Mexican food.

   c. It is not real Chinese food.

   d. It has more salt than the food she ate in Taiwan.

   e. People in America cook all types of food better than people do in foreign countries.

4. How did the citizens of Taipei know Carrie was an American?

   a. She dressed more formally than did the citizens of Taipei.

b. She spoke Chinese with an American accent.

c. Her attitude was different than that of other Chinese girls.

d. She spoke English with a Chinese accent.

e. She did not care for Chinese food.

5. Taipei is a city in what country?

a. China

b. Taiwan

c. Japan

d. America

e. Hakka

6. What is the main idea of this passage?

a. China was a foreign country to Carrie.

b. Carrie's parents were not foreigners in Taiwan.

c. Carrie is a foreigner no matter where she lives or visits.

d. American schools should do a better job of teaching world history.

e. Taiwan is a foreign country.

7. What cartoon character does Carrie compare herself to?

a. Lucy

b. Sally Forth

c. Peppermint Patty

d. Cathy

e. Wonder Woman

8. How old is Carrie?

a. 18

b. 21

c. 25

d. 23

e. 20

9. What about Carrie do transfer students from Taiwan envy?

   a. The wealth that allows her to live in America and visit Taiwan

   b. Her American citizenship

   c. The ability to speak both English and Chinese fluently

   d. Her home and parents in the United States

   e. Her English language skills

10. How does Carrie feel about Taiwan at the end of her visit?

    a. It's a nice place to visit but she doesn't want to live there.

    b. It's a place she'd like to live after she attends graduate school.

    c. America is a richer, more-educated country than Taiwan.

    d. Taiwan's citizens are less violent and more friendly than Americans.

    e. Her grandparents should move from Taiwan to the USA.

READ: Keys Activity 4.3

Examine each of the numbered phrases or sentences and complete the following on a separate sheet of paper or in your notebook.

(a) Write the boldfaced, italicized word. Identify one or two words that you can put in the place of the boldfaced, italicized word without changing the meaning of the phrase or sentence and write this synonym or synonymous phrase (words that have the same meaning) beside the word. (b) Identify the part of speech of this word as used in the sentence. (c) Look up the boldfaced, italicized word in a dictionary and write the dictionary definition. How does this compare with the definition from context? (d) List the parts of speech this word can sometimes be. (e) Write a complete sentence with each word.

1. Whenever one thinks of an American, one usually ***conjures*** up an image . . .

2. I wasn't a pale-faced, yellow-haired foreigner. Instead, the differences were much more ***subtle.***

3. Only the "native-born" Chinese and Taiwanese had the 3-D glasses that illuminated a *waiguo ren* among a ***homogenous*** crowd of dark heads.

4. We simply couldn't communicate very well with my limited Mandarin and their speaking a different ***dialect,*** Hakka.

5. ***Inadvertently,*** my parents were the intermediaries in the conversation, spanning the language gap . . .

6. Inadvertently, my parents were the ***intermediaries*** in the conversation, spanning the language gap . . .

7. They always say, "Wow, just like an American!"—as if I've successfully ***assimilated*** into a culture they long to be a part of.

8. My summer in Taiwan was fascinating not only because of the ***novelty***—but rather learning about my culture, and, in retrospect, learning about myself . . .

9. My summer in Taiwan was fascinating not only because of the novelty—but rather learning about my culture, and, in ***retrospect,*** learning about myself.

10. I got a glimpse of the future. Taiwan's ***burgeoning*** economic, social, and political aims give the nation a lot of potential in becoming a force in Asia and the world.

READ: Keys Activity 4.4

In Part A, use the following list of words to fill in the blanks. In Part B, use the information from Part A to complete the analogies.

Part A

identical	slight	unintention	growing
noticeable	calls	various	newness
deliberate	go-betweens	hindsight	absorbed
foresight	lessening	dismisses	superiors
standard	routine	separated	accent

Synonym	**Word**	**Antonym**
_____	**1.** conjures	_____
_____	**2.** subtle	_____
_____	**3.** homogenous	_____
_____	**4.** dialect	_____

_____   **5.** inadvertently   _____

_____   **6.** intermediaries   _____

_____   **7.** assimilated   _____

_____   **8.** novelty   _____

_____   **9.** retrospect   _____

_____   **10.** burgeoning   _____

Part B

1. _____ : retrospect :: slight : subtle

2. growing : _____ :: newness : novelty

3. go-between : intermediaries :: absorbed : _____

4. _____ : dialect :: different : homogenous

5. deliberately : _____ :: burgeoning : lessening

6. hindsight : retrospect :: calls : _____

7. accent : _____ :: routine : novelty

8. subtle : noticeable :: burgeoning : _____

9. intermediaries : _____ :: homogenous : different

10. conjures : dismisses :: retrospect : _____

READ: Keys Activity Posttest

Rate each of the following words according to your knowledge of them.

Word	Stage 0 *I don't know this word.*	Stage 1 *I've seen this word but I know nothing of its meaning.*	Stage 2 *I've seen this word and can make associations with it.*	Stage 3 *I know this word.*
1. conjures				
2. subtle				
3. homogenous				
4. dialect				
5. inadvertently				
6. intermediaries				
7. assimilated				
8. novelty				
9. retrospect				
10. burgeoning				

Answers to Test Anxiety Scale in Exercise 4.1.

1. T	5. T	9. T	13. F
2. T	6. T	10. F	14. T
3. T	7. T	11. T	15. T
4. T	8. T	12. T	16. T

Grade your response to the Test Anxiety Scale. If your answers match eleven or more times, then anxiety might be a problem for you.

Vocabulary Development

Chapter Map Exercise

Complete the following chapter map by filling in the blanks with the sub-headings in the chapter.

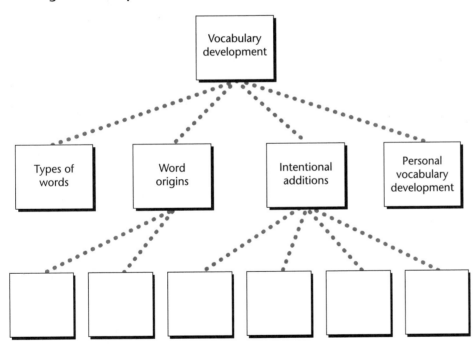

Objectives

After you finish this chapter, you will be able to do the following:

1. Compare different types of vocabulary.
2. Identify how words originate.
3. Describe ways that words are intention-ally added to the language.
4. Summarize your personal vocabulary development process.

Chapter Outline Exercise

Complete the following chapter outline by filling in the blanks with the sub-headings in the chapter.

I. Types of words

II. Word origins

    A. _____

    B _____

III. Intentional additions

    A. _____

    B. _____

    C. _____

    D. _____

IV. Personal vocabulary development

Do your thoughts decide the words you use? Or, do the words you have decide your thinking? When George Orwell wrote the novel *1984* in 1949, he described a society that controlled what people did and even thought. In fact, people were taught a new language called Newspeak. In this new language, no words existed for thoughts like *freedom.* In Orwell's words, such thoughts were "literally unthinkable" because there were no words to express them.

So, do thoughts determine words? Or, do words determine thoughts? The answers to these questions are *yes . . .* and *yes.* When people think of a new concept, they create a new word to name it. However, the words you personally know often determine how you think about a subject. This chapter looks at the words of our language—the types of vocabulary you'll find in your college courses, how language develops in general, and ways to develop your personal vocabulary.

Types of Words

If you look at the **glossary** in a typical freshman-level college text, you'll probably find more new words than you would find in a freshman level foreign language text. Thus, each course you take has a language of its own. Part of the course goal is for you to communicate in that subject's language. Not only are you learning the meaning of the words, you're also learning to think in those terms. The text glossary is a useful resource because it defines essential terms needed for understanding course content. Three types of words are found in college courses: general, technical, and specialized vocabulary.

General vocabulary words form the building blocks of language. These common words apply to many subjects. They include words like *one, exam, buy, forget,* and *different.* When you add general words to your vocabulary, you build your knowledge and communication in all subjects.

Technical vocabulary words or phrases apply to a specific subject. They have no meaning outside the context of the subject. Although each subject has its own technical terms, such words appear most often in science and applied technology courses. Examples include *ion* (science), *treble clef* (music), *sauté* (food and nutrition), and *polynomial* (math). Technical vocabulary words often pose problems because you need to learn them quickly. This speed is necessary because often you need these words to understand other concepts.

Sometimes general words have special meanings in specific content areas. These are termed **specialized vocabulary.** For instance,

> A person growing up with Newspeak as his sole language would no more know that . . . free had once meant "intellectually free," than, for instance a person who had never heard of chess would be aware of the secondary meanings attached to queen and rook. There would be many crimes and errors which would be beyond his power to commit, simply because they were nameless and therefore unimaginable.
>
> —George Orwell
> *Twentieth century American novelist*

READ Exercise 5.1

the general word *set* has specific meanings for theater (a stage *set*), math (a *set* of numbers) and printing (to *set* type). Humanities texts use specialized vocabulary when they use symbolic or figurative language (see Chapter 6). Specialized vocabulary words often appear in social science and science texts. Such words present problems because the meaning you know may hinder your understanding and learning a new meaning. *Exercise 5.1 provides practice in identifying types of vocabulary in context.*

Word Origins

> **Words have their genealogy, their history, their economy, their literature, their art and music, as too they have their weddings and divorces, their successes and defeats, their fevers, their undiagnosable ailments, their sudden deaths.**
>
> —Virgilia Peterson
> *Twentieth century writer and TV critic*

The study of word histories is called **etymology.** A word's etymology is its genealogy. It tells when and how a word was born. It tells how the word is used now. Why should you learn about word histories? The more you know about a word, the more you understand and recall it.

Etymologies show that English is a living and growing language. Although many words have been in our language for many years, new words join all the time. Dictionary entries often include information (see Figure 5.1) about a word's etymology. In this example, *bedlam* is a variation of the word *Bethlehem.* Just as we often shorten a lengthy name of a place to something easier, people probably referred to the Hospital of St. Mary of Bethlehem (a hospital for the insane) as simply *Bethlehem*—or in this case, *Bedlam.* The date in parentheses tells approximately when the word originated. *Bedlam* can be traced to 1522. When used to describe a maniac (see meaning 1), *bedlam* is an obsolete meaning. When capitalized, *Bedlam* refers to an asylum for the mentally ill. The history of the word clarifies the meaning. Now it's easy to see why people describe an out-of-control situation as *bedlam.*

How do words become part of the vocabulary of English? In *The Mother Tongue: English and How It Got That Way* (1990), Bill Bryson says that words were often borrowed from other languages or created by accident. In addition, some are purposefully created.

Incorporating Foreign Words

READ Exercise 5.2

Do you speak a foreign language? If you speak English, then you probably use words each day that came from a foreign language. Most of our language has ancient Greek, Anglo-Saxon, or Latin origins. Words from other languages have also been added to our vocabularies. Table 5.1 shows some examples of foreign words and their sources. *Exercise 5.2 gives you an opportunity to identify the country of origin for common English words.*

Figure 5.1   Dictionary Entry Example

bed·lam \'bed-ləm\ n [Bedlam, a popular name for the Hospital of St. Mary of Bethlehem, London, an insane asylum] (1522) **1** *obs* : a maniac; **2** *often cap* : a lunatic asylum; **3** a place, scene, or state of confusion.

Table 5.1   Examples of Foreign Words and Their Countries of Origin

abolish, jury, larceny, mackerel, massage, olive	France
chino, bonanza, bravado, ranch, spaniel	Spain
whim, reel, shrivel, queer, rift, baffle, scraggy	Scandinavia
jilt, nab, bog	Scotland
hold, howitzer, toot, yacht, yawl, aardvark, wilt	Holland
sauerkraut, strudel	Germany
salami, cameo, balcony, macaroni, opera	Italy
arsenal, harem, alcohol, algebra	Arabia
cocoa, coyote, arroyo, chocolate	Mexico
tank, molasses, albino, caste, banana	Portugal
tangerine, canary, chimpanzee, zombie	Africa
hickory, hammock, tobacco, succotash	American (Indian)

Accidental Creation of Words

When conditions are exactly right, a substance can burst into flames without fire or heat. Similarly, words—when the conditions are right—burst into being. Such words often reflect the background from which they originated. Others occur when ideas get to be known more by the letters that stand for them than by the words that name them.

History affects words as well as people. The time, place, and circumstances surrounding an event influence meaning. New words explain or define these events or meet new needs. For instance, the word *mailman* was coined to describe postal service workers who delivered mail. History continues to change the meanings of these words through use. For example, in response to the demand to make words less sexist, *mailman* became *letter carrier*. The words live in our language. *Exercise 5.3 lets you practice finding word histories in a dictionary.*   *READ Exercise 5.3*

Some people, such as 'NSync's J.C. Chasez, poet e.e. cummings, musical group LFO, female vocalist J Lo, and musician Master P, often choose to use initials rather than names. Their initials become so well connected with them that people even forget their names. The same thing can happen with items, concepts, or groups. The initials eventually replace the names, and they represent the item, concept, or group. Common words from letters include *SUV*—sport utility vehicle; *PC*—Personal Computer; *TV*—TeleVision; *DUI*—Driving Under the Influence; *VD*—Venereal Disease; *UPC*—Universal Product Code; and *DVD*—Digital Video Disc.

Acronyms are words formed from the first letters or first few letters of several words. Acronyms sometimes aid your memory (see Chapter 4). Other acronyms now replace the words for which they once stood. Common words from acronyms include RAM—Random Access Memory, SNAFU—Situation Normal All Fouled Up (in polite terms), NABISCO—NAtional BIScuit COmpany; M*A*S*H—Mobile Army Surgical Hospital, and SIDS—Sudden Infant Death Syndrome.

READ Exercise 5.4 *Exercise 5.4 lets you practice using a dictionary to find the meanings of words that are abbreviations or acronyms.*

Intentional Additions

What do you call the screw that holds a lampshade in place? The *doodad* or the *finial?* What is the hinged flap on the wing of an airplane called? The *thingamabob* or the *aileron?* What would you call the fluid in rubber trees? The *whatchamacallit* or *latex?* Faced with such choices, inventors, authors, and others have created names for every product, process, and item they developed, found, or described. Because these developments occur every day, our language changes daily with the addition of new words. *The essay in Exercise 5.5 helps you see how some intentional additions begin at home. Exercise 5.6 lets you see how your definitions for new words to our language compare with their dictionary definitions. Exercises 5.7 through 5.9 give you opportunities to identify the etymology of selected words from three of the READ Keys excerpts.*

READ Exercise 5.5
READ Exercise 5.6

READ Exercises 5.7–5.9

Words from Products

In the summer of 1881, an assassin tried to kill U.S. President James Garfield. Garfield slipped in and out of consciousness for more than two months before he died. To provide him some relief during the summer heat, military engineers were asked to invent something that would cool his room. Using ice, water, salt, filters, and a fan, they

Table 5.2   Examples of Words from Common Products

yo-yo	cornflakes	thermos	Kleenex
Band-Aid	sheetrock	aspirin	zipper
Xerox	Walkman radio	nylon	trampoline
linoleum	Velcro	Jacuzzi	hamburger

Table 5.3   Examples of Contemporary Additions from Science and Technology

astronaut	V-chip	terminal	satellite
space shuttle	output	splashdown	monitor
countdown	programmer	microwave	call waiting
solar cell	user-friendly	byte	compact disk

managed to cool Garfield's room to 81 degrees. Garfield finally died in mid-September. But this is not just an historical account. This is also a story of the etymology of the term *air conditioner* (*American Heritage*, 1964).

It makes sense that the invention of new products requires the invention of new names. But, in some cases, the products become so well known that all similar products became known by the same name. Table 5.2 lists common words from products.

Words from Science and Technology

Scientists are in the business of finding and identifying new elements and processes. Things we take for granted now were once exciting new discoveries. The 1600s brought us *magnetism* (1616), *gravity* (1642), and *electricity* (1646), among others. Contributions during the next two centuries included *oxygen* (1789), *atom* (1801), and *evolution* (1832). *Hormone* (1904), *vitamin*, (1905), and *penicillin* (1928) are early twentieth century additions. New words such as *e-mail, Internet, designer genes,* and *in vitro fertilization* continue to reflect current interests, trends, and innovations. Innovations in technology and the sciences have been some of the most recent contributors. Words from these areas appear in Table 5.3.

Table 5.4   Examples of Contemporary Additions from Social Science and Humanities

Watergate	hype	rollerblade	lifestyle	culture
food processor	built-in	fast foods	X-rated	feminist
zit	hijack	close-captioned	Heimlich maneuver	gridlock
strip search	the Web	street people	go postal	downsize
trophy wife	focus group	family leave	reality check	urban legend

Words from Social Sciences and the Humanities

Scientists are not the only people who devise, describe, and name new ideas. For example, William Shakespeare (Brandeth, 1980) coined more than 1,700 words including *assassinate, bump, critical, hurry,* and *lonely.* Contemporary events such as wars also produced new words. For instance, *binge, camouflage,* and *zoom* came from World War I, and World War II produced *blackout, blitz,* and *bulldozer.* The Vietnam War gave us *defoliate* and the verb form of *napalm.* The Persian Gulf War also contributed a variety of new words and phrases to our vocabulary such as *airborne sanitation* and *smart bombs.* The human condition provides a wealth of new terms, including the words in Table 5.4.

Words from Math

In math, the focus of vocabulary is less on how a word came into being and more on how it is used in the context of math. Whether specialized or technical vocabulary (see Tables 5.5 and 5.6), math terms require exact meanings. Synonyms or approximate definitions are not good enough. The meaning of a word sometimes differs by topic within the subject of math. For example, *base* has a different meaning in geometry than it does in algebra.

Write to Learn

Twentieth century Supreme Court Justice Oliver Wendell Holmes, Jr., said, "A word is not a crystal, transparent and unchanged; it is the skin of a living thought and may vary greatly in color and content according to the circumstances and time in which it is used." Respond to the following on a separate sheet of paper or in your notebook: Using a collegiate dictionary, identify three words, other than those identified in the section on etymology, and describe how the color and content of the words have changed according to circumstances and time.

Table 5.5   Examples of Math Words with Specialized Meanings

base	point	square	ray	union	ruler
tangent	locus	compass	function	intercepts	coordinates
axis	domain	radical	even	value	angle
log	inequality	negative	slope	intervals	equilateral
null	parallel	inverse	variable	infinity	symmetrical
equation	difference	product	quadrant	paradox	reciprocal

Table 5.6   Examples of Math Words with Technical Meanings

parabola	asymptotes	logarithm	pi	hyperbola	sine
cosine	theorem	topology	scalene	hypotenuse	integer

Personal Vocabulary Development

The language we speak grew as words joined, left, and changed to meet new needs. Growth was both accidental and intentional. Similarly, your vocabulary grows as you encounter new subjects and situations. Some words will be added to your vocabulary without deliberate effort. But, you may need to intentionally collect others to grow the words you need to understand and be understood in the subjects you take.

Awareness forms the first step in your vocabulary development. Choose to notice unfamiliar words that you hear or see. When you come upon them, make a mental or written note to check their meanings.

Verification is a second step in learning new words. Look at the word's context (see Chapter 6) to see if it gives clues to meaning. When you hear or see a word in the context of a specific course, check a text glossary to identify specialized or technical meanings. Then, check the dictionary to see if it also has general meanings.

Third, decide if this is a word you want to add to your vocabulary. Some words have limited meaning or usage. Others are essential to the subject. Focus on learning the most important words first. How will you know if a word is important or critical? Terms identified by the author in either a list or in context (e.g., by boldface) are important. Words that repeatedly appear in either the text or the lecture are also critical to your understanding.

> **The words! I collected them in all shapes and sizes, and hung them like bangles in my mind.**
>
> —Hortense Calisher
> *Twentieth century American novelist and educator*

Fourth, if the word is one you want to add, decide how well you want to understand and use it. Is general understanding enough or do you need precise meanings? For instance, you might only need to know that *serotonin* is a kind of brain chemical in biology; however, you probably need to know the exact meaning of *union* in math.

Fifth, put the word in writing. You can use word lists, notecards, concept maps, or other forms as you want. Include the definition of the word in context and **paraphrase** (put in your own words) the definition as well. If you don't understand the original definition, look up words within it until you know what it means well enough to rephrase it. When possible, give examples of the word or include related concepts. The more connections you have with a word, the more easily you can recall it. Make sure you know how the word is pronounced. The look and sound of some words differ.

Last, use the words in writing and speaking. This helps you assimilate the words in your thinking. Nineteenth-century American poet Emily Dickinson said, "A word is dead when it is said, some say. I say it just begins to live that day." Using words to communicate brings your vocabulary to life and helps it grow.

Chapter Summary Exercise

On a separate sheet of paper or in your notebooks, complete the chapter summary by filling in the blanks:

Words determine thoughts and thoughts determine words. Three types of words are often found in college courses. Words common to all courses are called (1) _____ vocabulary. Words that apply to a specific subject are (2) _____ vocabulary. (3) _____ vocabulary refers to those general vocabulary words that have a different meaning in a specific subject. (4) _____ is the study of word histories. Many of the words that we consider to be English really come from (5) _____ languages. Some words are created by accident. For example, some concepts become better known by their initials or as special words called (6) _____. Some words are intentionally created. For instance, the names of some products became so well-known that all similar products are also known by that name. Examples of these products include (7) _____, (8) _____, and

(9) _____. Some words come from inventions, discoveries, and events. Examples of these include (10) _____ (from science and technology), (11) _____ (from humanities and social science), and (12) _____ (from math).

Personal vocabulary development is a process. The first step is (13) _____. This means (14) _____.

Step 2 is (15) _____. This involves (16) _____

_____. In Step 3, you decide

(17) _____.

This is important because (18) _____.

In Step 4, you decide (19) _____.

Step 5 involves (20) _____. You

can use different forms to record the word. In addition to the word,

you can also include (21) _____ and (22) _____

_____. Last, it's important to use the word in (23) _____

_____ and (24) _____.

Chapter Review

Respond to the following on a separate sheet of paper or in your notebook.

1. Using the content of a course in which you are now enrolled, provide an example of general, technical, and specialized vocabulary in your course text or notes.

2. How can a text glossary help you learn course terms more efficiently than a dictionary can?

3. What is a word's etymology? How can it help you remember new words?

4. Name and give an example of each source of new words described in the chapter.

5. List the steps in developing your vocabulary. Check the ones you already do. Underline the steps that were new to you. Put a star by the one you think is most important to you.

Terms

Terms appear in the order in which they occur in the chapter.

glossary
**general
    vocabulary**
**technical
    vocabulary**
**specialized
    vocabulary**
etymology
acronyms
paraphrase

Exercises

Exercise 5.1   The following words are underlined in Sample Chapter 11, "Opportunities to Work in the Theater," at the end of this text. On a separate sheet of paper or in your notebook, identify if the words are general, specialized, or technical terms in the context of the subject. Define each word in context.

1. an <u>avocational</u> interest

2. whose <u>sole</u> responsibility

3. <u>plays</u> sometimes are directed

4. from the <u>immediate</u> community

5. the production program is treated as <u>extracurricular</u>

6. <u>bachelor</u> of fine arts degree

7. participation in productions is often restricted to <u>majors</u>

8. who will become teachers, <u>dramaturges,</u> theatre historians, critics, and scholars

9. some <u>mingle</u> students and professionals

10. from many <u>periods</u>

11. hold <u>joint</u> auditions

12. more <u>prosperous</u> groups

13. They should be <u>diplomatic</u>

14. only a <u>nucleus</u> company

15. receive room and <u>board</u>

16. a major <u>clearinghouse</u>

17. actors in each <u>company</u>

18. Eligible Performer's <u>Card</u>

19. <u>principal</u> stage managers

20. for <u>aspirants</u> to look to theatres

Exercise 5.2   On a separate sheet of paper or in your notebook, match the following words with their country or language of origin. This information can be found in a large collegiate dictionary.

1.	moose	A.	Dutch
2.	snoop	B.	Spanish
3.	bagel	C.	Algonquian (American Indian)
4.	detour	D.	Yiddish
5.	khaki	E.	Chinese
6.	tycoon	F.	Arabic
7.	safari	G.	Japanese
8.	avocado	H.	French
9.	chowchow	I.	Hindi

Exercise 5.3   Look up the histories for the following words in the etymology section of the entries of a large collegiate dictionary. On a separate sheet of paper or in your notebook, identify the word's history, then define it.

1. bonfire

2. assassin

3. chauvinist

4. hooligan

5. jumbo

6. namby-pamby

7. derby

8. dunce

9. spoonerism

10. leotard

Exercise 5.4   Look up the etymologies of each of the following words in a large collegiate dictionary. On a separate sheet of paper or in your notebook, identify if the word is an acronym or derived from initials and what each letter stands for. Then, define the meaning of the word.

1. GI
2. FYI
3. LASER
4. SCUBA
5. RADAR
6. MTV
7. CD
8. SONAR
9. e-mail
10. bit (in computer science)

Exercise 5.5   Read the essay and answer the questions that follow on a separate sheet of paper or in your notebook.

A Family Has a Slang All Its Own

Let's call it family slang: words invented by you and yours that don't appear in any dictionary but that convey your meaning just fine.

If you don't think you have any, think again.

I never considered this phenomenon until I hear my brother, an IBM manager, use a weird word to address his 13-year-old son, who grabbed the last piece of bacon off the breakfast platter.

"Aww!" My brother groaned to his boy. "What a *peckinjivinwood!*" That's pronounced like peck-and-jive-in-wood, but real fast.

His son knew exactly how to take that. It's Dad's word for anyone who's a little sleazy, a little selfish, but still mostly lovable. My brother can't remember when or why or how he made up that word, but it's as much a part of his vocabulary as "jerk" and "loser" and "doofus"—all of which were coined by one human being, then migrated into the mainstream.

It's tough for an average dad to get his words into widespread circulation. It helps to be a writer. Not long ago a colleague wandered into my office to say that a friend of his, a columnist at the *Santa Rosa (Calif.) Press Democrat,* is credited in the new edition of the Oxford English Dictionary with having coined the phrase "bad hair day." She told her friends she thinks she picked it up from her daughter.

Envy filled my heart. I grew up wanting to change the world but have only changed clothes, changed gears, and changed light bulbs. To change the language would be very satisfying.

But I've invented only a couple of words. "Yikesarooni!" is my response when I hear an amazing story of troubles. "Woweekazowee" is what I say when I'm very excited. When I pull open the veggie drawer and find that the zucchinis have deteriorated to slime, I call it "smuchneyeh"—pronounced the way it looks—a word that's good to describe any icky mess. (I think I adapted it from the Polish "smaczne"—smach-nyeh—which means delicious). To "squoosh" something, like a tomato, is to squeeze it till it collapses. And when my husband goes grocery shopping, he knows what I mean when I ask if he got any "tasties," my word for free food samples.

I inherited "yejeboat" from my family, a word Mom or Dad hollered whenever it was time to go and we kids were dawdling. It rhymes with edge-a-boat and we understand it as "Hurry up!" But it's a mix of Polish and English that literally means "the boat is leaving." I'm guessing it goes back generations.

An old boyfriend taught me that a car with a burnt-out headlight is a "padiddle." I've heard other people use it, too, but it hasn't made Merriam-Webster's yet.

Food is a favorite for coined words. That hodgepodge of macaroni, hamburger and tomato sauce? One family calls it "ooblek." Another calls it "hooshmie." At college we called it Johnny Marzetti, whoever he was.

What a happy mystery, how the playful brain finds sounds to make meaning.

Some of the words might catch on, now that they're in print. The author of *Alice in Wonderland,* Lewis Carroll, gave us "squawk" a clever blend of squall and squeak. And in the late 1960s, according to Merriam Webster, somebody gave us "humongous," a gorgeous word that is scarier than the sum of its parts: huge and monstrous.

Could have been a 13-year-old boy. Maybe he was talking fast, describing a creature in his nightmares. And maybe a writer was listening.

From Susan Ager, Knight Ridder Newspapers, Appeared in the *Kansas City Star* on Sunday, September 9, 2001.

1. Define each of the following underlined words in the essay from context: peckinjivinwood, doofus, yikesarooni, woweekazowee, smuchneyeh, smaczne, squoosh, tasties, yejeboat, padiddle, ooblek, hooshmie, Johnny Marzetti, squawk, humongous. Put a check by the words that can be found in a dictionary (English or other).

2. What is the main idea of the essay?

Exercise 5.6   The tenth edition of *Merriam Webster's Collegiate Dictionary* identifies the following words as recent additions to our language. On a separate sheet of paper or in your notebook, answer the following questions for each word: What does the word mean to you? What is the word's dictionary definition? How do the two definitions compare?

1. glass ceiling

2. couch potato

3. date rape

4. hip-hop

5. significant other

6. voice mail

   7. ozone hole

   8. downsize

   9. spin doctor

   10. safe sex

   11. buffalo wing

   12. abs

   13. home schooling

   14. secondhand smoke

   15. scrunchie

Exercise 5.7   Respond to the following on a separate sheet of paper or in your notebook. Provide the etymology and definitions of the following italicized words in the READ Keys excerpt in Chapter 8 ("Being Appropriate" from *Building a Speech):* *elevator, fluffy* (see *fluff), vowels, consonants, dialect, patronizing, fax, bottom line, silly, negotiations.*

Exercise 5.8   Respond to the following on a separate sheet of paper or in your notebook. Provide the etymology and definitions of the following italicized words in the READ Keys excerpt in Chapter 3 ("The Most Precious Gift"*):* *muses, banjo, grin, county, ramshackle, hamlet, movie, whim.*

Exercise 5.9   Respond to the following on a separate sheet of paper or in your notebook. Provide the etymology and definitions of the following italicized words in the READ Keys excerpt in Chapter 6 ("Entunese Mañana"): *soap operas, hippies, earth mother, wayward, buddy, smooches, fans, slurs, norm, baldness* (see *bald), restaurants, bus*

Web Exercise

A variety of information related to you, the reader, is available on the World Wide Web. For this exercise, search using the word *etymology.* Choose a Web site related to word histories and answer the following questions on a separate sheet of paper or in your notebook.

   1. What is the title and URL for the Web site you chose?

   2. What kind of information does the Web site provide?

   3. How can this Web site help you learn new words?

   4. Use the Web site to identify and summarize the etymology for three words.

READ: Keys

READ: Keys Activity Pretest

Rate each of the following words according to your knowledge of them.

Word	Stage 0 *I don't know this word.*	Stage 1 *I've seen this word but I know nothing of its meaning.*	Stage 2 *I've seen this word and can make associations with it.*	Stage 3 *I know this word.*
1. obscurely				
2. apprehensively				
3. oblige				
4. detachment				
5. scorn				
6. giddy				
7. solitude				
8. draught				
9. indulge				
10. phial				

READ: Keys Activity 5.1

Read the following excerpt and keep track of your reading time.

The Chaser
John Collier

Alan Austen, as nervous as a kitten, went up certain dark and creaky stairs in the neighborhood of Pell Street, and peered about for a long time on the dim landing before he found the name he wanted written **obscurely** on one of the doors.

He pushed open this door, as he had been told to, and found himself in a tiny room, which contained no furniture but a plain kitchen table, a rocking chair, and an ordinary chair. On one of the dirty buff-colored walls were a couple of shelves, containing in all perhaps a dozen bottles and jars. An old man sat in the rocking chair, reading a newspaper. Alan, without a word, handed him the card he had been given.

"Sit down, Mr. Austen," said the old man very politely. "I am glad to make your acquaintance."

"Is it true," asked Alan, "that you have a certain mixture that has—er—quite extraordinary effects?"

"My dear sir," replied the old man, "my stock in trade is not very large—I don't deal in laxatives and teething mixtures—but such as it is, it is varied. I think nothing I sell has effects which could be precisely described as ordinary."

"Well, the fact is—" began Alan.

"Here, for example," interrupted the old man, reaching for a bottle from the shelf. "Here is a liquid as colorless as water, almost tasteless, quite imperceptible in coffee, milk, wine, or any other beverage. It is also quite imperceptible to any known method of autopsy."

"Do you mean it is a poison?" cried Alan, very much horrified.

"Call it a glove-cleaner if you like," said the old man indifferently. "Maybe it will clean gloves. I have never tried. One might call it a life-cleaner. Lives need cleaning sometimes."

"I want nothing of that sort." said Alan.

"Probably it is just as well," said the old man. "Do you know the price of this? For one teaspoonful, which is sufficient, I ask five thousand dollars. Never less. Not a penny less."

"I hope all your mixtures are not as expensive," said Alan **apprehensively.**

"Oh dear, no," said the old man. "It would be no good charging that sort of price for a love potion, for example. Young people who need a love potion very seldom have five thousand dollars. Otherwise they would not need a love potion."

"I am glad to hear that," said Alan.

"I look at it like this," said the old man. "Please a customer with one article, and he will come back when he needs another. Even if it is more costly, he will save up for it, if necessary,"

"So," said Alan, "you really do sell love potions?"

"If I did not sell love potions," said the old man, reaching for another bottle, "I should not have mentioned the other matter to you. It is only when one is in a position to *oblige* that one can afford to be so confidential."

"And these potions," said Alan. "They are not just-just-"

"Oh, no," said the old man. "Their effects are permanent, and extend far beyond casual impulse. But they include it. Bountifully, insistently, everlastingly."

"Dear me!" said Alan, attempting a look of scientific *detachment.* "How very interesting!"

"But consider the spiritual side," said the old man.

"I do, indeed," said Alan.

"For indifference," said the old man, "they substitute devotion. For *scorn,* adoration. Give one tiny measure of this to the young lady—its flavor is imperceptible in orange juice, soup, or cocktails—and however gay and *giddy* she is, she will change altogether. She will want nothing but *solitude,* and you."

"I can hardly believe it," said Alan. "She is so fond of parties."

"She will not like them any more," said the old man. "She will be afraid of the pretty girls you may meet."

"She will actually be jealous?" cried Alan in rapture. "Of me?"

"Yes, she will want to be everything to you."

"She is, already. Only she doesn't care about it."

"She will, when she has taken this. She will care intensely. You will be her sole interest in life."

"Wonderful!" cried Alan.

"She will want to know all you do," said the old man. "All that has happened to you during the day. Every word of it. She will want to know what you are thinking about, why you smile suddenly, why you are looking sad."

"That is love!" cried Alan.

"Yes," said the old man. "How carefully she will look after you! She will never allow you to be tired, to sit in a *draught,* to neglect your food. If you are an hour late, she will be terrified. She will think you are killed, or that some siren has caught you."

"I can hardly imagine Diana like that!" cried Alan, overwhelmed with joy.

"You will not have to use your imagination," said the old man. "And, by the way, since there are always sirens, if by any chance you should, later on, slip a little, you need not worry. She will forgive you, in the end. She will be terribly hurt, of course, but she will forgive you in the end."

"That will not happen," said Alan fervently.

"Of course not," said the old man. "But, if it did, you need not worry. She would never divorce you. Oh, no! And, of course, she herself will never give you the least, the very least, grounds for uneasiness."

"And how much," said Alan, "is this wonderful mixture?"

"It is not as dear," said the old man, "as the glove-cleaner, or life-cleaner, as I sometimes call it. No. That is five thousand dollars, never a penny less. One has to be older than you are to *indulge* in that sort of thing. One has to save up for it."

"But the love potion?" said Alan.

"Oh, that," said the old man, opening the drawer in the kitchen table and taking out a tiny, rather dirty-looking ***phial.*** "That is just a dollar.

"I can't tell you how grateful I am," said Alan, watching him fill it.

"I like to oblige," said the old man. "Then customers come back, later in life, when they are rather better off, and want more expensive things. Here you are. You will find it very effective,"

"Thank you again," said Alan. "Good-by!"

"*Au revoir,*" said the old man.

Originally from *The New Yorker.* Copyright 1940 by John Collier.

1059 words / _____ minutes = _____ words per minute

Calculate your reading time by dividing the number of words in the article by the amount of time it took to read it. Then mark your reading time on the chart located on page 338.

READ: Keys Activity 5.2

On a separate sheet of paper or in your notebook, answer the following questions about the excerpt you just read:

1. Who is Diana?

    a. the old man's daughter

    b. a woman that Alan likes

    c. Alan's mother

    d. none of the above

2. How might the old man's apartment be described?

    a. bright and cheerful

    b. small and dingy

    c. well-furnished and clean

    d. small but attractive

3. The old man says, "Young people who need a love potion very seldom have five thousand dollars. Otherwise they would not need a love potion." He means

    a. it's easy to find love if someone has money.

b. lovers don't care about money.

c. there's no relationship between love and money.

d. love makes you wealthy.

4. When the old man says that Alan might "slip a little," he means Alan might

a. fall.

b. have an affair with another woman.

c. be clumsy

d. become forgetful.

5. The real danger in Diana's taking the old man's love potion is that

a. it will also clean her life.

b. it won't work.

c. it can also kill her.

d. Diana will smother Alan with attention.

6. The old man is most like a _____

a. doctor.

b. lawyer.

c. minister.

d. pharmacist.

7. Which word best describes the old man's inventory?

a. extensive

b. expensive

c. limited

d. ordinary

8. What is the effect of the life cleaner?

a. It makes someone tell the truth.

b. It makes a person who takes it more wealthy.

c. It kills anyone who takes it.

d. It has the same effect as a love potion.

9. In this story, a *siren* refers to _____.

   a. a loud noise

   b. a flashing light

   c. another woman

   d. Diana

10. Which of the following describes Diana before she takes the potion?

   a. Diana does not know Alan.

   b. Diana is fun-loving and not attracted to Alan.

   c. Diana is reclusive and serious.

   d. Diana adores Alan and wants to get married.

READ: Keys Activity 5.3

Examine each of the numbered phrases or sentences and complete the following on a separate sheet of paper or in your notebook.

(a) Write the boldfaced, italicized word. Identify one or two words that you can put in the place of the boldfaced, italicized word without changing the meaning of the phrase or sentence and write this synonym or synonymous phrase (words that have the same meaning) beside the word. (b) Identify the part of speech of this word as used in the sentence. (c) Look up the boldfaced, italicized word in a dictionary and write the dictionary definition. How does this compare with the definition from context? (d) List the parts of speech this word can sometimes be. (e) Write a complete sentence with each word.

1. Alan Austen, as nervous as a kitten, went up certain dark and creaky stairs in the neighborhood of Pell Street, and peered about for a long time on the dim landing before he found the name he wanted written ***obscurely*** on one of the doors.

2. "I hope all your mixtures are not as expensive," said Alan ***apprehensively***.

3. "If I did not sell love potions," said the old man, reaching for another bottle, "I should not have mentioned the other matter to you. It is only when one is in a position to ***oblige*** that one can afford to be so confidential."

4. "Dear me!" said Alan, attempting a look of scientific ***detachment***.

5. "For indifference," said the old man, "they substitute devotion. For ***scorn,*** adoration.

6. Give one tiny measure of this to the young lady—its flavor is imperceptible in orange juice, soup, or cocktails—and however gay and ***giddy*** she is, she will change altogether.

7. She will want nothing but ***solitude,*** and you."

8. She will never allow you to be tired, to sit in a ***draught,*** to neglect your food.

9. One has to be older than you are to ***indulge*** in that sort of thing. One has to save up for it."

10. "Oh, that," said the old man, opening the drawer in the kitchen table and taking out a tiny, rather dirty-looking ***phial.***

READ: Keys Activity 5.4

In Part A, use the following list of words to fill in the blanks. In Part B, use the information from Part A to complete the analogies.

Part A

contempt	fearfully	box	indifference
bottle	serious	isolation	displease
enthusiasm	deny	breeze	satisfy
pamper	bravely	indistinctly	gust
frivolous	clearly	admiration	inclusion

Synonym	Word	Antonym
_____	**1.** obscurely	_____
_____	**2.** apprehensively	_____
_____	**3.** oblige	_____
_____	**4.** detachment	_____
_____	**5.** scorn	_____

_____ **6.** giddy _____

_____ **7.** solitude _____

_____ **8.** draught _____

_____ **9.** indulge _____

_____ **10.** phial _____

Part B

1. phial : _____ :: solitude : inclusion

2. giddy : serious :: indulge : _____

3. oblige : _____ :: apprehensively : fearfully

4. scorn : contempt :: detachment : _____

5. solitude : _____ :: draught : breeze

6. enthusiasm : _____ :: frivolous : giddy

7. box : bottle :: breeze : _____

8. obscurely : _____ :: indulge : satisfy

9. apprehensively : _____ :: draught : gust

10. clearly : _____ :: isolation : interest

READ: Keys Activity Posttest

Rate each of the following words according to your knowledge of them.

Word	Stage 0 *I don't know this word.*	Stage 1 *I've seen this word but I know nothing of its meaning.*	Stage 2 *I've seen this word and can make associations with it.*	Stage 3 *I know this word.*
1. obscurely				
2. apprehensively				
3. oblige				
4. detachment				
5. scorn				
6. giddy				
7. solitude				
8. draught				
9. indulge				
10. phial				

Using the Context

Chapter Map Exercise

Construct a chapter map from the major headings and subheadings in the chapter.

Objectives

After you finish this chapter, you will be able to do the following:

1. Demonstrate how to use context to identify part of speech.

2. Demonstrate how to use stated, bridging, and experiential context clues.

3. Identify types of figurative language.

Chapter Outline Exercise

Create a chapter outline from the major headings and subheadings in the chapter.

Ladle Rat Rotten Hut

Wants pawn term, dare worsted ladle gull hoe lift wetter murder inner ladle cordage honor itch offer lodge dock florish. Disc ladle gull orphan worry ladle cluck wetter putty ladle rat hut, end fur disc raisin pimple caulder ladle rat rotten hut. Wan moaning rat rotten hut's murder colder inset: "Ladle rat rotten hut, heresy ladle basking winsome burden barter and shirker cockles. Tick disc ladle basking tudor cordage offer groin murder hoe lifts honor udder site offer florist. Shaker lake, dun stopper laundry wrote, end yonder nor sorghum stenches dun stopper torque wet strainers."

"Hoe-cake, murder," resplendent ladle rat rotten hut, end tickle ladle basking an stuttered oft. Honor wrote tudor cordage offer groin murder, ladle rat rotten hut mitten anomalous woof.

"Wail wail, wail," set disc wicket woof, "evanescent ladle rat rotten hut! Wares or putty ladle gull goring wizard ladle basking?"

"Armor goring tumor groin murder's," reprisal ladle gull. "Grammars seeking bet. Armor ticking arson burden barter end shirker cockles."

"O hoe! Heifer blessing woke," setter wicket woof, butter taught tomb shelf, "Oil tickle shirt court tudor cordage offer groin murder. Oil ketchup wetter letter, an den—O bore!"

By permission. From a May 1953 issue of *Word Study* (c) 1953 by Merriam-Webster, Inc.

The story you just read is one your parents probably told you many times. Do you recognize it?

The story is "Little Red Riding Hood" written in a way that makes its subject difficult to grasp immediately.

Reread the story aloud and listen to the rhythm of the words. Does it make more sense? Now that you know story's subject, you more easily recognize the words that compose it. That's because your mind now supplies some of the standard words for the dialect. You can do this because you know how the words fit together in the story. For instance, you know all fairy tales begin "Once upon a time," so you translate "wants pawn term" for the standard opening. Your skill in identifying something, then, depends on your skill in figuring out its connection with its surroundings—its **context.**

As you may have discovered, using the context to define unknown words takes practice. But it is the easiest and most efficient way to identify words. In addition, using the context is the only way to figure out the exact use of the word in a particular sentence, passage, or chapter.

Consider the word *bar. Bar* is a common word. But without surrounding words, you don't know if it describes soap, a place that serves beer, a sand formation, a way to lock the door, or whatever. Readers often misunderstand because they identify the **literal** but incorrect meaning of a word when they should identify the meaning based on the way it was used.

Using Context to Identify Part of Speech

In "The Hunting of the Snark," twentieth century author Lewis Carroll writes, "The snark was a boojum." Although you might not know what *snark* or *boojum* means, you do know that both are nouns because an article (*the, a*) precedes each one. Thus, as nouns, they must be persons, places, or things. One consideration in using context, then, is the unknown word's **part of speech.** A word's function in a sentence helps determine its meaning. Consider the following sentences:

1. I hurt my *back* at work today.
2. Move *back* three spaces.
3. The *back* room needs painting.
4. Can you *back* your car out of the driveway?

The meaning of *back* depends on its use in each sentence. Although each sentence contains *back,* the word functions as a noun, adverb, adjective, and verb, in that order. Its meaning in the first sentence refers to a part of the body. In the second sentence, *back* indicates the direction in which movement should occur. The third sentence uses *back* to describe which room is to be painted. In the fourth sentence, *back* is an action to be taken by the driver. Thus, the meaning of *back* depends on its part of speech. Table 6.1 provides a review of the parts of speech. *Exercises 6.1 and 6.2 provide practice in working with parts of speech.*

READ Exercises 6.1 & 6.2

Using Context Clues to Determine Meaning

Police often block off the scene of a murder to search for clues. Such clues usually consist of three kinds. First, police look for obvious physical evidence—a smoking gun, a knife, and so on. Second, police search for clues that are less noticeable, such as threads from clothing or fingerprints. These are physical clues, but the police must figure out if and how they relate to the crime. Finally, investigators consider the

Table 6.1   Parts of Speech

Part of Speech	Definition	Function
Noun (n.)	Identifies persons, places, or things; collections or groups of persons, places, or things; qualities; actions; conditions; processes; ideas	Names
Pronoun (p.)	Replaces a noun	Names
Verb (v.)	Shows action or state of being	States, asks, or commands
Adjective (adj.)	Modifies or limits a noun or pronoun	Clarifies or describes
Adverb (adv.)	Modifies or limits a verb, adjective, or other adverb	Clarifies or describes
Preposition (prep.)	Connects the noun or pronoun following it to some other word in the sentence relationships	Clarifies or modifies
Conjunction (conj.)	Joins words or groups of words	Connects
Interjection (intj.)	Expresses strong or sudden feeling	Exclaims

situation: Was there a jealous lover? Did the victim owe large sums of money? Had the victim been involved in a quarrel of some kind? Each scenario could produce a murder. Putting all the clues together helps investigators figure out who did it.

Just as a detective uses clues to solve crimes, you use context clues to determine the meanings of new words. Some clues resemble the obvious physical clues found at the scene of a crime. They are stated within the sentence. Others parallel the less noticeable clues. They're there, but you must look for them and use your experience to bridge the gap between what is stated and unstated. Finally, sometimes you must look at a situation and use your background knowledge to figure it out.

Stated Context Clues

Stated context clues consist of written clues to the meanings of unknown words. They are found directly within text in sentences, paragraphs, passages, or chapters. Stated context clues can be punctuation marks or **linking verbs.** These marks and words point to the meanings

Table 6.2   Stated Context Clues: Types, Clues, and Examples

Types	Clues	Examples
Punctuation	commas, dashes, parentheses, brackets	The determination of physical characteristics like hair color is the result of *polygenic* (multiple gene) influence. *Aspiration*—the act of breathing—was explained in the CPR course.
Definition	is, was, are, means, involves, is called, that is, i.e., which means, resembles	*Statistics* involves using math to make predictions. *Mitosis,* i.e., the equal division of chromosome material, is a necessary step in cell division.

you need. Knowing the clues helps you define new words in context more effectively. Table 6.2 provides a summary of stated context clues and examples.

Punctuation text-based clues consist of commas, parentheses, brackets, or dashes. The information contained within the punctuation marks usually means the same or nearly the same as the unknown word. For example, "Atmospheric cooling leads to the formation of clouds and precipitation (moisture in the form of rain, fog, dew, hail, or snow)." Here, the word's meaning appears in parentheses. Thus, precipitation means moisture in the form of rain, fog, dew, hail, or snow. Or, sometimes the definition is given in the sentence and the word is set off by punctuation marks. Thus, the preceding example could be written, "Atmospheric cooling leads to the formation of clouds and moisture in the form of rain, fog, dew, hail, or snow (precipitation)." Punctuation marks are not always reliable indicators of meaning. In some cases, information set off by punctuation clarifies or explains the word rather than defines it. Or it may simply provide additional information. For example, "Atmospheric cooling leads to the formation of clouds and precipitation (in some cases)."

Definition text-based clues directly join the unknown word with the word or words that rename it or tell its meaning. The clues precede or follow words that are or act like linking verbs. A linking verb shows no action. Rather, it indicates being. Examples of these clues include *is, was, are, means, involves, is called,* and *resembles*. For example, "The art, science, or profession of teaching is pedagogy." In this sentence, pedagogy means "art, science, or profession of teaching."

READ Exercises 6.3 & 6.4   Exercises 6.3 and 6.4 allow you to practice determining word meanings from punctuation and definitional clues.

Table 6.3   Bridging Context Clues: Types, Clues, and Examples

Types	Clues	Examples
Contrast	however, on the contrary, while, but, instead of, on the other hand, although, nevertheless, yet	Students often *cram* at the last minute; however, spaced study proves more effective.
		ET was an *extraterrestrial* creature; on the other hand, the children with whom he lived were all from our planet.
Comparison	similarly, both, as well as, likewise	Many *atolls* can be found in the Pacific Ocean; similarly, other coral islands are found in the Caribbean Sea.
		Both spaghetti and *tortellini* are common pasta dishes.
Example	e.g., other, such as, such, like	*Unguents,* such as first aid cream, Cortaid, Vick-Salve, and Deep Heat, are found in most homes.
		Psychosomatic disorders, e.g., ulcers and tension headaches, are physical illnesses that result from psychological stress.

Bridging Context Clues

Bridging context clues use words within the text to signal the kinds of conclusions to draw. These clues point to meanings that are the same as or the opposite of words or meanings you already know. Such clues can also signal that the unknown words are examples of a group. Table 6.3 summarizes types of bridging context clues and provides examples for each type.

Contrast clues use a combination of word(s) found within a sentence and your background knowledge. Thus, although these clues are not as exact as stated clues, they help you use background knowledge more efficiently. Connecting words—such as *however, on the other hand, instead of, but, while,* and *although*—point to meanings that are the opposite of those you know. For example, "Some business disputes can be settled out of court; on the other hand, others require litigation." If litigation is the opposite of out of court (signaled by "on the other hand"), then litigation means in court. *You can practice using contrast clues in Exercise 6.5.*

READ Exercise 6.5

Like contrast clues, **comparison clues** form a bridge between the text and what you know. Here, they show likenesses between two or more things. A comparison is possible because the known and unknown words are alike in some way. Such words as *similarly, as well as, both,* and *likewise* signal you to look for similarities. For example,

"Periodicals as well as other reading materials sometime become out-dated." The clue *as well as* tells you that periodicals are probably types of reading materials. *Exercise 6.6 provides practice in using comparison clues.*

READ Exercise 6.6

Example clues tell you that an example of an unknown word follows. Using background knowledge, you derive the meaning of the unknown word by determining what the stated examples have in common. Example clues are usually introduced by the following words and phrases: *such as, such, other, for example,* and *like.* For example, "Various means of conveyance—for example, cars, subways, and ships—are used around the world." Cars, subways, and ships are means of travel. Therefore, conveyance must also refer to a form of travel. *Exercise 6.7 provides practice in using example clues.*

READ Exercise 6.7

Experiential Clues

Experiential context is more difficult to use than other context clues are. As in many crimes, there might be no physical evidence. Like an investigator, you rely on your experience and knowledge to determine meaning. Likewise, experiential context has no specific written clues to assist you. Instead, you must examine the whole situation and sentence and draw your conclusions based on what you already know. Your knowledge of the meanings of surrounding words helps you decide how to use the background knowledge you have. Common sense and your knowledge of parts of speech also help in determining the meanings of unknown words. You combine your experience with what the text contains to determine meaning. For example, "The angry driver shouted vehemently during his quarrel with the other driver."

What does *vehemently* mean? You know what angry means, and you know how people feel when they quarrel. From this, you can figure out that *vehemently* has something to do with strong emotion or intense feeling. This is an example of using experiential context to find the meanings of new words. The meaning you find comes from your personal experience. *Practice using various context clues in Exercises 6.8 and 6.9.*

READ Exercises 6.8 & 6.9

Write to Learn

Tomorrow you will be participating in a debate concerning the value of using the context. Your opponent advocates the use of a dictionary for determining the meaning of unknown words. On a separate sheet of paper or in your notebook, construct an argument for using context instead of the dictionary.

In and Out of Context: Figurative Language

A physics professor once lectured about motion and then assigned several homework problems. One question described the departure angle and velocity of a baseball hit during a game, as well as the field and wall dimensions, and then asked, "Will the ball be a home run?" During the next class, the professor asked if the class had trouble with any of the homework problems. A foreign student inquired about the baseball question. The professor launched into a discussion about the relationship between velocity, departure angle, and distance. When the professor finished, the student said, "I understand that part." "Then what is your question?" the professor asked. "What is a *home run*?" replied the student.

The student's problem was that the words *home* and *run* were not in the context she expected. When combined, the words form an expression of **figurative language** whose meaning is out of its literal context. For this reason, figurative language can be difficult for all students, and it is especially difficult for English as a Second Language (ESL) students who might not have the specialized background knowledge to decode it.

Figurative language describes the intentional use of words in contexts other than those that provide literal meanings. Such expressions compare an idea with another to form distinctly different meanings. These meanings become understood through use. For example, to understand the expression *turning green with envy,* you must first understand that the phrase doesn't mean that a person turns green. If you know from background knowledge that green symbolizes jealousy, then you understand that the phrase describes someone who is very jealous.

Although a variety of types of figurative language exist, some, like **symbols,** depend most on context for understanding. Others—such as **similes, metaphors,** and **allusions**—retain meaning whatever the context.

Identifying Symbols

Symbols are based on your own background knowledge and experiences. In general, symbols are universally understood. This is because of years of association between a symbol and the object it represents.

Some symbols, however, mean different things in different cultures. For example, in Western countries, white is a symbol of purity. In Eastern cultures, such as Japan or India, white is a symbol of death or mourning.

Table 6.4   Common Symbols and Their Meanings

Color

yellow: fear

green: jealousy, money, growth

purple: royalty

red: anger, danger

blue: sadness

white: innocence, purity, death

black: death

Animals

owl: wisdom

fox: cunning, trickery

lion: strength, bravery

hawk: war

dove: peace

stork: babies

elephant: memory, Republican party

donkey: Democratic party

crow/buzzard/vulture: death

dog/faithfulness

Objects

heart: love, soul

rose: love

cross: Christianity

red cross: first aid

skull and crossbones: danger, poison, piracy

four-leaf clover: good luck

horseshoe: good luck

Uncle Sam: United States

white hats: good guys

black hats: bad guys

flag: patriotism

tree: life

rainbow: promise

cloud: trouble

olive branch: peace

laurel wreath: victory

winter: old age, death

spring: youth

Other symbols have no strong meaning for a specific culture. Think of how you feel about the flag of another country. You might recognize the flag of Great Britain when you see it; however, it does not fill you with the same sense of patriotism as the American flag does. In the United States, the American flag (or the colors red, white, and blue) symbolizes our country. It evokes a patriotic feeling.

The meaning of the symbol depends on the context. It also depends on the time and place in which it is used. For instance, the swastika was originally a religious sign in ancient India. Mayans and American Indians also used it. Its meaning changed when Hitler adopted it as a symbol. It became one of the most hated symbols in history because it stood for the evil associated with Nazi Germany.

Table 6.4 lists common symbols and meanings. Symbols can be used alone or as parts of other figurative language. The symbol lends its meaning to the overall image as shown in the following examples:

- green-eyed monster (someone who is jealous)
- a yellow streak down his back (someone who is a coward)
- broken heart (a failed romance)
- resting on her laurels (relying on earlier victories or successes)

Recognizing Similes and Metaphors

Writers often use simile or metaphors to compare something unfamiliar with something familiar. At first, the two ideas appear to have nothing in common. However, a closer look reveals a basic relationship between them.

The words *like* or *as* signal that a simile is being used. In a metaphor, one idea is described as if it were another, without the use of *like* or *as*. Sometimes it is difficult to remember that similes, not metaphors, are cued by like or as.

Some similes and metaphors are used so often they lose their freshness. When this happens, they no longer add vividness to language. Such similes and metaphors are called **clichés.** Phrases like *pretty as a picture, hard as a rock,* and *slept like a baby* lost their imagery through overuse.

```
A
S I M I L E
    I
    K
    E
```

Grasping Allusions

Allusions are somewhat like symbols. Both express ideas in a shortened form. Both require background knowledge for understanding. Both use commonly known information to be understood. Symbols draw from similes and metaphors that have become well-known over time. Allusions refer to works of literature, history, and the arts. Thus, allusions are aptly named. They allude (refer) to some character, writing, event, music, and so on.

Consider a cross-reference in a dictionary or an encyclopedia. It tells you where to get more information. Allusions comprise a kind of cross-reference that does not tell you where to go for more facts. Instead, when authors use allusions they want you to connect the allusion to its source from memory. Grasping allusions, then, requires vast amounts of background information.

Authors, as well as speakers, often allude to characters, phrases, terms, or places. These come from mythology (*Pandora's* box, *Herculean* strength, a *Siren* song) and history (honest as George Washington, as beautiful as Helen of Troy, as traitorous as Benedict Arnold). The Bible (Garden of Eden, patience of Job, wise as Solomon) and other works of literature (grinning like a Cheshire Cat, "I'll think about that tomorrow," a Scrooge) also provide allusions. Finally, allusions come from media sources like television ("You are the weakest link."; "Dude, you're getting a Dell!") and movies ("Show me the money"; "Play it again, Sam"; "May the Force be with you.").

If you do not recognize an allusion at once, there is hope. First, you look carefully at the context. For example, perhaps someone says, "I thought he was my friend, but he was just a Benedict Arnold." Although allusions can be used in any context, the sentence they reside in can provide clues to the allusion's meaning. Here, because you know that *but* is a contrast clue, you know that whoever Benedict Arnold was, he was no friend. Then you search your memory for possible links with other information. Perhaps you recall the name Benedict Arnold from history. If so, you know that he was infamous as a traitor during the American Revolution. But, if nothing comes to mind, you can attempt to look it up. Dictionaries of all sorts and books of quotations provide the sources of some allusions. In this case, you would look up *Benedict Arnold.*

READ Exercises 6.10 & 6.11

Practice using figurative language and context clues in Exercises 6.10 and 6.11.

Chapter Summary Exercise

On a separate sheet of paper or in your notebooks, complete the chapter summary by filling in the blanks:

Using the _____ involves figuring out the connection between a word and its surroundings. Context helps identify part of speech, as well as the meaning of the word through _____, _____, and _____ clues. _____ results from a special use of context in which a word or phrase is taken out of its literal context and used in a new way. _____ and _____ are types of figurative language that depend on context and background knowledge for meaning. _____, _____, and _____ are figures of speech that retain meaning, no matter the context.

Chapter Review

Answer the following questions on a separate sheet of paper or in your notebook.

1. Using examples other than those provided in the chapter, explain how confusion occurs when meaning is taken out of context.
2. Why would using context to define words be particularly difficult for nonnative speakers?
3. Construct one or more sentences and label any five parts of speech.
4. How are adjectives and adverbs alike? How are they different?
5. Of the three kinds of context—stated, bridging, experiential—which kind do you think would cause an ESL (English as a Second Language) speaker most difficulty? Why?
6. In what ways do stated context clues differ from other types of context clues?
7. Choose ten symbols from Table 6.4. Categorize the symbols according to positive and negative association.
8. Create a concept map for the topic of context.

Terms

Terms appear in the order in which they occur in the chapter.

context
literal
part of speech
stated context clues
linking verbs
punctuation text-based clues
definition text-based clues
bridging context clues
contrast clues
comparison clues
example clues
experiential context
figurative language
symbols
similes
metaphors
allusions
clichés

Exercises

Exercise 6.1   On a separate sheet of paper or in your notebook, use context to identify the part of speech of each nonsense word in the sentences below. Then revise the sentence using actual words so that each sentence makes sense.

1. Ertyuss accidents often pqwst from sdfel.

   a. Ertyuss

   b. pqwst

   c. sdfel

2. In xuio places, weplms travel with sdgtp.

   a. xuio

   b. weplms

   c. sdgtp

3. The typlm of apples has mcyopo.

   a. typlm

   b. mcyopo

4. Poikmn cutbacks ppleds my retlk completely.

   a. Poikmn

   b. ppleds

   c. retlk

5. Last srplmo I uipolshed the first ikljr.

   a. srplmo

   b. uipolshed

   c. ikljr

Exercise 6.2   On a separate sheet of paper or in your notebook, select the letter of the correct definition for each italicized word in the sentence below. Use parts of speech to help you find the correct definition.

Flush

a. to flood with water (v.)

b. in poker, five cards of the same suit not in sequence (n.)

   c. having a ruddy, healthy color (adj.)

   d. abundant (adj)

   e. arranged edge to edge (adj.)

1. The carpenter hammered the nail *flush* with the board.

2. Jack tried to bluff when he saw the *flush* in his hand.

Order

   a. members of a religious group (n.)

   b. an arrangement or sequence of objects (n.)

   c. a rule of law (n.)

   d. a written direction to pay money to someone for something (n.)

   e. state or condition of functioning or repair (n.)

   f. demand (v.)

3. My telephone was out of *order.*

4. When I dropped the pages of my paper, they got out of *order.*

5. I *ordered* flowers from the florist.

Post

   a. a pole fixed in an upright position (n.)

   b. the place or task where a soldier is stationed (n.)

   c. to put something up for public notice (v.)

   d. to mail (v.)

   e. a place of trade (n.)

6. Carl *posted* the announcement in the dean's office.

7. Phong *posted* the letter two days before Jan received it.

8. Kay leaned on a *post* in the field.

Call

   a. a brief visit (n.)

   b. to speak of or address by a specified name (v.)

   c. to shout (v.)

    d.   to warrant (v.)

    e.   to suspend (v.)

9.   The ball game was *called* because of the rain.

10.   The situation *called* for legal action.

Exercise 6.3   On a separate sheet of paper or in your notebook, identify the meaning of the italicized term. Then identify the words that gave you clues to meaning.

1.   Family violence has varied forms: *Protective-reactive violence* (spouse strikes mate to stop an anticipated attack) is just one of many.

2.   Most of the earliest computer systems used *serial* processing—one at a time, one after the other.

3.   Each cell contains a *homologue,* an identical chromosome with complementary alleles.

4.   Astronomers characterize the energy emitted by a star as *luminosity* [energy emitted per second].

Exercise 6.4   On a separate sheet of paper or in your notebook, use definition clues to find the meaning of the italicized word. List the meaning and the words that helped you find meaning.

1.   Money is used to buy goods and services; hence, it is a *medium of exchange.*

2.   The science of measuring star positions is called *astrometry.*

3.   The idea that a child's understanding of his or her social world shapes concepts of gender is known as *self-socialization.*

4.   The motor neuron and the muscle fibers stimulated by it are referred to as a *motor unit.*

Exercise 6.5   On a separate sheet of paper or in your notebook, identify the meaning of the italicized word or phrase by using contrast clues. Identify contrast clue words.

1.   In this case, *contact* does not refer to direct physical touching but to a symbolic meeting of the minds through imagination.

2.   Whereas clinical studies isolate patterns of genetic variation one trait at a time, *multivariate* studies focus more on the "big picture."

3.   Galaxies often form in *superclusters,* rather than in a uniform distribution.

4.   Although fission splits a single nucleus, *fusion* results in the creation of a new chemical element.

Exercise 6.6   On a separate sheet of paper or in your notebook, identify the definition for the italicized word by using comparison clues. Then identify the comparison clues.

1.   Jail time is often shorter for youths who steal ten dollars or other *petty* amounts.

2.   Social influence often sways opinion; similarly, *conformity* encourages appropriate behavior.

3.   Like lungs in mammals, *gills* serve a critical function in fish.

4.   Just as a storm eventually subsides, energy finally *flags.*

Exercise 6.7   On a separate sheet of paper or in your notebook, identify the meanings of the italicized words in the following sentences based on the example clues. Then identify the words that clued you to the meaning.

1.   Arguing, cursing, striking, and other kinds of *antagonistic* behavior is typical of some gang members.

2.   Regular checkups, balanced diets, and other principles of *wellness* are advised for all age groups.

3.   *White-collar crime,* such as bribery, embezzlement, and fraud seems to be increasing.

4.   Such *bureaucracies* as community colleges, corporate giants, and military organizations share the same basic features.

Exercise 6.8   Use experiential context to decide what the italicized word means. On a separate sheet of paper or in your notebook, write your definition beside the word. Then explain your definition on the line below it.

1.   After discovering an incident of plagiarism, the professor was more *vigilant.*

2.   *Scathing* reviews forced the play to close after only one performance.

3.   Although its members came from across the country, the group *coalesced* into a strong force.

4.   I was *disconsolate* when I discovered I didn't have enough money for tuition this term.

5.   What is the address of your *abode?*

Exercise 6.9   On a separate sheet of paper or in your notebook, use the text on astrology and astronomy in the READ Keys in Chapter 2 to define the following words from context. After you have defined these words, identify the words that cued the definition and the kind of context clue each is.

1. gods

2. currying

3. celestial

4. realms

5. antiquity

6. astrology

7. natal astrology

8. treatise

9. horoscope

10. house

11. horoscopes

12. Examine the definitions in numbers 9 and 11. What accounts for the differences between them?

Exercise 6.10   Read the short story found in the Chapter 5 READ Keys. Then answer the questions that follow it on a separate sheet of paper or in your notebook.

1. Identify each of the following as either a simile or metaphor. Explain them literally.
   a. *nervous as a kitten*

   b. *colorless as water*

   c. *a life-cleaner*

2. Identify the source of the allusion *siren* as it used in the story. What is its literal meaning? To what does the old man mean when he makes reference to *sirens?*

3. Explain the significance in the old man's saying *"Au revoir"* as Alan leaves.

4. The title of this story is also an allusion. Identify the source of the allusion and explain its relevance.

Exercise 6.11   Read the chapter excerpt found in the Chapter 10 READ Keys Activity 10.1. Then define each of the following words and phrases from context. Identify the type of context clue you used to find meaning.

1. status quo

2. Reagan Democrats

3. tangled

4. détente

5. "Evil Empire"

6. glasnost

7. perestroika

8. ". . . communist governments in Eastern Europe fell like dominoes."

Web Exercise

New environments form contexts for words. You can virtually visit a number of new environments through the World Wide Web.

Global Village Tour of the Internet
http://www.logiconline.org.ve/sites/MTWS/Globalvillage/tour.html

Virtual Tours: 300 Tours (choose one tour)
http://www.virtualfreesites.com/tours.html

Greatest Places Online
http://www.sci.mus.mn.us/greatestplaces/ or http://www.greatestplaces.org/

Click on the location of your choice within the Web site and answer the following questions on a separate sheet of paper or in your notebook:

1. Which Web site and location did you choose?

2. Why did you choose this site/location?

3. Identify and define 10 words in the Web site that a user needs to understand in this environment:

4. What did you see and use in this Web site that helped you obtain meaning from context?

READ: Keys

READ: Keys Activity Pretest

Rate each of the following words according to your knowledge of them.

Word	Stage 0 *I don't know this word.*	Stage 1 *I've seen this word but I know nothing of its meaning.*	Stage 2 *I've seen this word and can make associations with it.*	Stage 3 *I know this word.*
1. novellas				
2. hiatus				
3. startle				
4. hysterical				
5. provocative				
6. alienating				
7. conspicuous				
8. pretentious				
9. affluent				
10. glitches				

READ: Keys Activity 6.1

Read the following essay and keep track of your reading time.
Note: Underlined, italicized words are used in Chapter 5, Exercise 5.9.

Entunese Mañana (Tune In Tomorrow)
Lelia Loban Lee

In English, they're *soap operas*. In Spanish, they're histories or ***novellas*** (stories). I discovered them when I tuned into the Spanish-language stations Univision and Telemundo to brush up on my rusty, outdated Spanish. (Imagine what your English would be like if you'd learned it from *hippies* in 1965, and hadn't spoken it since.)

I tuned in to *Rebelde (Rebel); Maria, Maria; Cantare Para Ti (I'll Sing For You); Simplemente Maria; Venganza De Mujer (Woman's Vengeance,* which uses a Spanish-language version of "Memories" from the musical Cats as its theme song); *La Revancha (Revenge);* and *Amandote II.* There are many more, including *Carusel (Carousel)* and other soaps specifically made for children. These programs come from all over the Hispanic world, from as far as Peru and as near as Los Angeles. Most Spanish soaps run every day for only a few weeks or months at a time, then conclude or go on ***hiatus,*** the way our nighttime series do.

At first, I couldn't understand the dialogue, but the characters and plots seemed so familiar that I could still follow the stories. Soon I began to recognize common phrases. One day, I realized I wasn't just hearing the words anymore. I understood.

Hispanic soaps focus on love and family, the same as Anglo soaps. Even a viewer who can't speak any Spanish will be able to identify the hero, the villain, the *earth mother,* the loving father, the bitch, the *wayward* daughter, the meddlesome aunt, the scheming uncle, the headstrong son, the hero's clownish *buddy* and the fragile innocent, and, of course, the super couple. Murder mysteries, revenge stories and Romeo-and-Juliet romances between members of rival families are as popular in Spanish as they are in English.

Some cultural differences may ***startle*** Anglo viewers at first. Men hold hands with men. Women hold hands with women and kiss each other on the lips. Such behavior doesn't suggest homosexuality to Hispanic audiences. And remember the scene in "Twin Peaks," when Leland Palmer discovered his daughter, Laura, was dead? Anglo viewers didn't quite know how to react to his ***hysterical*** sobbing, but Hispanic viewers probably thought, "Finally, a man who acts normal." On Hispanic soaps, men cry as freely as women.

The sex and violence on Hispanic soaps are somewhat less graphic than what is routinely seen on Anglo shows. Although there are plenty of *smooches* and ***provocative*** clothes, sex scenes usually end at the bedroom door. The programs available for viewing in the U.S. aren't a completely representative sampling of Latin American soap operas. "Entertainment Tonight" recently reported that audiences in Brazil, for example, expect nudity and sex scenes far too explicit for North American television.

Characters on Spanish-language soaps discuss morality, sin and their religious beliefs more often than characters on *All My Children* or *The Young and the Restless.* While Anglo soaps don't treat abortion, divorce or illegitimate pregnancy lightly, these subjects get far graver treatment from Hispanic writers. The reason may be that Anglo soaps reach viewers who practice many different religions. The audience for Spanish soaps is so overwhelmingly Roman Catholic that the producers can make nearly all their characters outspoken Catholics without worrying about **alienating** viewers.

Although Hispanic soaps promote Catholic ideas as best, they also reinforce the "love will find a way" theme familiar to *fans* of the mixed marriage of Cruz and Eden on Santa Barbara. The children's soap *Carusel* recently showed Hispanic children from different racial and religious backgrounds learning not to taunt each other with ethnic *slurs*.

Anglo viewers may also notice that the Hispanic entertainment industry sees fashion and beauty differently. Many performers wear blond or red wigs, or bleach their hair. Because many of these Hispanic women have olive or brown skin and many leave their eyebrows dark, the lightened hair is more **conspicuous** than on Anglo actresses.

Characters dress quite differently on Hispanic soaps, too. Although some Hispanic soap opera characters do dress outrageously, wild styles are not the *norm*. On a fair number of Spanish-language soaps, women favor dresses with lots of gathering and ruffles (a style popular for many years among Hispanics that never caught on for long among Anglo women) and men wear shinier fabrics, brighter colors and bolder patterns than their Anglo counterparts. But most Hispanic soap characters wear affordable, department store clothing, in the same fashionable but not extreme styles that middle-class viewers would wear.

Set decoration looks less **pretentious** on Telemundo and Univision. Offices seem smaller and more like real offices, and homes are more down-to-earth, not like the extravagant palaces of *Santa Barbara*'s Capwells or *General Hospital*'s Quatermaines. Hispanic soap characters don't hide their TVs off-camera. A living room setting often includes a gigantic television in an impressive cabinet, along with other electronic gear of all kinds, including huge console stereos and elaborate telephones. The less-**affluent** characters seem to furnish their homes from moderate-priced chain stores, such as Levitz and Sears, while furniture in the homes of wealthy characters looks as if it came from Bloomingdale's or Ethan Allen, not from design shows in Italy.

This difference in appearance is probably less a reflection of taste than of money—most Hispanic shows look low-budget. The sets resemble those of network soaps in the United States from the late 1960s. Expect fewer camera angles and more production **glitches;** however, the acting is so professional, you won't hear many flubbed lines.

You'll feel right at home during the commercials. Watch for Madge, selling Palmolive in Spanish with a terrible accent. One big difference: Commercials on Hispanic soaps address men and women equally. You'll see ads for *baldness* cures, automotive services and electronic equipment. Most of the ads are local rather than national. They promote neighborhood *restaurants* (this is a great way to find out where to get authentic ethnic food), Hispanic civic organizations, language and citizenship classes and professional offices where doctors and lawyers speak Spanish.

Some Hispanic viewers think of soap opera characters as real people, the same way Anglo viewers do. If you watch Univision and Telemundo long enough, the day may come when you can't help understanding a conversation in Spanish on the <u>bus</u> or in a restaurant. Suddenly, you realize you know those people that your neighbors are gossiping so happily about. That's right—they're talking about characters from Spanish-language soaps.

From Lelia Loban Lee, "Entunese Mañana (Tune in Tomorrow)," *Soap Opera Digest,* January 22, 1991. Used with permission of Lelia Loban Lee, Falls Church, Virginia.

1025 words / _____ minutes = _____ words per minute.

Calculate your reading time by dividing the number of words in the article by the amount of time it took to read it. Then mark your reading time on the chart located on page 338.

READ: Keys Activity 6.2

On a separate piece of paper or in your notebook, answer the following questions about the essay you just read:

1. What is Telemundo?

　　a. a city in Mexico

　　b. a Spanish dialect

　　c. a Spanish language TV station

　　d. a Spanish soap opera

2. Which Spanish soap opera uses "Memories" as its theme song?

　　a. *Rebelde*

　　b. *Maria, Maria*

　　c. *La Revanch*

　　d. *Venganza De Mujer*

3. According to the article, which of the following is NOT true of Spanish soap operas?

　　a. Some are made in the United States.

　　b. Some are made for children.

c. Some last only a few months.

d. Some have no commercial interruptions.

4. According to the article, which of the following correctly describes the way female characters dress on Hispanic soap operas?

   a. coats with more buttons

   b. skirts that are shorter

   c. dresses with more ruffles

   d. suits that are more formal and tailored

5. According to the article, which of the following characterizes the production of Hispanic soap operas?

   a. more camera angles than Anglo soaps

   b. fewer production glitches than Anglo soaps

   c. few missed lines by actors

   d. rich and expensive set décor

6. Typical viewers of Spanish-language soaps

   a. are members of a single religion.

   b. do not believe in God.

   c. are more tolerant of divorce.

   d. actively support abortion rights groups.

7. Which of the following is rarely seen in Anglo soaps?

   a. an office

   b. a television

   c. a bed

   d. a living room

8. Which of the following is NOT an example of a typical soap opera character identified in the article?

   a. the aging grandmother

   b. the earth mother

   c. the wayward daughter

   d. the meddlesome aunt

9. According to the article, how do commercials on Hispanic soaps differ from commercials on Anglo soaps?

   a. There are more commercials that advertise women's products on Hispanic soaps.

   b. On the average, commercials are longer on Anglo soaps.

   c. On Spanish language soaps, more commercials advertise community products and services.

   d. Spanish soap opera actors perform in the commercials for their programs.

10. Which of the following would you expect to see on Hispanic soap operas?

   a. women with dark skin tones and red or blond hair

   b. men wearing dark suits in "earth" tones

   c. expensive designer furniture and clothing

   d. few plots concerning love and family

READ: Keys Activity 6.3

Examine each of the numbered phrases or sentences and complete the following on a separate sheet of paper or in your notebook.

(a) Write the boldfaced, italicized word. Identify one or two words that you can put in the place of the boldfaced, italicized word without changing the meaning of the phrase or sentence and write this synonym or synonymous phrase (words that have the same meaning) beside the word. (b) Identify the part of speech of this word as used in the sentence. (c) Look up the boldfaced, italicized word in a dictionary and write the dictionary definition. How does this compare with the definition from context? (d) List the parts of speech this word can sometimes be. (e) Write a complete sentence with each word.

1. In Spanish, they're histories or ***novellas*** . . .

2. Most Spanish soaps run every day . . . then conclude or go on ***hiatus,*** the way our nighttime series do.

3. Some cultural differences may ***startle*** Anglo viewers . . .

4. Anglo viewers didn't quite know how to react to his ***hysterical*** sobbing.

5. Although there are plenty of smooches and ***provocative*** clothes, sex scenes usually end at the bedroom door.

6. . . . producers can make nearly all their characters . . . Catholic without . . . **alienating** viewers.

7. Because . . . Hispanic women have olive or brown skin . . . , the lightened hair is more **conspicuous** than on Anglo actresses.

8. Set decoration looks less **pretentious** on Telemundo and Univision. . . . smaller and more like real offices . . . down-to-earth.

9. The less-**affluent** characters . . . furnish their homes from moderate-priced chain stores . . .

10. Expect fewer camera angles and more production **glitches**; however, the acting is so professional, you won't hear many flubbed lines.

READ: Keys Activity 6.4

In Part A, use the following list of words to fill in the blanks. In Part B, use the information from Part A to complete the analogies.

Part A

subtle	frantic	narratives	poor
joining	expect	continuance	calm
obvious	modest	separating	surprise
sexy	showy	mistakes	reserved
wealthy	essays	break	corrections

Synonym	Word	Antonym
_____	**1.** novellas	_____
_____	**2.** hiatus	_____
_____	**3.** startle	_____
_____	**4.** hysterical	_____
_____	**5.** provocative	_____
_____	**6.** alienating	_____

_____   **7.** conspicuous   _____

_____   **8.** pretentious   _____

_____   **9.** affluent   _____

_____   **10.** glitches   _____

Part B

1. glitches : _____ :: affluent : wealthy

2. pretentious : showy :: conspicuous : _____

3. hysterical : frantic :: _____ : separating

4. startle : _____ :: novella : narrative

5. _____ : hiatus :: poor : affluent

6. calm : _____ :: joining : alienating

7. _____ : essays :: provocative : modest

8. subtle : _____ :: expect : startle

9. mistakes : _____ :: breaks : hiatus

10. fiction : nonfiction :: poor : _____

READ: Keys Activity Posttest

Rate each of the following words according to your knowledge of them.

Word	Stage 0 *I don't know this word.*	Stage 1 *I've seen this word but I know nothing of its meaning.*	Stage 2 *I've seen this word and can make associations with it.*	Stage 3 *I know this word.*
1. novellas				
2. hiatus				
3. startle				
4. hysterical				
5. provocative				
6. alienating				
7. conspicuous				
8. pretentious				
9. affluent				
10. glitches				

Analyzing Vocabulary Through Structure

Chapter Map Exercise

Construct a chapter map from the major headings and subheadings in the chapter.

Objectives

After you finish this chapter, you will be able to do the following:

1. Define and use structural analysis.

2. Identify prefixes, suffixes, and roots.

3. Create meaning through association.

4. Describe the limitations of structural analysis.

Chapter Outline Exercise

Create a chapter outline from the major headings and subheadings in
the chapter.

The quote "It's Greek to me"—an allusion from Shakespeare's *Julius Caesar*—has come to mean that a person doesn't understand. That's because Greek is considered to be a language that's not widely used today. This is ironic, however, because Greek is spoken in every English-speaking country. How can that be? Greek—and Latin—word parts compose a large percentage of the English language. Knowing these word parts, then, helps you identify the meanings of many words you hear or read each day. Indeed, learning these word parts puts words that seem Greek to you into your vocabulary.

Cassius: Did Cicero say anything?

Casca: Ay, he spoke Greek.

Cassius: To what effect?

Casca: Nay, and I tell you that, I'll ne'er look you in the face again; but those that understand him smiled at one another and shook their heads; but, for mine own part, it was Greek to me.

—William Shakespeare
*Sixteenth century
British playwright*

Structural Analysis

Each word part has its own meaning with each part contributing to the total meaning of a word. Thus, you can often find the meaning of an unknown word by analyzing its parts. In this process—**structural analysis**—**bases** or **roots** provide basic meaning. Some roots may be used alone. Others must be used with other bases or **affixes** (**prefixes** or **suffixes**). They help identify the subject area of the unknown word. Affixes also help determine the part of speech of the unknown word. For example, consider the following sentence:

The doctor used a cast to immobilize the patient's arm.

Can you tell what *immobilize* means in this sentence? Several meanings, such as *injure, cover,* or *heal* are possible. Look at the parts of this word.

im	mobil	ize
not	**movable**	**to make (verb)**

The word parts tell you that the arm was "made not movable" by the cast. *Immobilize* means to make something immobile (that is, not movable). The suffix *ize* is a verb suffix. That tells you that the word *immobilize* shows some sort of action or being.

Identifying Prefixes, Suffixes, and Roots

When present, prefixes always occur at the beginnings of words. Suffixes are found at the ends of words and indicate the part of speech of a word. Bases or roots come after prefixes, before suffixes, or between prefixes and suffixes. Bases or roots can also be used alone. If you think you might have trouble recalling where each word part occurs, remember this trick.

Think of the placement of the letters *P, R,* and *S* in the alphabet. They occur there in the same order as in words.

P	(Q)	R	S
R		O	U
E		O	F
F		T	F
I			I
X			X

Table 7.1 List of Prefixes

Negative	Example	
a (not)	asexual	_____
anti (against)	antisocial	_____
contra (against)	contraceptive	_____
il (not)	illegal	_____
in (not)	incorrect	_____
ir (not)	irregular	_____
mis (not)	misconception	_____
neg (not)	negation	_____
un (not)	unknown	_____

Position	Example	
ad (to)	adjourn	_____
auto (self)	automobile	_____
be (by)	beloved	_____
circum (around/round)	circumference	_____
co (with)	coauthor	_____
col (with)	collusion	_____
com (with)	combustion	_____
con (with)	conjunction	_____
cor (together)	correlation	_____
de (away/down)	devalue	_____
dis/di (apart)	disarm/divide	_____
en (in)	enroll	_____
extra (beyond)	extraterrestrial	_____
inter (between)	interstate	_____
para (beside or equal)	parallel	_____
post (after/later than)	postmortem	_____
pre (before)	precook	_____
pro (in front/favor of)	proceed	_____
re (back/again)	return	_____
sub (under)	submarine	_____
super (above/greater than)	superstar	_____
tele (far)	television	_____
trans (across/through)	translucent	_____

Study the lists of prefixes, suffixes, and roots in Tables 7.1, 7.2, and 7.3. They are by no means complete. However, these lists give some of the most common affixes and roots, grouped for ease of learning. *Exercises 7.1 through 7.4 provide practice identifying prefixes, suffixes, and roots.*

READ Exercises 7.1, 7.2, 7.3, & 7.4

Table 7.2   List of Suffixes

Noun	Example	
ance/ence (state of being)	disturbance/absence	_____
ation (act of)	information	_____
hood (state of being)	childhood	_____
ism (state of being)	consumerism	_____
ist (one who does)	chemist	_____
ity/ty (state/condition)	community	_____
ment (action or state of)	government	_____
ness (state of being)	happiness	_____
or/er (that/one who does/is)	visitor/Westerner	_____
ory (place or thing for)	directory	_____
ship (state of being)	leadership	_____
sion (act of)	confusion	_____
sis (process or action)	paralysis	_____
tion (state of being)	irritation	_____

Adjective	Example	
able (able to/capable of being)	desirable	_____
al (pertaining to)	comical	_____
ful (full of)	beautiful	_____
ible (able to)	divisible	_____
ic (pertaining to)	alcoholic	_____
ive (having the quality of)	creative	_____
ous (having)	courageous	_____

Verb	Example	
en (belonging to/cause to be)	roughen	_____
fy (to make)	glorify	_____
ize (to become/to make)	minimize	_____

Adverb	Example	
ly (in the manner of)	quickly	_____

Table 7.3 List of General and Math and Science Roots

General Roots

Root	Example	
cede (go)	precede	_____
flect/flex (bend)	reflect	_____
dict (say)	dictate	_____
ject (throw)	interject	_____
junct (join)	junction	_____
kinesis (movement)	kinetic	_____
mem (mind)	memory	_____
monitor (warning)	admonition	_____
path (feeling)	sympathy	_____
percept (observe)	perceptive	_____
phil (love)	philanthropy	_____
port (carry)	transport	_____
pseudo (false)	pseudonym	_____
psych (soul; mind)	psychotic	_____
rupt (break)	interrupt	_____
script (write)	manuscript	_____
sens (feelings)	sensitive	_____
soph (wisdom)	sophisticated	_____
theo (god)	theology	_____
vert (turn)	extrovert	_____
vis (see)	vision	_____

Math and Science Affixes and Roots

Root or Affix	Example	
acro (height; top)	acrobat	_____
animate (breathing)	animated	_____
aqua (water)	aquarium	_____
astro (star)	astronaut	_____
bi (two)	bicycle	_____
bio (life)	biology	_____
botan (plant)	botany	_____
centi (hundred; hundredth)	centimeter	_____
dec (ten)	decade	_____
equi (equal)	equivalent	_____
geo (earth)	geology	_____
hemi (half)	hemisphere	_____

> **Return to the root and you will find the meaning.**
>
> —Sengstan
> *Ancient Chinese Zen master*

Table 7.3   *Continued*

hetero (different)	heterosexual	_____
homo (same)	homogenized	_____
hydro (water)	hydroplane	_____
kilo (thousand)	kilogram	_____
mega (large)	megaphone	_____
meter (measure)	diameter	_____
micro (small)	microfilm	_____
milli (thousand; thousandth)	millimeter	_____
octa (eight)	octagon	_____
ology (study of)	geology	_____
onomy (science of)	astronomy	_____
pan (all)	panacea	_____
ped (foot)	pedestrian	_____
pod (foot)	tripod	_____
quad (four)	quadrangle	_____
semi (half)	semicircle	_____
sphere (ball; globe)	atmosphere	_____
tele (far off)	telescope	_____
temp (time)	temporary	_____
thermo (heat)	thermodynamic	_____
tri (three)	triangle	_____
uni (one)	universe	_____

Write to Learn

On a separate sheet of paper or in your notebook, create an acrostic to help you recall the order in which roots, suffixes, and prefixes occur in words.

Creating Meaning Through Association

Like other types of vocabulary, you learn word parts in various ways. One way is to memorize a list of them. However, people sometimes memorize information without really understanding it. Rather, the

All words are pegs to hang ideas on.

—Henry Ward Beecher
Nineteenth century American preacher

READ Exercise 7.5

words you learn should become, as Beecher suggested, pegs on which you hang other words. For this reason, you need to relate the word parts to what they mean. Our lists include examples to help you. However, these words might not be those you use. *Exercise 7.5 gives you an opportunity to list your own examples.*

How can you use word parts to find meaning? Suppose you need the definition of *genocide* for a sociology class. You recall these words: *suicide, homicide,* and *pesticide.* What do you think these have in common? They all concern a kind of killing. What part is shared by the words? The common part is *cide.* Therefore, you conclude that *cide* generally means *killing* and *genocide* has to do with killing. Then, you add *genocide* and your idea of its meaning to your vocabulary. *Exercises 7.6, 7.7, and 7.8 provide more practice with words and word parts.*

READ Exercises 7.6., 7.7, & 7.8

Limitations of Structural Analysis

Using word parts seems to be an easy and accurate way to define new words. However, this is not always true. For example, the word *colt* comes from a Middle English word. In colt, *col* is not a word part. How can you know the difference? Sometimes you find meaning by splitting the word into parts and looking for affixes or roots that you can identify. Fortunately, most common affixes and roots are Greek and Latin. Thus, using word parts works most of the time. Your skill in determining when to use structural analysis improves with practice. *Exercises 7.9 and 7.10 provide practice determining word meaning through structual analysis.*

READ Exercises 7.9 & 7.10

> ### Write to Learn
>
> **The person who sits behind you had a flat tire on the way to class and missed the discussion on structural analysis. On a separate sheet of paper or in your notebook, describe what structural analysis is and how it differs from using the context.**

Chapter Summary Exercise

Proof the following summary for errors. Cross out incorrect words and replace them with your corrected version.

> Many common French and Roman word parts often combine to form other words. These word parts consist of affixes (profixes and suffixes) and roots. Synthesizing, or breaking down, the structure of an unknown word often helps you identify all or part of its meaning. Effective use of structural analysis depends more on your ability to memorize, rather than associate, the meanings of the word parts.

Chapter Review

Answer the following questions on a separate sheet of paper or in your notebook.

1. Compare and contrast bases, prefixes, and suffixes.
2. What information about a word can word parts give you?
3. How does structural analysis help you generalize the meanings of words?
4. Your reading instructor asks you to learn the word parts in Table 7.2. According to your text, how might you go about doing this?
5. Complete the following analogy—*big : large :: base :* _____
6. Describe the limitations of structural analysis.
7. From what two languages do most word parts come?
8. List five suffixes that identify nouns.
9. Which suffix commonly identifies an adverb?
10. What trick helps you remember the order in which word parts occur?

Terms

Terms appear in the order in which they occur in the chapter.

**structural
    analysis**
bases
roots
affixes
prefixes
suffixes

Exercises

Exercise 7.1   On a separate sheet of paper or in your notebook, write the letter of the correct word. Do not look up the words in a dictionary. Use the prefix meanings in Table 7.1 to find the answer.

1. The events were linked one with another. The events were _____.
   a. contracatenated
   b. concatenated
   c. supercatenated

2. Because of the poor living conditions under which they were forced to exist, the citizens were against the reelection of their president. They had feelings of
   a. sympathy.
   b. empathy.
   c. antipathy.

3. The criminal was a repeat offender, having been convicted again and again. She was a
   a. recidivist.
   b. negidivist.
   c. autodivist.

4. A bird's beak performs the same function as a human's mouth. A beak is _____ to a mouth.
   a. homologous
   b. cormologous
   c. contramologous

5. The actions taken by the defendant were not permitted under the current laws. They were _____ activities.
   a. prolicit
   b. illicit
   c. interlicit

6. If an emergency arises, a special news bulletin will air before anything else is shown. It will _____ all other programming.
   a. subempt
   b. circumempt
   c. preempt

7. Neville Chamberlain, the British prime minister in the late 1930s, stepped between the Germans and Czechoslovakians in an attempt to stop World War II. Chamberlain _____ to prevent the war.

a. interceded

b. preceded

c. superceded

8. Sunlight does not reach the deepest part of the ocean. The deepest part of the seas is _____.

a. antiphotic

b. aphotic

c. disphotic

9. The queen found that the morals of the nation were falling down. She described the citizens as

a. procadent.

b. retrocadent.

c. decadent.

10. After about fifty miles, the atmosphere is described as _____. It is composed of several layers, each differing in chemical content from the others.

a. homospheric

b. circumspheric

c. heterospheric

Exercise 7.2   Directions: Using the suffix clues from Table 7.2, identify the part of the speech for each word on a separate sheet of paper or in your notebook. Select from the following responses: ***noun, adverb, verb, adjective.***

1. imposition

2. pasteurize

3. abrasion

4. provincial

5. androgynous

6. anesthesiologist

7. hedonism

8. effervescence

9. exploitation

10. gentrify

11. undeniably

12. fortification

13. organizer

14. perceptive

Exercise 7.3 Using the suffixes in Table 7.2, supply a word for each of the following definitions on a separate sheet of paper or in your notebook.

1. one who studies geology

2. having beauty

3. pertaining to biology

4. act of being animated

5. state of being sad

6. one who governs

7. to turn into a liquid

8. state of being futile

9. capable of being predicted

10. having the quality of invention

Exercise 7.4 On a separate sheet of paper or in your notebook, complete the sentence by combining the given definitions of roots and affixes to form words. You might have to rearrange some of the word parts to form the appropriate word. Check the spelling.

1. This semester Maria is enrolled in English, history, psychology, and _____ (stars + science of).

2. The solid part of the earth is called the _____ (earth + globe).

3. _____ (the act of + seeing + from far away) was first shown at the New York World's Fair.

4. _____ (pertaining to + life + global) issues concern all people in all countries.

5. _____ (the act of + breaking + together) often results from the greed for power and money.

6. The author was most famous for her _____ (study of + three) of the American frontier.

7. Cellular phones are the most recent evidence of the American need to be _____ (carry + able to).

8. Washing the windshield increases _____ (state of being + able to + see).

9. The marriage counselor agreed to _____ (go + between) to help the couple.

10. Today's _____ (heat + measure) are digital.

Exercise 7.5   For each prefix, suffix, and root in Tables 7.1, 7.2, and 7.3, provide a personal example on the blank lines beside each given example.

Exercise 7.6   Each of the following sets of words contains three words from the same word-part family and the definition of each word. Identify and define the common word part in each set on a separate sheet of paper or in your notebook.

1. prehistoric—before history

   precede—to come before

   predecessor—one who comes before

2. regiment—governmental rule

   regime—a form of rule

   regimen—a prescribed rule

3. cohabitate—to live together

   habitat—a place where someone or something lives

   inhabitant—person who lives in a certain place

4. malignant—bad in nature

   malady—bad condition

   malice—bad feelings

5. telegram—written information sent from a distance over wire

   graphic—written

   grapheme—smallest unit of written language

Exercise 7.7   On a separate sheet of paper or in your notebook, write the letter of the response that is unrelated to the others. Provide an explanation for your choice.

1. a. hemisphere
   b. semicircle
   c. earth
   d. half moon

2. a. biology
   b. astronomy
   c. astrology
   d. geology

3. a. hydrophobia
   b. aquarium
   c. hydrology
   d. geodesy

4. a. irrelevant
   b. irrational
   c. irradiate
   d. irreparable

5. a. geology
   b. geomorphology
   c. geometry
   d. geophysics

6. a. cent
   b. century
   c. centigrade
   d. docent

7. a. equidistant
   b. equipped
   c. equilateral
   d. equity

8. a. vista
   b. envision
   c. invisible
   d. visualize

9. a. tricycle
   b. triad
   c. trial
   d. trio

10. a. unbelievable
    b. understand
    c. unwilling
    d. unwise

Exercise 7.8   Use Table 7.2 to identify the words from the READ Keys excerpt in Chapter 8 ("Being Appropriate" from *Building Speech*) according to their descriptions. The words are found in the indicated paragraphs.

1. adverb meaning "in the manner of being certain" (paragraph 1)

2. noun meaning "state of being not appropriate" (paragraph 1)

3. noun meaning "condition of being diverse" (paragraph 2)

4. adjective meaning "having number" (paragraph 2)

5. adjective meaning "pertaining to dictators" (paragraph 3)

   6. adjective meaning "having the quality of including" (paragraph 4)

   7. state of being sensitive (paragraph 4)

   8. adjective meaning "able to have comfort" (paragraph 4)

   9. verb meaning "to make emphatic" (paragraph 5)

   10. noun meaning "that which disclaims" (paragraph 7)

Exercise 7.9   On a separate sheet of paper or in your notebook, use structural analysis to define the following words from the READ Keys excerpt in Chapter 2 ("Astrology and Astronomy"). Each word is boldfaced and underlined in the excerpt. Then look up each word in a dictionary and write that definition. In a short paragraph, describe how structural analysis helped or failed to help you identify meaning.

   1. supernatural

   2. displeasures

   3. unaided

   4. pantheon

   5. astrology

   6. astronomy

   7. natal astrology

   8. *Tetrabiblos*

   9. constellation

   10. predictions

Exercise 7.10   Respond to the following on a separate sheet of paper or in your notebook. First, use structural analysis to define the following words from the READ Keys excerpt found in this chapter ("Does a Falling Tree Make a Sound When No One Is There to Hear It?"). Second, define the words in context. How do the definitions compare? Finally, write a paragraph that compares these methods in identifying the meaning of words.

   1. philosophers (phil/soph)

   2. perception (percept/tion)

   3. inflections (in/flect/tion)

   4. phrenology (phren/ology)

   5. contemporary (con/temporary)

Web Exercise

A variety of information related to vocabulary development is available on the World Wide Web. For this exercise, go to one of the following Web sites and answer the questions below on a separate sheet of paper.

World Wide Words
http://www.quinion.com/words

Etymology
http://ancienthistory.miningco.com/library/weekly/aa052698.htm

yourDictionary.com
http://www.yourdictionary.com/

1. Write the name and the URL of the Web site you chose.

2. Describe the kinds of information the Web site contains.

3. Choose three articles or topics at the Web site and identify the article or topic of each one.

4. Using one of the articles or topics, identify either five or more words you learned and their meanings or describe how that information could help you learn new words.

READ: Keys

READ: Keys Activity Pretest

Rate each of the following words according to your knowledge of them.

Word	Stage 0 *I don't know this word.*	Stage 1 *I've seen this word but I know nothing of its meaning.*	Stage 2 *I've seen this word and can make associations with it.*	Stage 3 *I know this word.*
1. stimulus				
2. perception				
3. inflections				
4. integrated				
5. correlation				
6. vague				
7. immense				
8. dissected				
9. revealed				
10. emerges				

READ: Keys Activity 7.1

Read the following textbook excerpt and keep track of your reading time.
Note: Underlined, italicized words are used in Chapter 7, Exercise 7.10.

Does a Falling Tree Make a Sound When No One Is There to Hear It?

A. J. Tobin and J. Dusheck

Philosophers and philosophically minded students have argued about this question for century. We now know that the answer is "no." A falling tree makes the air vibrate, but it makes no sound. Sound is a perception, the recognition and interpretation of an outside **stimulus.** In the case of a falling tree, the stimulus is a series of pressure waves, or vibrations, which arrive at the ear and are interpreted by the brain.

As humans, the air vibrations to which we have the strongest and most varied reactions are patterns that we perceive as words. English speakers know that the vibration pattern we hear as "ma" conveys a particular meaning. Remarkably, people who speak many different languages also recognize slight variations of this particular vibration pattern as meaning "mother." But both the **perception** of the sound and the interpretation of its meaning depend on the experience of the hearer: a Chinese speaker, for example, hears tonal **inflections** in the vibration pattern that an English speaker might miss. To a Chinese speaker, "ma" can mean "mother" or "horse" or a fiber-producing plant, depending on how the word is said.

We hear with our brains, not our ears. People with excellent hearing may be unable to understand language. Most English speakers do not understand Chinese language. And people who have suffered strokes on the left side of the brain may be unable to recognize or form words.

For the last 150 years, researchers have been trying to understand the basis of word recognition and hearing in general. Early researchers knew enough to look beyond the ears to the brain itself, the site of perception and learning. But they could not agree whether the brain worked as an **integrated** whole or a set of parts, more like the cogs of a machine.

The notion that the brain is subdivided into specialized parts first gained prominence in the early 19th century from the work of Franz Joseph Gall, a German physician and neuroanatomist who worked in Vienna. Gall tried to establish a **correlation** between the size of a brain area and a particular emotional or intellectual capacity.

Gall estimated these traits, moreover, not from the brain anatomy of people who had died but from the ridges and bumps on the skulls of his living subjects. This practice came to be known as *phrenology* (Greek, *phren* = hear, mind), an exercise that captured the imagination of many 19th-century intellectuals, including the writers George Eliot and Charles Dickens. While phrenology was more of a social than a scientific endeavor, it helped stimulate interest in the physical basis of the mind.

In the early 1820s, a young scientist subjected Gall's ideas to actual experiments. Pierre Flourens, who had recently graduated from medical school, studied what happened when he damaged specific parts of the brains of experimental animals. Flourens found, for example, that destroying the cerebellum, a structure in the lower part of the brain, led to a loss of coordination. But when he removed slices of the *cerebral cortex,* the convoluted surface layer of the brain, he did not find any specific loss of particular traits, but rather a ***vague,*** general loss of mental function.

In humans, the cerebral cortex is far larger than in other animals. Indeed, like our upright posture and hairlessness, our ***immense*** cerebral cortex is one of the handful of traits that sets us apart from other primates. Flourens argued that his studies supported the idea that humans have a single, integrated mind and a single soul.

Though many scientists shared his opposition to the idea that the brain consisted of a collection of independent machines, other neurologists continued to try to associate specific functions—such as touching or hearing—with specific regions of the brain. For example, the French neurologist Pierre Paul Broca described a patient who could understand words but could not speak. After the patient's death, Broca found damage near the front, also on the left side of the cerebral cortex. Similarly, the British neurologist John Hughlings Jackson showed in 1870 that specific parts of the cerebral cortex were responsible for different types of sensation and movement.

In 1876, a young German neurologist named Carl Wernicke described a patient who was able to speak, but who could not understand what he himself was saying. After the patient died, Wernicke ***dissected*** his brain and found that the cerebral cortex had been damaged in a single place, probably by a stroke. Wernicke knew about the area Broca had described and its importance for language. He also knew that the cerebral cortex contained another area where damage led to a general failure of hearing.

Wernicke realized that word perception involved several different elementary processes, each of which occurred in a different region of the brain. His work became the basis for the now-accepted idea of *distributed processing,* in which different regions of the brain together perform specific components of a complex process such as word perception. Even today, Wernicke's model of how the brain processes language still influences the thinking of neuroscientists.

Today, neuroscientists can actually light up the different regions of the brain involved in word recognition and other thought processes. For example, researchers can compare the metabolic activity of different regions of the cerebral cortex as human subjects perform various tasks, as ***revealed*** by such techniques as positron emission tomography (PET) and functional magnetic resonance imagining (FMRI).

If a person has heard a single word read aloud, metabolism increases in the very areas predicted by Wernicke. When a person reads the same word silently, however, metabolism increases in a totally different region. When the person speaks the word, the researchers observed metabolic increases in still different regions, including Broca's area. And when the person is asked to merely think about the word, a new pattern ***emerges*** that includes not only Wernicke's and Broca's areas but also other areas of the cortex.

Contemporary neuroscientists accept the view that individual regions of the brain perform specific functions and that complex functions of the brain require cooperation and information flow between several regions.

From Tobin, A.J. & Dusheck, J. (2001). _Asking About Life._ Philadelphia: Harcourt, pp. 862–863.

1021 words / _____ minutes = _____ words per minute.

Calculate your reading time by dividing the number of words in the article by the amount of time it took to read it. Then mark your reading time on the chart located on page 338.

READ: Keys Activity 7.2

On a separate sheet of paper or in your notebook, answer the following questions about the excerpt you just read:

1. Which of the following is true of sound?

  a. Hearing and understanding are the same.

  b. Neither pressure waves nor vibrations can be heard.

  c. Falling trees make sounds even when no one is around.

  d. Spoken language is a kind of air vibration.

2. According to the text, which of the following is true of Franz Joseph Gall?

  a. He was a French doctor.

  b. He was critical of the practice known as phrenology.

  c. He tried to find a relationship between the size of brain areas and emotional or intellectual abilities.

  d. He was close friends with George Eliot and Charles Dickens.

3. Pierre Flourens

  a. performed scientific experiments to study Broca's ideas.

  b. used human subjects for his experiments.

  c. was a twentieth-century scientist.

  d. argued that humans have an integrated mind and a single soul.

4. The cerebral cortex in humans

   a. is deep within the brain.

   b. is smaller than the cerebral cortex in other animals.

   c. is larger than that of other primates.

   d. is the same as the cerebellum in animals.

5. Metabolic activity is an indicator of

   a. brain function.

   b. phrenological activity.

   c. brain uniformity.

   d. emotional stability.

6. Which pair of sentences correctly compares the patients of Broca and Wernicke described in the article?

   a. Broca's patient could understand, but not produce, spoken language. Wernicke's patient could speak, but did not understand his own speech.

   b. Broca's patient could neither understand nor produce spoken language. Wernicke's patient could understand, but not produce, spoken language.

   c. Broca's patient could understand and produce spoken language. Wernicke's patient could not speak and did not understand spoken language.

   d. Broca's patient could not understand speech, but could speak. Wernicke's patient could speak, but not understand speech.

7. According to the text, whose model of brain processing still influences the thinking of neuroscientists?

   a. Gall

   b. Eliot

   c. Wernicke

   d. Dickens

8. If a physician wanted to assess the metabolic activity in a patient's brain, _____ would be best to use.

   a. distributed processing

   b. surgical dissection

   c. positron emission tomography

   d. phrenology

9. Which view of brain function is generally accepted by today's neuroscientists?

   a. Individual regions of the brain do not perform specific functions because complex processes of the brain require cooperation and information flow between regions.

   b. Individual parts of the brain have specific functions and even more complex processing is confined to one section of the brain or another.

   c. Different kinds of functioning occur in specific areas of the brain; however, complex brain functions are processed cooperatively among several regions.

   d. There are no differences between the way the brain processes simple and more complex functions.

10. Which of the following is true of reading and brain processing?

   a. Metabolically, the same part of the brain is used for reading aloud, silently reading, and mentally thinking about the same word.

   b. Metabolically, different parts of the brain are used for reading aloud, silently reading, and mentally thinking about the same word.

   c. Metabolically, the same part of the brain is used for silently reading and mentally thinking about the same word, but a different part of the brain is used in reading it aloud.

   d. Metabolically, different parts of the brain are used for reading words aloud and reading words silently. The same part of the brain used for reading a word aloud is also used in mentally thinking about it.

READ: Keys Activity 7.3

Examine each of the numbered phrases or sentences and complete the following on a separate sheet of paper or in your notebook:

(a) Write the boldfaced, italicized word. Identify one or two words that you can put in the place of the boldfaced, italicized word without changing the meaning of the phrase or sentence and write this synonym or synonymous phrase (words that have the same meaning) beside the word. (b) Identify the part of speech of this word as used in the sentence. (c) Look up the boldfaced, italicized word in a dictionary and write the dictionary definition. How does this compare with the definition from context? (d) List the parts of speech this word can sometimes be. (e) Write a complete sentence with each word.

1. Sound is a perception, the recognition and interpretation of an outside ***stimulus.***

2. But both the ***perception*** of the sound and the interpretation of its meaning depend on the experience of the hearer:

3. . . . a Chinese speaker, for example, hears tonal ***inflections*** in the vibration pattern that an English speaker might miss.

4. But they could not agree whether the brain worked as an ***integrated*** whole or a set of parts, more like the cogs of a machine.

5. Gall tried to establish a ***correlation*** between the size of a brain area and a particular emotional or intellectual capacity.

6. . . . he did not find any specific loss of particular traits, but rather a ***vague,*** general loss of mental function.

7. Indeed, like our upright posture and hairlessness, our ***immense*** cerebral cortex is one of the handful of traits that sets us apart from other primates.

8. After the patient died, Wernicke ***dissected*** his brain and found that the cerebral cortex had been damaged in a single place, probably by a stroke.

9. For example, researchers can compare the metabolic activity of different regions of the cerebral cortex as human subjects perform various tasks, as ***revealed*** by such techniques.

10. And when the person is asked to merely think about the word, a new pattern ***emerges*** that includes not only Wernicke's and Broca's areas but also other areas of the cortex.

READ: Keys Activity 7.4

In Part A, use the following list of words to fill in the blanks. In Part B, use the information from Part A to complete the analogies.

Part A

excluded	departs	thought	hidden
issues	shown	action	soundless
joined	pitch	small	included
huge	disconnection	clear	separated
unclear	damper	motivation	relationship

Synonym	Word	Antonym
_____	**1.** stimulus	_____
_____	**2.** perception	_____
_____	**3.** inflections	_____
_____	**4.** integrated	_____
_____	**5.** correlation	_____
_____	**6.** vague	_____
_____	**7.** immense	_____
_____	**8.** dissected	_____
_____	**9.** revealed	_____
_____	**10.** emerges	_____

Part B

1. emerges : _____ :: revealed : shown

2. stimulus : _____ :: dissected : joined

3. _____ : integrated :: inflection : pitch

4. correlation : relationship :: vague : _____

5. immense : huge :: dissected : _____

6. emerges : departs :: _____ : action

7. revealed : _____ :: inflection : soundless

8. stimulus : motivation :: perception : _____

9. included : excluded :: joined : _____

10. integrated : _____ :: correlation : disconnection

READ: Keys Activity Posttest

Rate each of the following words according to your knowledge of them.

Word	Stage 0 *I don't know this word.*	Stage 1 *I've seen this word but I know nothing of its meaning.*	Stage 2 *I've seen this word and can make associations with it.*	Stage 3 *I know this word.*
1. stimulus				
2. perception				
3. inflections				
4. integrated				
5. correlation				
6. vague				
7. immense				
8. dissected				
9. revealed				
10. emerges				

Reading and Thinking Critically

Chapter Map Exercise

Construct a chapter map from the major headings and subheadings in the chapter.

Objectives

After you finish this chapter, you will be able to do the following:

1. Draw valid conclusions.

2. Find the author's perspective.

3. Differentiate between fact and opinion.

4. Assess problems and issues.

Chapter Outline Exercise

Create a chapter outline from the major headings and subheadings in the chapter.

Thinking does not occur in a vacuum. Your perception of a problem affects the information you need to help you solve it. People influence you and the information available to you. The information you find determines the kinds of choices you think you have. Thus, problems, people, and information interact. Practice in critical thinking helps you find, sort, evaluate, and choose wisely. **Critical thinking** involves drawing valid conclusions, finding the author's perspective, and assessing problems and issues. Through practice, you learn to make more informed and better choices.

Reading is a logical forum in which to practice critical thinking skills. Reading lets you vicariously experience a variety of situations and work through thought processes. Identifying problems, examining options, and making decisions are skills you can then apply to other areas of your life.

Drawing Valid Conclusions

For better or worse, you are responsible for the valid **conclusions,** or reasoned judgments, you draw, even if the author provides you with false, incomplete, or misleading information. Because conclusions are based on both implied (hinted) and literal (stated) information, it's not always easy to draw the right conclusion.

Much of the reading you do is based on literal information or specific facts. The answer to a literal question is found in the text. You can physically point to the word or phrase that answers that question. Answers to literal questions are the stated details of a text.

Inferred information is not found directly in the text. You must make mental connections to determine the meaning implied by the author. This answer might be a detail or a main idea. Inferences and implications relate to drawing conclusions. A reader or listener makes inferences based on information implied by a speaker or author.

A variety of conclusions can be drawn from almost any situation. Sometimes the right conclusion will be easy to make. Sometimes it will be hard. Sometimes you will consider all the facts, both stated and hinted, and still reach the wrong conclusion. Drawing conclusions improves with practice. Using the knowledge you have and thinking actively helps you draw two kinds of valid conclusions—logical inferences and assumptions.

Logical Inferences

A **logical inference** is an unavoidable conclusion. Based on the stated or implied information, nothing else can be inferred. For instance, if you skip class and fail every course exam and assignment, you logically conclude that you will fail the course. Or, if you make an *A* on every test and project and fulfill all other course requirements, you logically conclude that you will pass the course. This inference, then, is somewhat like the geometric theorem that states, "If a = b and b = c, then a = c."

Logical inferences form the basis for understanding analogies (like those you might have completed in the READ Keys sections of this text). That is, analogies ask you to infer points of comparison. Although this is true in all analogies, such inferences become more complex when found in paragraph format. For instance, consider the analogy in the following excerpt:

> Old western movies often included a scene with a scraggly old gold miner standing in water, panning for gold. He would put his tin pan through the water, pull it out, swish it around, and then look to see if there were any tiny nuggets in it.
>
> In this chapter, we do much the same kind of thing. Although we are not panning for gold, we are panning for the essence of the payments to capital, land, and entrepreneurship. These payments are interest, rent, and profits, respectively.
>
> You may think you know all there is to know about interest, rent, and profits. You may say interest is what you pay when you get a loan from the bank; rent is what you pay for your apartment; profits are what a big corporation earns in a good year.
>
> In truth, there is more—much more. Let's go panning.

From *Economics* by R. A. Arnold. Copyright © 1989 by West Publishing Company. All rights reserved. Reprinted with permission.

What items or processes form the basis of the analogy? Here, the author compares panning for gold and panning for the essence of the payments to capital, land, and entrepreneurship (interest, rent, and profits). How do these compare? First, both require human intervention. A miner pans for gold. Perhaps a businessperson pans for interest, rent, and profits. Second, you must know what is important to your goal. To pan for gold, you separate important from unimportant materials. To pan for interest, rent, and profits, you separate important economic choices from those that fail to result in interest, rent, or profits. Time, patience, and effort are required for both processes.

To form standard analogies, you first identify the processes you want to compare. You examine the relationships. Next, you form comparisons. You check for correspondence between the processes. You infer missing elements in the process. Then you convert the written analogy to standard form. For example, miner : businessperson :: gold : profits. Here the analogy compares the two people involved in panning with the material for which they pan. The analogy could also be expressed as the following: miner : gold :: businessperson : profits. Now the analogy compares two examples of a person with the product for which he or she pans. Thus, analogies allow you to think of concepts in a variety of ways and relationships through the logical inferences you make. *Exercise 8.1 lets you practice drawing valid conclusions.*

READ Exercise 8.1

Assumptions

When you assume something, you draw a conclusion based on your background knowledge with no other supporting facts or proofs. For example, if an instructor is assigned to teach a particular course, you assume that he or she has the expertise and knowledge to do so. Or, if you find a particular textbook is required reading for a course, you assume that the text's author is knowledgeable about the topic. Such inferences are based on your **assumptions** (expectations or generalizations) about a topic. Assumptions are often true, but can also be false.

In some cases, your assumptions become over-generalizations in which you believe all examples of a certain type share the same characteristics or behaviors. For example, if you bought a car that turned out to be a lemon, you might generalize that all cars of that type are lemons. When you hold such generalizations about a particular group of people, you are thinking in **stereotypes.** Stereotypes can be based on gender, ethnic background, religious affiliation, age, occupation, location, or any other factor. For example, some people think that everyone who lives in California is a beach-loving surfer. Some people think that everyone over age 65 is retired. Some people think that all college presidents are men. None of these statements is true of everyone who lives in California, is over the age of 65, or is a college president.

Assumptions can also be used to entertain new options. Creativity expert Edward De Bono (1992) invented the word *po* to describe such assumptions. Extracted from words such as *hy(po)thesis, sup(po)se,* and *(po)ssible,* De Bono uses *po* to explore the possibilities of an assumption that is not logically possible. It shows that the absurdity of the assumption is understood. For instance, *"Po,* cats and dogs could mate to form a hybrid animal." Even though you know this could not logically occur, it allows you to explore the possibilities of the situation. Such exploration leads to the development of new ideas and methods.

Authors and instructors sometimes use such statements or questions (although without the clue *po*) to allow consideration of "what ifs." Thus, if an author or instructor asks, "What would happen if the judicial, executive, and legislative branches of the government were merged?" that individual is asking you to consider what would happen based on that assumption.

Finding the Author's Perspective

Authors, like people in other professions, are goal-oriented. They write because they have something to say. They have objectives and purposes in mind. They write to influence the understanding, emotions, beliefs, or actions of their readers through the words they use and the facts and opinions they include. Sometimes, either by accident or design, an author's bias affects the form and content of the information that is presented.

Establishing Purpose

Because writing is purposeful, an author seeks to obtain a desired response from you. For example, if an author writes to inform, then you could learn information you have not known before. If an author writes to persuade, then your belief may sway in that direction. If an author writes to entertain, you might feel amused or interested. These, then, constitute the three purposes authors have when writing—to inform, persuade, or entertain. Although one purpose may dominate, an author sometimes mixes the three. For instance, an author might provide information in a humorous way. Or an author might support a persuasive paper with information. Because texts usually contain humorous passages only to capture your interest, only the persuasive and informative types will be discussed in this section.

Informational Passages. Informational passages seek to educate. Usually, an author tries to present material in a way that readers will easily understand. Such writing often consists of explanations, analyses, descriptions, demonstrations, and definitions. It also includes examples, statistics, comparisons, contrasts, and expert opinions. Although most often found in textbooks, newspapers and magazines also include informative writing.

Persuasive Passages. An author writes a persuasive passage to bring about a change in either your opinion(s) or your behavior(s). Authors change your opinion by convincing you to agree with what they think—they seek to make you believe their points of view. For instance, an author might try to convince you that conserving resources is necessary for survival. Authors try to change your behavior in two ways: First, they change your beliefs. Then, they ask for a promise of action on your part. For example, an author might convince you that conservation is necessary. Then, you'd be asked to recycle waste products to conserve resources.

Persuasive writing is found in educational, cultural, or historical documents. Like informative writing, persuasive writing includes examples, statistics, comparisons, contrasts, and expert opinions. *Exercise 8.2 helps you learn to tell the difference between informational and persuasive passages.*

READ Exercise 8.2

Identifying Author Bias

Republicans, Democrats, believers, atheists, pro-choice advocates, gays, environmentalists, spendthrifts, men, women, liberals, buyers, adolescents, adults, elderly, conservatives, and on and on and on. The number of groups to which authors could belong or give support is almost endless. And because any given individual can hold membership in several groups, that person's beliefs and attitudes combine in a variety of ways to form perspective—a way of looking at issues, problems, information, and people.

An author's perspective affects the form and content of what he or she writes. When authors allow their perspectives to slant meaning, they **bias** the information. The words that authors choose and the ways in which they write can affect both your understanding and your beliefs.

An author chooses words carefully. This choice is critical because words form the means by which a message is conveyed. Choosing a wrong word can result in a reader's being confused or alienated. And the way one person perceives a word often differs from the ways in which others perceive that same word.

Connotations are implied meanings you derive from hearing, reading, speaking, and writing words in everyday life. They are your personal associations with the word. Denotations are the opposite of your personal perceptions of words. They consist of the literal, or dictionary, definitions of a word.

The way authors use words depends on their connotations, just as the way you understand words depends on your connotations. For instance, consider how you describe an odor and the effects of your description on others. Do you describe it as *fragrant* or *musty? Pungent* or *putrid? Aromatic* or *smoky?* The denotation of all the words relates to smell, but the connotations help differentiate among kinds of smells.

Euphemisms and **loaded words** are other ways of assigning meanings to words. The word *euphemism* comes from two Greek word parts—*eu*, which means good, and *pheme*, which means voice—which translate literally into "good voice." Euphemisms substitute "good" or pleasant phrases for "bad" or unpleasant phrases. Authors use them to soften the reality of negative statements or to disguise the truth. For instance, describing a person as "careful with details" sounds better than saying the person is "picky."

Loaded words, on the other hand, make people, issues, and things appear worse than they might really be. Because of the connotations carried by loaded words, a word that seems OK to you might trigger an emotional response in another person. For example, *accused murderer* has a different impact than *convicted felon* because you have definite feelings about murder and less definite ideas about felonies.

READ Exercise 8.3 *Exercise 8.3 provides practice in identifying an author's choice of words.*

Write to Learn

On a separate sheet of paper or in your notebook, respond to the following: Imagine you are a spy and have to pass along the secret of denotation and connotation to your superiors. You cannot give a definition or actually explain the differences between the two. You can, however, identify a word as a denotation and provide several connotations for it. Provide three to five examples of denotations and related connotations so your superiors will be sure to understand what you mean.

Differentiating Between Fact and Opinion

Is everything you read true? Can you trust experts? Do you accept as fact everything you see? Should you believe everything you hear?

P. T. Barnum is often quoted as having said, "There's a sucker born every minute." Barnum owned a circus he described as "The Greatest Show on Earth." He often used exaggeration and deception to create interest in his show. It follows that he might have thought a sucker is born every minute. Thus, many people accept this as his spoken opinion. However, no record exists of Barnum making this statement. Indeed, the word *sucker* was not commonly used in this context in Barnum's day.

In a free country like the United States, almost anything anyone thinks can be printed or said somewhere. Whether those thoughts begin as fact or not, distortions occur. You are responsible for determining if information is fact or opinion. You control whether you exist as a critical judge of information or just another sucker.

Facts

Witnesses sworn in during trials promise to tell all the **facts** they know about a crime. Their **opinions** are immaterial, or not important. The judge wants to hear what the witnesses know to be true. Thus, they describe what they actually saw or heard. They cannot add to, subtract from, or change the facts in any way. It is the judge's job to determine how closely each witness sticks to the bare facts.

What is a bare fact? A fact is a statement of reality. For instance, there are seven days in a week. That's a fact. Canada is in North America. That's also a fact. Facts also exist in the form of events known to have occurred. For instance, George Washington was the first president of the United States. The bombing of Pearl Harbor occurred on December 7, 1941. These are facts. Facts are truth.

Facts are based on direct evidence or on actual observation or experience. These are called primary sources and consist of original documents or first-person accounts of an event. Secondary sources also provide facts. These sources interpret, evaluate, describe, or otherwise restate the work of primary sources. Because information can be lost in translation, primary sources are preferred.

Words telling about facts are descriptive. They give details but are not judgmental. They express absolutes. They represent concepts that can be generally agreed upon. Words like *dead, freezing,* and *wet* are examples of such words. Other words limit a statement of fact. They show the possibility of other options. Look at the difference between these two statements: "I make good grades." "At times, I make good grades." The words *at times* limit the truth of the first sentence. Words like *frequently, occasionally,* and *seldom* are examples of such limiting words.

Opinions

Like facts, opinions are also a form of truth. The difference between the two lies in whose reality is represented. Facts belong to all people. They are universally held. An opinion belongs to one person. An opinion is what someone thinks about a subject. It is a viewpoint, belief, or judgment. Opinions reflect personal attitudes or feelings. Words describing opinions are interpretive. Consider the word *pretty.* One person may think that a dress is pretty. Someone else might think it is not pretty. It depends on what you think—your opinion. Objectivity refers to an author's skill in reporting facts without including personal opinions, feelings, or beliefs. Inclusion of biased material undermines the validity and value of what you read.

Words expressing opinions are qualitative. They tell about the value of something. For example, a three-year-old child might think that 500 pennies (five dollars) is a large amount. That would be his opinion. To a millionaire, however, 500 pennies is small change. That would be her opinion. Some examples of qualitative words are *cute, bad,* and *sour.*

Some phrases indicate an opinion is forthcoming. These help you recognize opinion for what it is. Examples of such phrases are *in my opinion, I believe,* and *I think. Exercise 8.4 provides practice in distinguishing fact from opinion.*

READ Exercise 8.4

Expert Opinions

The background of the person giving an opinion affects the value and validity of the opinion. Anyone can give an opinion, but some are **expert opinions.** Your dentist might say, "This is a good car." An auto mechanic might say, "This is a good car." Which person would you trust to know more about cars?

How do you know if an author's opinion is an expert one? First, you judge an author's educational and professional backgrounds. This includes occupation, years and kinds of experience, degrees, and source(s) of the degrees. Often an author's background affects his or her point of view, what is said about a topic, and the way in which facts are reported. For instance, an Army general who graduated from West Point and served in WWII might view the military differently than would an Army general who rose through the ranks following the Vietnam War. Both provide different, yet still expert, opinions. You find background information about an author in the preliminary or concluding statements of an article or a book. A biographical dictionary or an encyclopedia also contains such information. You also gain this knowledge through discussions with others in the field. You judge where the author works and the reputation of that institution, company, or organization.

You also judge the reputation of the author. However, this works both as an advantage and a disadvantage. Sometimes authors who are well-known authorities in one field write below their standards in another. For example, perhaps a best-selling mystery author might write a cookbook. The fact the author writes well may or may not mean that she knows how to cook. As a critical reader, you need to know the difference.

Sometimes information about the author's credentials is missing. You then need another way to judge the information. For example, suppose an article in *Today's Science* compares the incidence of cancer in the United States with that of France. The author, who is unknown to you, concludes that the air in France is cleaner than that in the United States and that this keeps the French in better health. If you

---

Write to Learn

On a separate sheet of paper or in your notebook, respond to the following: In your American history class, a graduate student in history guest lectures. She asserts that Grover Cleveland was the most effective president. Do you consider hers an expert opinion? Justify your answer.

---

have no information about the author's background, you cannot evaluate the author's qualifications or bias. In this case, you judge the standards and credibility of the journal containing the article. *Exercise 8.5 provides practice in finding facts, opinions, and expert opinions.*

READ Exercise 8.5

Propaganda

Propaganda is a form of persuasion used to change or sway opinion. Propaganda is one-sided, telling only one side of an issue to make you believe that side is the right one. Propaganda tries to make you think a certain way or believe or desire a certain thing.

You can be wary of the effect of propaganda by knowing what it is. Common types of propaganda include **image advertising, bandwagoning, testimonial, plain folks, name calling,** and **weasel words** (see Figure 8.1). Because propaganda is more obvious in advertising, it is easier to recognize it there. However, once you know what to look for, you also can find propaganda fairly easily in other written work.

In image advertising, a person, product, or concept is linked with certain people, places, sounds, activities, or symbols. This connection creates a positive mental picture. The new concept is tied to feelings about the old concept. For instance, an ad for a kind of cereal might show a famous athlete eating it. Now the image of the cereal is linked with that of the athlete.

In bandwagoning, the theme is "join the crowd." If you, as a child, said, "Everyone buys hightop tennis shoes. I want some, too," then you used this technique to convince your parents to let you buy what you wanted. You, like others who use bandwagoning, implied that you would be left out by not being like everyone else. Bandwagoning is a form of peer pressure. Because you conform to the wishes or beliefs of the group, bandwagoning tends to suppress individualism.

In a testimonial, a famous person or authority on the subject says a product, person, or idea is good. A testimonial suggests that if a famous person likes it, you should, too. However, you rarely see famous people selling soap or mouthwash. Because they are famous, you don't really think they need those kinds of things. Besides, it might be bad

Figure 8.1   Examples of Propaganda

Image Advertising

Examples: Fine wines and rich people; cars and western and outdoor settings; politicians and American symbols.

Plain Folks

Examples: Politicians shaking hands and kissing babies; a young woman advertising wart remover.

Testimonial

Examples: Tiger Woods and Nike; Jerry Lewis and muscular dystrophy; Brittney Spears and Pepsi; Shaquille O'Neal and Burger King.

Name Calling

Examples: One soft drink challenging another in a taste test; aspirin or cold remedies (eight of these, four of these, one of ours); competitions between hamburger chains.

Bandwagoning

Examples: Soft drink advertisements; generalization, such as, "*Everybody* in college is a genius."

Weasel Words

Examples: "Leaves your dishes *virtually* spotless"; "Cleans your teeth as white as *they* can be"; politicians promise not to ask for *unneeded* taxes; *almost* no poisons were found in the water supply.

for their images. Celebrities also give testimonials for good causes, such as campaigns for environmental issues or medical research.

When the plain folks technique is used in advertising, people in ads seem to be average and ordinary. The ad gives the impression that a friend or neighbor endorses a product. This is almost the opposite of testimonial. This ad wants you to trust the judgment of an average person.

An old English proverb goes, "Sticks and stones will break my bones, but names will never hurt me." Unfortunately, this is not true in advertising. Name calling is a form of propaganda that forms unfair comparisons. In name calling, a product or cause is made to appear better in relation to a competing product or cause. This is accomplished by the use of unpopular or unflattering language about the competition. You are led to believe that one product or cause is superior to another. Name calling can be either obvious or subtle. Often, advertisers use obvious name-calling techniques, whereas politicians use these techniques more indirectly.

Weasels are animals with keen sight and smell that are known for their quickness and slyness. Because of these characteristics, evasive words that lack exact meanings are called weasel words. Their meanings cannot be pinned down. Implications are made but promises are not assured. Weasel words leave the speaker with a quick and sly way out. As Theodore Roosevelt said, "When a weasel sucks eggs, the meat is sucked out of the egg. If you use a 'weasel word' after another there is nothing left over." *Exercise 8.6 helps you identify bias and propaganda.*

READ Exercise 8.6

Write to Learn

On a separate sheet of paper or in your notebook, respond to the following: You are the advertising manager of a company that manufactures a new kind of school notebook. Devise a television advertising campaign for your product. Justify the type of propaganda technique you decide to use.

Assessing Problems and Issues

To decide what you want from life, you must first assess yourself and determine what options are available to you and which are important to pursue. Similarly, to get what you want from information, you must be able to assess problems and issues and discover their importance to

Table 8.1   Assessing Problems and Issues
1. What is the point?
2. Why am I interested in this problem or issue?
3. What is my purpose in solving this problem or addressing this issue?
4. Who or what is affected by this problem or issue?
5. What is the best question I can ask about this problem or issue?
6. What additional questions do I have about this problem or issue?
7. What assumptions do I have about this problem or issue?
8. Where can I get additional information about this problem or issue?

you. You accomplish this by identifying central questions and issues, determining which are most important, and finding relevant information about them. Table 8.1 identifies some of the questions to ask when assessing problems and issues. *Exercise 8.7 provides practice in assessing problems and issues.*

READ Exercise 8.7

Relevancy means separating what is important from what is unimportant. Relevancy, like opinion, is in the eye of the beholder. What is relevant to one person may or may not be relevant to another. In addition, what is relevant in one situation may or may not be relevant in another.

Anderson and Pichert (1978) conducted a research study in which they examined the effect of point of view on recall. Subjects read a passage about what two boys did at one boy's home while playing hooky from school. Some readers were asked to read as if they were burglars. Others were asked to read as if they were home buyers. A third group read from no particular viewpoint. Researchers found that the reader's point of view affected what was relevant and later recalled. For example, those readers who read as burglars were more likely to recall where money was kept. That's what was relevant to them. Readers who read as home buyers recalled more about the house's landscape. That's what was relevant to them. Relevancy, then, depends on your point of view or your purpose for reading. *Exercise 8.8 provides practice in identifying relevancy.*

READ Exercise 8.8

Chapter Summary Exercise

Proof the following summary for errors. Cross out incorrect words and replace with your corrected version.

Critical thinking helps you make reasonable, informed decisions about learning, relationships, and life. Applying critical thinking skills to reading provides actual experiences in a variety of situations. In jumping to conclusions, you think critically about both implied and literal information. Four types of conclusions—illogical inferences, assumptions, and nonsensical conclusions—are possible. Critical thinking also involves finding the author's organization in terms of purpose (philanthropic or mercenary), expert opinions versus opinionated information, and bias. Finally, as a critical thinker, you identify minor questions, determine importance, and find irrelevant information when assessing problems and issues.

Chapter Review

Answer the following questions on a separate sheet of paper or in your notebook.

1. On a separate sheet of paper, create a chart that defines and provides an example of each type of conclusion (logical inferences and assumptions) for the topic of test preparation.
2. Compare and contrast primary and secondary sources.
3. Identify another example for each of the types of propaganda identified in Figure 8.1.
4. Create and label three statements of opinion and three statements of fact concerning the last exam you took in this course.
5. Explain the idea that relevancy is in the eye of the beholder.
6. What is the role of background knowledge in drawing conclusions?
7. Choose any one of the groups or organizations listed in the first paragraph of the section "Identifying Author Bias." Relative to the topic, "higher education," describe how you think membership in the group could result in bias.
8. Again choose one of the groups or organizations listed in the first paragraph of the section "Identifying Author Bias," and provide your connotation of what that word means. Look up the word in a dictionary and provide its denotation. Does your connotation show bias? If so, how?
9. Compare and contrast euphemisms and loaded words. Provide an example of each other than those included in the chapter.
10. How would you describe the effect of background knowledge on your ability to assess problems and issues?

Terms

Terms appear in the order in which they occur in the chapter.

critical thinking
conclusions
logical inference
assumptions
stereotypes
bias
euphemisms
loaded words
facts
opinions
expert opinions
propaganda
image advertising
bandwagoning
testimonial
plain folks
name calling
weasel words
relevancy

Exercises

Exercise 8.1   Read each paragraph and answer the following questions.

To help a person who is choking, first ask this critical question: "Can you make any sound at all?" If the victim makes a sound, relax. You have time to continue with your questioning to see what you can do to help; you are not going to have to make a quick decision. But whatever you do; don't hit him on the back. If you do, the particle may become lodged more firmly in his air passage.

1. Why can you relax if a choking victim can make a sound?

Some people believe there are two kinds of body fat: regular fat and "cellulite." Cellulite is supposed to be a hard and lumpy fat that yields to being "burned up" only if it is first broken up by methods like the massage or the machine typical of the health spa. The notion that there is such a thing as cellulite received wide publicity with the publication of a book by a certain Madam R of Paris, which sold widely during the 1970s. The American Medical Association reviewed the evidence on cellulite (there was none) and concluded that cellulite was a hoax.

2. How many kinds of body fat are there?

3. Why is the first mention of cellulite in quotation marks?

4. What is the difference between regular fat and cellulite?

5. What is the writer's opinion of Madam R?

As with murder, a society can also have different attitudes about sex at different times. Kissing and intercourse before marriage were viewed differently during the colonial era than today. Kissing in public was considered unacceptable behavior. One historian recorded the event of a Captain Kemble who, returning from a long sea voyage, kissed his lady as he stepped on shore. As a result, he "was promptly closed in the stocks."

6. What is the purpose of stocks?

7. How have society's views toward murder changed?

Some doctors prescribe amphetamines ("speed") to help with weight loss (the best known are dexedrine and benzedrine). These reduce appetite—but only temporarily. Typically the appetite returns to normal after a week or two, the lost weight is regained, and the user has the problem of trying to get off the drug without gaining more weight.

8. Other than reducing appetite, how do amphetamines affect the human body?

Food can lodge so securely in the trachea that all air is cut off. No sound can be made because the larynx is in the trachea and makes sounds only when air is pushed across it. This has happened often enough so that the event has been given a name—*cafe coronary*.

9. Why is the event called *cafe coronary*?

10. What is the common name for this event?

People have varying needs to be recognized and valued by others and by themselves. We all like to receive "strokes" that say to us, "Your efforts are recognized, and you are regarded as a person of value." Work in organizations can often provide such esteem needs through the dispensing of organizational rewards. Even subtle rewards such as private offices, carpeting on the floor, or a more desirable location in the workroom can convey this recognition and sense of worth to an individual employee.

11. What are *strokes?*

The United States is moving away from sexual straightjackets, which assumed woman's natural place was at home while man's was out seeking fame and glory, to a broader participation of both parties. Today, more than half the American labor force is women. And a larger percentage of those women also function as mothers and homemakers in addition to their job responsibilities. The trend seems to be increasing, especially when economic difficulties make the two-paycheck family the norm rather than the exception.

12. What is meant by *sexual straightjackets?*

13. What proportion of today's American labor force is male?

14. In today's society, are there more one-paycheck or two-paycheck families?

15. What are some ways in which men can participate more broadly in the family?

Exercise 8.2   On a separate sheet of paper or in your notebook, indicate whether the purpose of each of these passages is to inform (*I*) or persuade (*P*).

1. To create a motivational climate, there must be openness between managers and subordinates. Each must have a clear understanding of both the organization's goals and, to the degree possible, the individual employee's goals. The manager must be flexible, creative, and receptive to new ideas from his or her subordinates. The only way this can be conveyed is through effective communication and positive interpersonal relationships.

2. Organizations exist for the purpose of accomplishing things that cannot be done by individuals working alone. From the day that the earliest cave dweller discovered that he or she could not move a large boulder alone but needed to enlist the help of others, people have organized efforts. As the tasks at hand became more and more complicated, the organization structure, too, became more complex. Today, with enormous tasks such as building elaborate missile systems, huge nuclear power generators, expansive water conservation systems, and ambitious space exploration programs, the need for sophisticated organizations is greater than ever.

3. Communication with workers can in itself be regarded as a form of reward. Positive communication with one's boss is often associated with job satisfaction. There are at least four ways that a supervisor can use communication to motivate and encourage employees. These include (1) "stroking" or giving recognition, (2) receptiveness to workers' ideas, (3) providing timely information, and (4) systematically reviewing employee performance.

4. Training includes activities that improve job performance. Training helps make a person more employable or promotable within the organization and teaches basic skills. It is specific learning and focuses directly on basic activities. For example, a typist may be trained to move from the typing pool to a secretarial position. A laborer could be taught to drive a truck and then to qualify as a driver. Training teaches people new basic techniques and introduces them to new methods related to their jobs. We all need to improve ourselves for our jobs at all times, by being as effectively trained as possible.

5. Ideally, periodic performance reviews combine information giving with information getting. They are not talking to subordinates, they're talking with them. The manager's role is and must be that of an evaluator, but the review should not be judgmental in matters going beyond the work context. Statements such as "The accuracy with which you write up your sales orders needs to be improved" would normally be appropriate in an appraisal interview. Statements such as "You need to change your hair style and stop living with your boyfriend" would probably be out of line. Stick to the work-related evaluations.

6. Identify the purpose of Chapter 1's Reading Keys passage.

7. Identify the purpose of Chapter 2's Reading Keys passage.

8. Identify the purpose of Chapter 3's Reading Keys passage.

9. Identify the purpose of Chapter 5's Reading Keys passage.

10. Identify the purpose of Chapter 6's Reading Keys passage.

Exercise 8.3   Read the following essay. On a separate sheet of paper or in your notebook, complete the following:

1. What is the author's purpose in writing this passage?

2. List 10 euphemisms found in the essay and provide your connotation for each.

3. Identify their denotations.

4. Describe how each euphemism softens the reality of each denotation.

5. Reread the last three paragraphs of the essay. Contrast Admiral McDonald's statement with that of General Powell.

By Any Name, War Is Still War
Clarence Page

These days the first casualty of war is its language. . . . You may have noticed that we don't "kill" anybody anymore. Instead, we have "weapons systems" that "visit" the enemy and deposit our "ordnance," sometimes with "collateral damage."

We don't bomb the enemy. We "suppress their assets." If our "targeting" was "ineffective," we "visit" the enemy again and "retarget" their "assets."

And a target isn't blown up. It is "degraded," "eliminated," "suppressed" or "neutralized," just to name a few of the ways military spokespeople nowadays describe the blowing of something or someone to smithereens.

Military people have long tried to fuzz up the language that describes what they do for a living, but the language of this war is more abstract than ever, says Rutgers University's William Lutz, chair of the Committee on Public Doublespeak of the National Council of Teachers of English.

"Unless you have some sort of a context, you simply don't know what it means," Lutz said in a telephone interview. In Vietnam, he explained, "air support" was not a tough term to figure out, and as evasive as such terms as "protective reaction strikes" or even "limited duration protective reaction strikes" may have seemed, you still could figure out from the sound of them what they meant, even if their emotional impact may have been softened somewhat.

But "airborne sanitation" in the Gulf "has something to do with the planes that go in ahead of the bombers to clean out the antiaircraft batteries," Lutz said. "Or at least that's what I think it means."

Today's military doublespeak triggers no mental picture, said Lutz. We don't have airplanes. We have a "weapons system." Weapons have become "assets," which sounds positive enough, particularly in the absence of "liabilities."

Even [such] standard military terms [as] "ordnance," which means explosives, have become a new form of doublespeak because of the way they are used, Lutz observed. "Delivery of ordnance" sounds like we have just loaded a bomb onto a truck and taken it somewhere. It really means we are bombing people.

In Lutz's 1989 book, *Doublespeak,* he traced how language designed to obscure and deceive, rather than enlighten or clarify, grew along with "technocrats" and "bureaucratization" in the military.

Lutz isn't alone in his concern. Retired Brigadier General William Louisell lamented the trend toward military doublespeak in the August 1988 issue of *Armed*

Forces Journal International. "Soldiers are beginning to obscure clear thinking with high-sounding, redundant, glittering generalities," he wrote.

The language of the . . . war seems to be characterized by military spokesmen and politicians who are trying conscientiously to replace language reminiscent of Vietnam with language that evokes World War II. "Body bags," for example, have become "human remains pouches."

General Norman Schwarzkopf, commander of the American and allied forces in the Gulf [during Operation Desert Storm], bristled when a reporter mentioned "carpet bombing," saying he didn't know what the reporter meant by the term, even though it has been a common military term for saturation bombing since World War II. Perhaps it simply has no convenient place in a war that emphasizes "precision targeting" and "smart bombs."

Accordingly, military officials are reluctant to talk about "collateral damage" or "incontinent ordnance," which are nice ways of describing bombs that miss their targets and perhaps blow to smithereens people we didn't want to hit.

Yet, clear language encourages clear thinking. Sanitized language about war can lead only to murky public perceptions of the whole bloody process.

Just as it has become extremely important for Pentagon officials to control media access to the war, it is important to control its language. But, unlike the debate over media access, the move toward military doublespeak seems a less tactical than political one that has less to do with fooling the enemy than with winning the hearts and minds of the American public.

The stark realities of war, delivered these days with unprecedented intensity by live television, should remind us of the fact that war kills lots of people in grisly ways and that we should be very clear about why and how we are fighting it and whether it is worth its horrible price.

When the price is worth it, precise language not only clarifies, it also can inspire. General Colin Powell, chairman of the Joint Chiefs of Staff [during Operation Desert Storm], apparently had that in mind when he described our strategy toward Iraqi forces as, "First we're going to cut it off, then we're going to kill it." Such candor has been strikingly rare in this war.

That's a far cry from Admiral Wesley McDonald's assessment of Grenada: "We were not micromanaging Grenada until about that time frame."

Let's hope our current time frame doesn't squeeze the intelligence out of our language.

From Tribune Media Services. Reprinted by permission.

Exercise 8.4

On a separate sheet of paper or in your notebook, distinguish between fact and opinion by placing an *F* for each phrase that is a fact and an *O* for each phrase that is an opinion.

1. a drab room

2. 60 cycles per second

3. the most popular candidate

4. an overripe banana

5. the best agency for the job

6. a liter of H_2O

7. the hottest day on record

8. black type on white paper

9. 0° C

10. a light photocopy

Exercise 8.5   On a separate sheet of paper or in your notebook, distinguish among facts, opinions, and expert opinions using the following key: *F*—facts, *O*—opinions, and *X*—expert opinions.

1. According to last term's grades, more people failed Dr. Jimenez's class than that of any other instructor in the department.

2. According to a periodic table of the elements, carbon has an atomic weight greater than that of hydrogen.

3. According to the person who sits behind me in English, our instructor is the best poet on campus.

4. According to our state senator, athletics have no place in higher education.

5. According to an editorial in our campus newspaper, most students fail to study adequately.

Exercise 8.6   Obtain copies of your student newspaper and any two of your favorite magazines. Select five advertisements from the publications that you think illustrate a propaganda technique. Glue or tape these ads to index cards or sheets of paper. In class, exchange your five advertisements with two other group members. Select the best examples from the 15 total advertisements. Try to find one example for each propaganda technique. You and your group mates may have to refer to the publications again.

Exercise 8.7   You are working your way through college. You want to keep the job you have because it is hard to find a job that works with your school schedule. The job pays minimum wage. You are considering applying for one or two credit cards to help you with your financial situation. You are looking for some information to help you make decisions about credit. Use Chapter 1's READ Keys passage as your source as you respond to the following questions from Table 8.1 "Assessing Problems and Issues." Elaborate on the scenario with specific details about your situation in responding to the questions on a separate sheet of paper or in your notebook.

Exercise 8.8   After reading this passage, respond to the following statements on a separate sheet of paper or in your notebook.

Houston was founded following the Texas battle for independence from Mexico in 1836. Two brothers from New York purchased 2,000 acres hoping to make Houston as great a city as New Orleans. It incorporated and became a town the following year. Houston takes its name from Sam Houston, a hero in the Battle of San Jacinto. Sam Houston was also the republic's first elected president. Houston served as the capital of the Republic of Texas for the next two years.

One hundred and fifty years passed. Houston grew from a pioneer town to become the largest city in Texas. It is also our country's fourth largest city. More than 1.5 million people make it their home. The Houston metropolitan area covers over 7,000 square miles. Houston is located in Harris County in the southeast part of the state. It is the county seat of Harris County.

Houston's climate is a mild one. The average winter temperature is about 55 degrees. The average summer temperature is about 85 degrees. Houston receives almost 50 inches of rain each year.

Oil was found in southeast Texas at Spindletop in 1901. Houston connects with the Gulf of Mexico through the Houston Ship Channel. The ship canal was completed in 1914. The canal was opened by President Woodrow Wilson. The discovery of oil combined with the opening of the ship canal stimulated industrial growth.

Today, over 200 industries—oil, chemical, steel, and others—line the canal. More than 6,000 ships dock along the canal each year. Indeed, Houston is the third largest port in terms of total tonnage. It ranks second in its handling of foreign tonnage. As a result, many foreign banks have representative offices in Houston. Many nations also maintain consular offices there.

NASA's Lyndon B. Johnson Space Center makes its home in Houston. Thus, Houston serves as one of the nation's premier space-age headquarters. The Space Center has been the headquarters for astronaut training, equipment testing, and flight control for Skylab and space shuttle missions.

Houston's Texas Medical Center is a major health complex. It serves the needs of the city, state, and region. It houses many medical research groups as well as providing health care. During the 1970s, numerous earth and physical scientists, as well as professionals in the life sciences, relocated in Houston.

Houston's culture attracts both tourists and hometown residents. The Astros baseball team and the Oilers football team are located there. Numerous high schools and universities also provide avenues of entertainment. Houston is home to a symphony orchestra, an opera company, and many other musical groups. Museums, art galleries, and parks complete Houston's cultural atmosphere. The Astrodome, Astroworld, and the battleship Texas provide both amusement and education for all.

---

1. You are a historian interested in writing about Texas history before 1900. List three relevant facts you could include in your account.

2. You are retired and planning to move. List three relevant facts that might encourage you to locate in Houston and the rationale for including each one.

3. You have just graduated with a degree in engineering. List three relevant facts that might encourage you to apply for jobs in Houston.

4. You are planning a vacation to Houston. List three attractions you might visit or activities you might pursue.

5. You are a native of Spain and are interested in opening a branch of your company in Houston. What relevant facts might encourage you to pursue this endeavor?

6. You like small towns and wide-open spaces. What relevant facts might discourage you from moving to Houston?

7. You are studying pollution and its effects on the environment. List three relevant facts about Houston that are indicators of possible pollution problems.

8. You have just received a degree in medical technology. List three factors that might encourage you to apply for a job in Houston.

9. You enjoy sports. What relevant facts about Houston would help you pursue this hobby?

10. You are a music major with a minor in theater. What three relevant facts about Houston might encourage you in this pursuit?

Web Exercise

Even people who are normally critical thinkers often get taken in by Internet hoaxes relating to cookie recipes, e-mail viruses, taxes on modems, and get-rich-quick schemes. For this exercise, access one of the following Web sites to help you think critically about what you find on the World Wide Web and respond to the following questions.

Urban Legends and Folklore
http://urbanlegends.miningco.com/library/blhoax.htm

Datafellows Hoax Warnings
http://www.Europe.Datafellows.com/news/hoax.htm

1. Describe the kind of information you find at the Web site.

2. What conclusions can you draw about the information at this Web site?

3. What is a hoax or urban legend?

4. How does someone use author's perspective and "expert opinion" in perpetrating a hoax?

5. Describe specifically how this Web site helps you become a more critical thinker.

READ: Keys

READ: Keys Activity Pretest

Rate each of the following words according to your knowledge of them.

Word	Stage 0 *I don't know this word.*	Stage 1 *I've seen this word but I know nothing of its meaning.*	Stage 2 *I've seen this word and can make associations with it.*	Stage 3 *I know this word.*
1. perceptive				
2. diverse				
3. dictatorial				
4. initiating				
5. profoundly				
6. convey				
7. patronizing				
8. complex				
9. tentative				
10. vengeful				

READ: Keys Activity 8.1

Read the following excerpt and keep track of your reading time.
Note: Underlined, italicized words are used in Chapter 5, Exercise 5.7.

Being Appropriate

Speech students often ask, "What exactly is inappropriate language? Shouldn't that decision be left up to the individual speaker?" Certainly each of us uses a different standard to define inappropriateness. But a speaker cannot simply make decisions in a vacuum. A speaker who wishes to have an impact must make **perceptive** decisions about the language he or she uses based upon the **diverse** members of the audience. Here are some suggestions that can help you become aware of your listeners and avoid words, terms, phrases, and expressions that listeners might consider ineffective or improper.

Be Aware of Cultural Differences

In most public speaking situations you encounter, there will be enormous differences in the cultural backgrounds of listeners. An audience of twenty people could include Hispanics, Caucasians, African Americans, Russians, Asians, southerners, westerners, or northeasterners. If you want to educate or influence individuals of such diversity, you need to understand the impact of culture upon language. Consider these examples. The word "submarine" is used throughout many parts of the United States to describe a large, overstuffed sandwich on an Italian roll. But terminology changes based on geography. Bostonians may call it a "grinder." New Yorkers may order a "hero." Philadelphians might ask for a "hoagie" and residents of New Orleans may want a "poor boy." Imagine the misunderstandings that can occur when individuals whose second language is English attempt to define "submarine," "hero," or "grinder" literally. An American asks, "Can I give you a lift?" but a British citizen defines the word "lift" as an "*elevator*." In the Eskimo language there are numerous words to describe varieties of snow such as "wet snow" or "*fluffy* snow;" and in Brazil, there are dozens of terms referring to the word "coffee." When several American car companies decided to use the term "Body by Fisher" as a selling point in foreign advertisements, they discovered in horror that in some foreign markets the term was translated as "Corpses by Fisher." And General Motors learned that one of the reasons their Chevrolet Nova models failed to sell in many Latin American countries was that *no va* means "does not go" in Spanish.[1]

If regional and ethnic differences can affect simple words and concepts, imagine how culture can influence more complicated language structures. In America, individuals with more knowledge about a topic tend to be direct and assertive, speaking in a straightforward manner. However, in a country such as Japan where people are concerned with saving face, those with greater knowledge tend to speak more indirectly and avoid direct statements that would appear **dictatorial.**[2] Americans enjoy talking and **initiating** conversation, but many Chinese use more silences within their language patterns.3 Some Hispanic, French, and Italian Americans complain that English does not allow them to express feelings as comprehensively as their own "romance" languages.4 The native Hawaiian language includes only five _vowels_ and seven _consonants_,5 and there are some American Indian languages that contain no past or future tenses.6

As you discover how **_profoundly_** culture influences language, you can develop speaking practices that **_convey_** greater sensitivity to the diverse members of your audience. Use language that is inclusive and avoid using "in-group" terms, jargon, and shorthand speech that excludes another individual's background or experience. Be clear and carefully define terms that listeners may not understand. Recognize that accents are not "wrong" or "bad," but speak slowly and distinctly and be aware that people of diverse backgrounds may need to listen to your _dialect_ or accent at a more comfortable speaking rate. Make an effort to understand the language of your audience. If you are speaking to listeners of another culture, take the time to learn greetings or important words that help you link your topic more successfully to them. Most important, respect the diversity of your audience. Avoid **_patronizing_** statements that insult or embarrass listeners and refrain from inappropriate humor that pokes fun at their culture or language. Recognize that the differences in language and culture can be a positive source for learning. As an effective speaker, you want to connect diverse cultures and languages by building bridges of understanding. 7

Recognize Differences Due to Gender

Do women talk more than men? Are men more direct than women? Are there distinct men and women's languages? The answers to these questions may surprise you. Before discussing differences in language, we must emphasize that the concepts being considered are based upon researched conclusions that have numerous exceptions. The language used by men and women can be influenced by family, education, or cultural socialization. Men and women can communicate differently or similarly based upon occupation, experiences, relationships, interests, needs, or social groupings. As men and women differ in size, color, age, shape, or interests, so can they vary in vocabulary, sentence structure, grammar, and language patterns.

First of all, it is a myth that women talk more than men. Studies indicate that men not only talk more, but control conversation and maintain their dominance by interrupting others more often.8 Men seem to be less concerned with grammatical errors and tend to use vocalized pauses to occupy center stage. Men use competitive and task-oriented language to take charge and get things done. Men will frequently issue orders and directives such as "You need to _fax_ this report," or "Let's get to the _bottom line_." Men have greater technical vocabularies and tend to be more fact-oriented than women. Men's language is more intense, and the language of some males includes more curse words and profanity. Men like to talk about topics such as sports, business, or current events. While they enjoy conversations with other men to escape, to share interests, and to experience "freedom," men seldom call each other simply to "talk."9

There are interesting differences in the language used by women. Women tend to speak with more qualifying words such as "possibly," or "maybe," and more disclaimers such as "this might be <u>silly</u>, but . . ." Unlike men, women don't interrupt conversations and use more polite forms for giving orders—"If you don't mind . . . ," or "If it isn't too much trouble . . ." Women tend to use more "tag" questions such as "That's the way it is, right?" and more descriptive words like "exceptionally," "adorable," "precious," and "lovely." Women use more **complex** sentence structures, prepositional phrases, and adverbs than men, and ask questions three times as often as men. Women also use more words and convey more comprehensive details than do men. Women tend to use more **tentative** phrases such as "I guess," or "I think," employ language that is less assertive than men, and make statements that express <u>negotiations</u> by describing what things are not. Unlike the more dominant males, women try to support conversation and keep it going. Women are more comfortable disclosing personal information and expressing emotional needs and psychological states. Women talk with other women to express empathy, to share feelings, or "just to talk."[10]

What can we learn from some of these conclusions and what are the implications for the speaker and listener? We must remember that differences in language patterns can depend on the situation, place, and environment. A businesswoman presenting a training lecture to new employees could use language that is direct, task-oriented, and to the point. At the same time, a man recounting a scuba diving experience in the Caribbean could use numerous details and descriptive adverbs. Much has been made about "the battle" of the sexes, and much has been written about the dominance of one gender or the **vengeful** role reversal of another. If we recognize that the rhetoric of confrontation is harmful, we can begin to listen honestly and genuinely learn from one another. We should enjoy the unique speaking patterns of women who can convey the depth and richness of language with expressive shades and images. We can also appreciate the directness of men who contribute power, intensity, and technical depth to language. If we avoid making judgments and understand that the language of one gender is not wrong and the other right, we can appreciate that our differences can actually complement each other. We can be more open when women or men need to alter their language patterns in response to different environments or roles. We can also be more accepting of the unique perspectives that each gender offers.[11]

---

1 R. Armao, "Worst Blunders: Firms Laugh Through Tears," *American Business* (January 1981), p. 11, cited by Ronald B. Adler and Neil Towne, *Looking Out, Looking In,* 8e (Ft. Worth: Harcourt Brace College Publishers, 1996), p 101.

2 Dodd, Intercultural Communication, p 150.

3 Ibid., p 149.

4 Ibid., p 148.

5 Ray Riegert, *Hidden Hawaii* (Berkeley: Ulysses Press, 1989), p 125.

6 Dodd, Intercultural Communication, p 134

7 Some of the suggestions used here are from the eleven-point plan for "Developing Skills in Language and Culture" in Dodd, *Intercultural Communication,* pp 149–150.

8 Sarah Trenholm and Arthur Jensen, *Interpersonal Communication,* 3e (New York: Wadsworth, 1996), p. 193.

9 Much of the information about gender differences in language was drawn from the following sources: Ronald B. Adler and Neil Towne, *Looking Out, Looking In,* 9e (Ft. Worth: Harcourt, 1999), pp 214–219; Roy M. Berko, Andrew D. Wolvin, *Communicating: A Social and Career Focus,* 6e (Boston: Houghton Mifflin, 1995), pp. 208–212; Sarah Trenholm and Arthur Jensen, *Interpersonal Communication,* 3e (New York: Wadsworth, 1996), p. 193–195; and Richard L. Weaver, *Understanding Interpersonal Communication,* 5e, (Glenview: Scott, Foresman/Little, Brown Higher Education, 1990), pp. 173–178.

10 Adler and Towne, *Looking Out Looking In,* 9th ed, p 216.

11 Weaver, *Understanding Interpersonal Communication,* p. 174, 177.

From Metcalfe, S. (2000). *Building Speech,* 4th ed. pp 307–309 and 310 lines 1–26. Ft. Worth, TX: Harcourt.

1390 words / _____ minutes = _____ words per minute.

Calculate your reading time by dividing the number of words in the article by the amount of time it took to read it. Then mark your reading time on the chart located on page 338.

READ: Keys Activity 8.2

On a separate sheet of paper or in your notebook, answer the following questions about the excerpt you just read:

1. Which of the following types of diversity was not addressed in this excerpt?

   a. race

   b. geography

   c. disabilities

   d. gender

2. _____ is an example of a romance language.

   a. Spanish

   b. Russian

   c. Japanese

   d. Eskimo

3. Which of the following is true?

   a. Residents of the United States and Great Britain easily understand each other because they all speak English.

   b. Some English terms mean different things in different parts of the United States.

   c. The effect of culture on language is minimal.

   d. Regional and ethnic/racial differences in language are the same.

4. According to the text, which sentence would not be found in some American Indian languages?

   a. I am hungry.

   b. Yesterday was a long day.

   c. I will buy a new car next week.

   d. I was hoping for a better grade in that course.

5. What is true of gender differences in speech?

   a. Women talk more than men.

   b. Men are more concerned with grammatical errors.

   c. Men rarely use vocalized pauses to gain attention.

   d. Women have less technical vocabularies.

6. Which of the following is NOT a common reason given for men's conversations?

   a. to escape

   b. just to talk

   c. sharing interests

   d. freedom

7. What would you expect to find in language used by women?

   a. fewer qualifying words

   b. fewer details

   c. more comments that support and facilitate conversation

   d. more interruptions

8. Which of the following comments would you most likely hear from a female speaker?

   a. I know exactly how you feel.

   b. Did you read today's newspaper?

   c. This is wasting time. We need to get busy and complete this project.

   d. I'll get right to it.

9. How is the Hawaiian language different from English?

   a. There is no difference.

   b. There are fewer vowels and fewer consonants.

   c. There are more vowels and more consonants.

   d. There is the same number of vowels but fewer consonants.

10. Based on language patterns, which nationality would probably be the quietest?

   a. Brazilians

   b. French

   c. Chinese

   d. Americans

READ: Keys Activity 8.3

Examine each of the numbered phrases or sentences and complete the following on a separate sheet of paper or in your notebook.

(a) Write the boldfaced, italicized word. Identify one or two words that you can put in the place of the boldfaced, italicized word without changing the meaning of the phrase or sentence and write this synonym or synonymous phrase (words that have the same meaning) beside the word. (b) Identify the part of speech of this word as used in the sentence. (c) Look up the boldfaced, italicized word in a dictionary and write the dictionary definition. How does this compare with the definition from context? (d) List the parts of speech this word can sometimes be. (e) Write a complete sentence with each word.

1. A speaker who wishes to have an impact must make ***perceptive*** decisions about the language he or she uses based upon the diverse members of the audience.

2. A speaker who wishes to have an impact must make perceptive decisions about the language he or she uses based upon the **diverse** members of the audience.

3. However, in a country such as Japan where people are concerned with saving face, those with greater knowledge tend to speak more indirectly and avoid direct statements that would appear **dictatorial.**

4. Americans enjoy talking and **initiating** conversation, but many Chinese use more silences within their language patterns.

5. As you discover how **profoundly** culture influences language, you can develop speaking practices that convey greater sensitivity to the diverse members of your audience.

6. As you discover how profoundly culture influences language, you can develop speaking practices that **convey** greater sensitivity to the diverse members of your audience.

7. Avoid **patronizing** statements that insult or embarrass listeners and refrain from inappropriate humor that pokes fun at their culture or language.

8. Women use more **complex** sentence structures, prepositional phrases, and adverbs than men, and ask questions three times as often as men.

9. Women tend to use more **tentative** phrases such as "I guess," or "I think," employ language that is less assertive than men, and make statements that express negotiations by describing what things are not.

10. Much has been made about "the battle" of the sexes, and much has been written about the dominance of one gender or the **vengeful** role reversal of another.

READ: Keys Activity 8.4

In Part A, use the following list of words to fill in the blanks. In Part B, use the information from Part A to complete the analogies.

Part A

hesitant	confident	condescending	greatly
bossy	withhold	easy	starting
varied	hardly	carry	homogeneous
unfeeling	unaffected	difficult	finishing
sensitive	kind	unforgiving	tolerant

Synonym	Word	Antonym
_____	**1.** perceptive	_____
_____	**2.** diverse	_____
_____	**3.** dictatorial	_____
_____	**4.** initiating	_____
_____	**5.** profoundly	_____
_____	**6.** convey	_____
_____	**7.** patronizing	_____
_____	**8.** complex	_____
_____	**9.** tentative	_____
_____	**10.** vengeful	_____

Part B

1. patronizing : _____ :: tentative : hesitant

2. perceptive : sensitive :: vengeful : _____

3. _____ : complex :: dictatorial : bossy

4. beginning : initiating :: carry : _____

5. unfeeling : _____ :: convey : withhold

6. _____ : perceptive :: easy : complex

7. homogeneous : _____ :: tolerant : vengeful

8. condescending : _____ :: beginning : ending

9. tentative : _____ :: profoundly : greatly

10. _____ : hardly :: initiating : ending

READ: Keys Activity Posttest

Rate each of the following words according to your knowledge of them.

Word	Stage 0 _I don't know this word._	Stage 1 _I've seen this word but I know nothing of its meaning._	Stage 2 _I've seen this word and can make associations with it._	Stage 3 _I know this word._
1. perceptive				
2. diverse				
3. dictatorial				
4. initiating				
5. profoundly				
6. convey				
7. patronizing				
8. complex				
9. tentative				
10. vengeful				

Reading in the Information Age

Chapter Map Exercise

Construct a chapter map from the major headings and subheadings in the chapter.

Objectives

After you finish this chapter, you will be able to do the following:

1. Compare the types of information found on the Internet.

2. Identify ways to find information on the Internet.

3. Evaluate information found on the Internet.

4. Document information from the Internet.

Chapter Outline Exercise

Create a chapter outline from the major headings and subheadings in the chapter.

The world has changed significantly in your lifetime. Everything—from classical literature to this week's Top Ten—is available online. People meet in chat rooms rather than in person. Viruses now infect computers as often as they do people. Everyone seems to have a personal Web page and get e-mail. What was uncommon—and practically unheard of—little more than a decade ago is the norm today.

Today's commodity is information—its acquisition, use, and delivery. Effective reading and learning in the information age requires the same skills as reading and learning in traditional formats. However, it also requires new skills in accessing, locating, and evaluating information from electronic formats. This chapter examines effective use of electronic formats for information and learning, efficient ways to find the information you need, and appropriate methods for evaluating and referencing what you find.

> When I took office, only high-energy physicists had ever heard of what is called the World Wide Web. . . . Now even my cat has its own page.
>
> —Bill Clinton
> *42nd U.S. President*

Internet: Information Superhighway

Roads have always been necessary for moving things around. The Roman Empire built roads to move goods and armies more efficiently. In the mid-1900s, the United States built interstate highways to transport manufactured goods and military forces more effectively. At the end of the twentieth century, the United States funded a network of computers to move knowledge more easily in an information-based society. This network between computers was called the **Internet.** Because the Internet moved information from place to place, it also became known as the **Information Superhighway.**

Like most things, the Internet started small. In 1969, only four computers in different places in the United State were linked for military purposes. The idea was that because government information was not in any one place, no single disaster could interfere with the operation of the United States. In 1984, the National Science Foundation improved the network so that more information could be shared. Scientists and educational institutions connected to exchange research results and information.

Today the Internet is a worldwide network of university, government, commercial, and personal computers in over 150 countries. Hundreds of thousands of computers and tens of millions of users now ride on the Information Superhighway. Others join each day. Currently, an estimated 2.1 billion separate publicly available Web pages are published, with seven million more added daily (*Cyveillance,* July 2000).

Although Internet use has grown exponentially, some things about it remain the same. First, it's still decentralized. That means that there's still no single place where the Internet exists. Thus, the Internet is everywhere a computer links to it. Second, no one owns or manages the Internet. Rather, people and organizations that provide information and interact with one another manage it cooperatively. As a result, quality or validity of information cannot be guaranteed. Internet information may be up-to-the minute weather reports, live camera views of important events, or the latest scientific and medical research. Or, it could be out-of-date, opinionated, or incorrect junk. Last, and most important, the Internet changes by the minute. The information that was available yesterday may be gone today. The information found today may be outdated by tomorrow. As a learner, you have to be an especially critical thinker to evaluate information effectively.

Several components enable a computer to access the Internet. First, the computer must have special communications software to link to other computers and send or get messages. These links are made through an Internet service provider, educational institution, business, or other organization. Connections are made with a modem that uses phone lines for access or through special direct links that are often only available at educational and other special locations. As a student, you'll use the Internet to locate information for your courses and communicate with your faculty and fellow students. To use its services and features effectively, you need to know the language that identifies and describes them. Table 9.1 provides a list of basic terms.

Write To Learn

On a separate sheet of paper or in your notebook, explain what the following sentences mean:

I was having a problem with my computer and I thought it might be a virus. But, when I searched for viruses, I got too many hits, so I decided to just surf the Net. While looking at some archives in a listserv, I checked the FAQ files. I found a URL in a post that looked like it had what I needed. When I went to that site, I read that I should check my ISP's homepage. When I did, I found a file that I could download to fix my problem.

Table 9.1   Basic Terms

Archives A file of past communications, history, or information.

Browse To follow links in a page or to explore without specific direction. Also called *surfing.* Less focused than *search.*

Browser A software program used to search for, view, and download information from the Web.

Bulletin Board Electronic message system for posting and reading information.

Chat Room Virtual location where several people can communicate at one time.

Cyberspace A general term that describes the virtual existence of Internet activities, communication, and culture.

Domain The last part of a URL that tells logical and sometimes geographical locations of Web pages. Common U.S. domains are .edu (education), .gov (government agency), .net (network related), .com (commercial business), .mil (U.S. military), .org (nonprofit and research organizations). Outside the United States, domains indicate country: .ca (Canada), .uk (United Kingdom), .au (Australia), .jp (Japan), .fr (France), and so forth.

Download To take information from the Internet and save to a hard drive or diskette; to transfer information from one computer to another.

E-Mail Abbreviation for *Electronic mail.* Private messages sent to an address on another computer.

E-Mail Address A unique code by which the Internet identifies you so that people can send you messages. Usually takes the form *specialname@hostname. Specialname* is a name you select (e.g., initials as in *JS,* part of your name as in *JSMITH,* or a name of your choice, *SPORTS-FAN). Hostname* is the name of your Internet Service Provider. Also called *address.*

FAQ Abbreviation for *Frequently Asked Questions.* A file on some Web pages that answers commonly asked questions about the site or information in it.

Hit One success in a keyword search using a search engine.

Home Page First screen of a Web site. Usually contains a site map or table of contents to other pages within the site.

Hyperlink A kind of shortcut referencing feature for selected words, phrases, or images in a Web site. These automatically go to another place within the page or to a different Web page that provides additional information about the word, phrase, or image. Also called *link.*

Hypermedia Images or other nontext information that allows users to link from one Web page to other pages.

Hypertext Words or phrases that allow users to link from one Web page to other web pages.

Internet Worldwide network of computers that provide information and communication. Also called the *net* or the *Information Superhighway.*

ISP Abbreviation for *Internet Service Provider.* A company that sells Internet access for a fee. May also provide Web page hosting services for individuals, companies, organizations, or other groups.

Keyword Words or phrases used to direct and focus searches.

Link "Rot" An error message that occurs when the information that a hyperlink references is no longer available.

Listserv A special interest e-mail list that facilitates exchange of information between large numbers of people. After joining the list, subscribers can view and respond to comments from others.

Modem Computer hardware that lets one computer link to others over telephone lines.

Netiquette Abbreviation for *Internet etiquette.* Commonsense rules for polite communications and behavior on the Internet.

Newsgroup A distributed bulletin board system on a particular topic.

Online Describes activities and information on the Internet. Users currently linked to the Internet are said to be *online.*

Continues

Table 9.1   *Continued*

Personal Page Web page created by an individual rather than by an institution, business, organization, or other group.

Post As a verb, to compose a message and place it on an electronic bulletin board. As a noun, messages on an electronic bulletin board.

Search Way to systematically look for information by using special programs called engines to identify all occurrences of a term. More focused and systematic than simply *browsing* or *surfing*.

Search Engine A special program used to look systematically for information.

Server, Web Server Also called a host. A computer running special software that allows it to provide or "serve" documents via the World Wide Web.

Subject Directory A set of topic terms hierarchically grouped that can be browsed or searched by using keywords.

Sub-Searching A search made only within the results of a previous search. This narrows the scope and refines the results.

Surf See *browse*.

Thread Specific topic of conversation on a listserv or bulletin board.

URL Abbreviation for *Uniform Resource Locator*. The unique address of any Web document. The URL appears in the "location" box on a browser once a connection has been made.

Virtual Reality Describes existence that is inferred from indirect evidence. For example, the existence of a virtual classroom is inferred from the evidence of students, teacher, and subject rather than by a physical location in which learning occurs. Opposite of *physical reality*.

Virus A destructive computer program that sometimes accompanies e-mail. It tries to impair normal computer operation, delete information from the computer memory, and in some cases, actually cause damage to the computer.

Web Page Document on the World Wide Web that can include text, images, sound, and video. Also called *page*.

Web Site A collection of several related pages; often incorrectly used as a synonym for *Web page*; a Web page is a single file rather than a collection of related files. Also called *site*.

World Wide Web Collection of Web pages connected by hyperlinks and accessed through the Internet. Also called the *Web* or *WWW*.

Information and the World Wide Web

The World Wide Web, also called the Web or WWW, is one kind of information on the Internet. Its introduction revolutionized Internet use. When the Internet first began, it contained only text information. Reading Internet materials was much like reading print materials. Information occurred in a definite, linear order. The reader could scan for information and skip sections within the text, but the reader always remained in the same document. The Web changed that through the use of hyperlinks. Hypertext has underlined or highlighted "hot words." When the reader clicks on one, the reader is automatically linked to another location—either within the document or to a different docu-

Table 9.2   URL Example

http://www.cmsu.edu/mydocs/ch1/terms.html

- **http://** transfer protocol (type of information being transferred)
- **www.** host computer name (or server name)
- **cmsu.edu** domain (or home) of the website. In this case, the first part shows that the computer home is Central Missouri State University. The last part indicates that it is an educational institution.
- **mydocs/ch1/terms** path of the files on the host computer. In this case, the document *terms* is in a subfolder called *Ch1* that is in another folder called *mydocs*.
- **html** file type

> Toto, I don't think we're in Kansas any more.
>
> —Dorothy
> *Twentieth-century fictional character in L. Frank Baum's* The Wizard of Oz

ment—that provides more information about that word. Readers no longer need to read in a linear way. Rather, as they read and have questions or want more details, they can quickly and easily get answers or additional text information. With hypermedia, the reader is no longer limited to text information. Now other forms of media such as pictures, audio clips, and video are just as immediately available.

Three different kinds of links are found on the Web. Text hyperlinks are words that are underlined and different in color. Graphic links are single pictures or **icons** used to link to other information. Imagemaps are larger images that have multiple links within them. For instance, in a diagram of a building, clicking on different locations on the building links to different information about the building.

How does a computer make these links? Each link has a unique address called a URL (Uniform Resource Locator). When a link is "clicked," the computer "calls" for the information from the computer that stores it. The new URL appears in the "location" box on the browser once a connection has been made. To form the unique URL, Web addresses use a specific form. Punctuation marks separate the parts of the address. Table 9.2 gives an example of a URL and the meaning of the address. *Exercise 9.1 allows you to practice reading URLs.*

READ Exercise 9.1

Internet addresses are often given verbally. To do so, you pronounce any recognizable word or name within the address. Otherwise, you spell that part of the address. The @ sign is said as *at*. A period is said as *dot*. A forward slash (/) is pronounced *slash*. For instance, you read *theprofesso@your-institution.edu/math* as "*the professor at your institution dot e d u slash math.*"

> ### Write to Learn
>
> Vannevar Bush, a twentieth century American scientist, said, "The human mind . . . operates by association. With one item in its grasp, it snaps instantly to the next that is suggested by the association of thoughts. . . ." Respond to the following on a separate sheet of paper or in your notebook. How does the quotation by Bush relate to the concept of hyperlinks on the Web?

Electronic Communication

As a learner in the Information Age, you may feel like Dorothy from *The Wizard of Oz*. Things just don't seem the same. And, you're probably right. Today's students obtain information from the Internet and communicate in electronic and virtual forms. These new mediums of **electronic communication**—e-mail, listservs, chat rooms, and newsgroups—require new skills to use them effectively.

The ease and speed at which electronic communications are made contribute to a feeling of informality. If you're accessing the Internet from your home or room, you can write e-mails to your instructors or chat with other students online wearing your pajamas—or less. Because your interactions are all virtual, it's easy to forget that you're dealing with real people. You can e-mail the President of the United States or the author of your textbook. The people who contribute to your listserv or newsgroup could be other students in your class or worldclass experts in their field. Therefore, you need to know how to communicate effectively and appropriately in each of these forms.

Netiquette. Every culture has its own standard of acceptable behavior. The culture of cyberspace is no different. Netiquette (short for *Internet etiquette*) refers to the practice of acceptable behavior in online communications. How do you know what's acceptable? When you enter a new area of cyberspace—class communications, chat room, listserv, or newsgroup, you need to get a sense of the attitude of the group before you interact. If you already have e-mails from your instructor or other students, you might read them for style and tone. If you enter a chat room, or join a listserv or newsgroup, you should **lurk** (listen or read without any other participation) or read the archives before participating. In each case, you need to get a sense of how the people who are already there act and tailor your responses accordingly.

Electronic communication, to some degree, creates an equal opportunity forum. Unless you use an online camera, no one can see you. Thus, you're not judged by physical characteristics such as age, skin color, clothing, or gender. But, people can and do make judgments about how you present yourself through your written communication.

First, be polite and use appropriate language. Use more formal language and correct spelling and grammar with faculty and classmates than you might use in correspondence to friends and family. Don't write comments that you wouldn't say in person (such rude or hateful messages are called **flames**). If you write in anger or frustration, reread what you have written *before* you hit the Send button.

Second, include your name in the body or subject line of your e-mails when corresponding with your instructor or classmates. They may not know you by your user name.

Third, make good use of electronic communication. Unless you're using real-time chat or instant messages, you have time to write, think, and revise before you send. In online classroom chats, you should feel free to offer answers and help to people who ask questions. Many students find that they contribute more freely in these formats than they do in traditional classroom settings.

Fourth, when using e-mail, use the subject line to label the contents of your correspondence. This will help the folks you are mailing gauge the response required to your message without having to open your note.

Last, never assume your e-mail or other electronic communications are private. Most electronic communications—even chats—are stored somewhere on your computer and can be accessed later. Don't write anything you would not want everyone to see.

E-Mail. E-mail is the fastest growing service on the Internet. The number of e-mails sent on an average day is expected to increase to an estimated 35 billion per day by 2005 (*IDC: Analyze the Future*, 2001). Like a postal service, e-mail is used for written communication. Unlike a postal service, you can send mail around the globe and get a response in minutes. In some ways, the informality of e-mails is more like a phone call than like postal mail. Some people e-mail back and forth several times a day or week to either discuss a project or common interest or just to stay in touch.

Just as you need a physical address or post-office box to get regular mail, you need an e-mail address to get e-mail. You often obtain an e-mail address from your college, business, Internet service provider (ISP), or other group. There are also free e-mail services available on the Internet that let you send and receive e-mail from any computer with access to the Internet—at a public library, a friend's home, or elsewhere.

E-mail addresses consist of two parts. The first part consists of the user name—your Internet nickname—followed by @. The second part is the domain name, the location of the person's account on the Internet. E-mail addresses have no spaces. For instance, the e-mail address *jsmith@university.edu* is read *"j smith at university dot edu."* All e-mail messages contain the e-mail address of the sender and the recipient, and a subject line that identifies the content of the message.

Listservs, Newsgroups, and Campus Bulletin Boards. Listservs, newsgroups, and electronic campus bulletin boards all perform the same function in different ways. A listserv is a special interest e-mail list that facilitates exchange of information between large numbers of people. A newsgroup is a special interest electronic bulletin board. Information in the newsgroup is accessed like a Web site rather than appearing automatically in your e-mail box. A campus bulletin board is for the special interests of students in a specific discipline or course at a specific educational institution. All three formats are designed for communication and interactions concerning special topics. *Exercise 9.2 provides an opportunity for you to examine listservs and newsgroups.*

READ Exercise 9.2

After joining a listserv, subscribers receive e-mails that other individuals send to the mailing list. In most cases, mail sent to the listserv address is automatically sent to all listserv subscribers. Some lists are moderated (screened by an individual for topics appropriate to the list). An active list can generate 50–100 e-mail messages each day. Some lists provide a digest option that compiles a week's mail in one message.

A newsgroup (also called Usenet) is like an Internet bulletin board. Like listservs, they may or may not be moderated. Some are very active with hundreds of postings or relatively inactive with only a few messages. Unlike listservs, you access information directly on the Internet rather than automatically receiving messages with your e-mail. Newsgroups are organized hierarchically in topics such as scientific and technical (*sci*), computers and computing (*comp*), and social issues and political discussions (*soc*). You can post your own questions or responses and search the newsgroup archives for information.

An electronic campus bulletin board is usually course or discipline specific. You access bulletin boards through the Internet. They appear as Web pages. Students enrolled in the subject can access comments and questions from other students and respond. In some cases, access to a specific bulletin board is restricted to students enrolled in a course. Thus, only students with the understanding of lecture and text content contribute to the topic. The instructor's role is to add to the discussion, clarify questions or comments, and post other messages for the entire class such as "Don't forget Tuesday's exam." or "Class cancelled on Monday." Course-specific bulletin boards accessed by password may also provide information about a student's test grades or other coursework.

Chat Rooms. Chat rooms provide virtual meeting places for conversations among two or more individuals at once. In education, an instructor often schedules an electronic chat for a specific time. At that time, everyone in the class goes online and accesses the chat space. The user name of each person that "enters" the room can be "seen" by everyone else. The instructor may initiate discussion by posing a question. Individuals in the chat room respond by typing their comments. As comments are made and sent, everyone in the chat room can read and respond accordingly. At times, it may seem like everyone is talking at once and the discussion can get very confusing. The informality of such communication encourages abbreviations (such as *btw* for *by the way*) and expression of emotion (such as :) to symbolize a "happy face"). However, as in other electronic communications, the formality of language depends on the course content, the instructor's style, and the tone of the other students.

Searching the Internet

In some ways, the Internet is the world's library. It contains more information than you could possibly find in your university's library. However, unlike a library, there's no systematic organization to help you find what you need. As a result, you need specialized search strategies. Once you have them, you use Internet tools to conduct an orderly search. Or, you locate a starting point and surf (also called browse) for information.

Search Strategies

Sometimes the best search strategy doesn't involve using special Internet tools at all. Often you find the best information in much the same way that you find information in print—from experts in the fields. Your instructor's recommendations are probably a good starting point. Next, if you've joined a listserv or newsgroup, ask members for suggestions. Third, printed materials such as professional journals, newspapers, and popular magazines often include valid Web sites for specific topics. Finally, academic institutions, professional organizations, and government Web sites are also good resources.

How you find information on the Internet depends on what you want to find. So, the first step is to identify your purpose. For instance, perhaps you are interested in *stress management.* Are you looking for a single piece of information? Do you need a broad overview or everything you can find? In general, search engines are best for well-defined or narrow topics. Do you need the latest news or research available? You may need to check newspapers or online journals. Does it matter if the source is biased or opinionated? You need a strategy for validating the information you find. Are you just looking around? Sometimes, you just get lucky. Next, identify what you want to know or do as clearly and precisely as possible. In this case, what exactly do you want to know about stress management? Do you want to know about stress in general? Are you specifically interested in stress for college students? Are you looking for a way to assess stress? Do you want techniques to manage stress? Maybe you're really thinking about the stresses of test-taking—test anxiety. Perhaps you're concerned about coping with a specific type of test anxiety, such as math anxiety. Thus, your question might be, "How do I manage math anxiety on tests?

Third, identify important concepts within the topic and keywords that might identify those concepts. In this example, words and phrases such as *stress, stress management, college stress, test-taking, test anxiety,* and *math anxiety* are possibilities. Finally, consider synonyms for the terms you identify. This might include *strain, hassle, tension, mathematics anxiety, exams,* and so on. Check spelling of the words you select. Enclose words that must go together (e.g., test anxiety) in quote marks.

Now you're ready to begin. Table 9.3 helps you identify some starting points for locating information. No matter where you start, analyze your results and learn as you go. Surprisingly, there's not much overlap among results of searches using differing search tools. For instance, if you search the Internet with two different tools, about one-third of the results will be the same (Feldman, 1998). Use of multiple search tools probably provides the best results. In addition to getting different results, search tools also differ in the way they are used. Take time to read any hints they provide. When available, use advanced options to refine your search. *Exercise 9.3 lets you compare advanced options for different search engines.*

READ Exercise 9.3

Search Tools

The Internet's changeable and independent nature does not lend itself to the traditional forms of indexing found in a physical library. Rather search tools index sites in ways that are more like electronic snapshots. There are two major types of tools: search engines and subject directories.

Table 9.3   Strategies for Locating Information

If You Use . . .	Try . . .	But Be Aware That . . .
Expert information	asking your instructor, campus librarian, or other professional; e-mailing someone you think is knowledgeable from a listserv or discussion group; thinking of a professional group or organization that might have relevant links on their Web sites	the individual may not be aware of the specific piece of information you need or may not have time to help you.
A search engine	narrowing your topics as much as possible; enclosing your search term with quotation marks to get more exact results; using different search engines and comparing results	you may get thousands of hits. If so, either choose another search engine, identify a different term, or conduct a sub-search from your original results.
A subject directory	making your topic more narrow to specify the category in which your information might be	you might not think of the correct category.
Surfing	following the links within the first few "hits" from your search engine or subject directory results	you may waste time or you may find something completely unexpected.

Each provides a slightly different way to locate information. *Exercise 9.4 lets you compare results for using two different kinds of search tools.*

READ Exercise 9.4

Search Engines. Search engines create databases of information by using electronic "spiders" or "robots" that comb the Internet and index sites word by word. Therefore, they are particularly useful when you need to find keywords, phrases, document, name, and other specific details in a site.

When you enter a search term, you get a list of ranked sites, or "hits," with best results appearing first. However, the tool looks through its current database, not the totality of sites currently available. Thus, what you want may be on the Internet, but not in that specific search engine's database. In addition, search engines vary in size, speed, and content. That's why different search engines get different results.

Which search engine gives the best results? It depends on what you want. Search Engine Watch (www.searchenginewatch.com) provides an overview of search engines.

Search Directories. Unlike search engines that look through every word in a site, search directories use humans—often experts in their fields—who look for the best and most relevant sites for each category and arrange them hierarchically. The resulting database is smaller and more general. However, the database is also more accurate because a human understands differences in meaning (for example, eye of a storm; eye of a person) that an electronic spider misunderstands or overlooks. In some cases, the information may also be more up-to-date because human researchers often update topics of special interest (such as updating football sites before the Super Bowl).

To use a search directory, you identify the broad category from a list or enter a search term. You continue browsing in subcategories or searching until you find the information you need.

Evaluating Web Sites

What you find on the Internet is a lot like what you find at a jewelry store. Some items are authentic gems. Others are worthless costume jewels. How do you know the difference? First, you check the source of the information to see if it is genuine. Second, you examine the content for credibility.

Checking the Source

Real people with real information generally don't mind admitting who they are. A reputable Web site generally identifies the name of the author, owner, or sponsor. If you are unfamiliar with the author, try using that person's name as your search term or search the *Library of Congress Online Catalog* (http://lcweb.loc.gov/catalog) or an online bookstore such as Amazon.com. A credible author probably has several articles or books on the topic. Check the domain of the site's owner or sponsor in the URL. Is the information just on someone's personal homepage, or is the site sponsored by a known group? Educational (.edu) and government (.gov) sites are usually reputable sources. Some, but not all, organizations (.org) and businesses (.com) provide credible information.

You need to be especially skeptical if a commercial site (.com) gives the impression that it is a different kind of site (e.g., an educational or government site). For instance, a site sponsor might be *The Government Agency for Internet Authenticity.* Although this sounds like it might be reputable, you notice that the URL is *gaii.com.* This may mean that the site is actually a company that is trying to sell something.

Finally, the site should also provide a way for you to reach the author, owner, or sponsor. This might be an address, phone number, or e-mail address. In checking the source, you might also need to know how current the information is. The relevancy of this factor depends on your purpose. Is what you need commonly known and unchanging information (e.g., biography of Shakespeare, algebraic formulas), or do you need the latest news? A reputable site often includes a *last date page updated* notation. This helps you identify how current the information is. In addition, look at the links within the page. If you find that several pages within the site or links to other sites no longer function, then the site is not regularly maintained.

Reputable sites also provide credentials or citations that support authority of the information. This might include a list of references or the professional experience or educational background of the author. If that information is unavailable, consider the sponsor's credentials. For instance, perhaps you find information written by J. Smith as part of the U.S. Department of Education Web site. Although you might not know who J. Smith is, you know that the U.S. Department of Education is a reputable source of information.

Just as people are often known by the company they keep, a Web page can also be known by the other pages that reference or link to it. To find the links to a page, use a search engine such as Google or AltaVista. Precede the URL you want to check with the term *link:* with no space after the colon. If you use the Google Advance Search option, type the URL in the *find pages that link to the page* box.

Checking the Content

The freedom of the Internet means that anyone can have a Web page, even a presidential cat. No one reviews or checks to see if information on the site is true. Even pages sponsored by reputable institutions may contain inaccurate or flawed information. Thus, you have to evaluate the information for yourself. To do so, you seek answers to some basic questions.

First, what is the purpose of the site? Does it appear to be informational or commercial? Determine if informational articles have any kind of hidden commercial intent. Consider the tone. Is the content serious with specific facts and figures or humorous with outrageous details and suggestions? Is it written to incite emotions such as fear, anger, or sorrow? Is a spoof or a hoax? Next, determine if the author has anything to gain. Is what you find designed to provide information or enhance the reputation of the author or sponsor? What does the author or sponsor want you to do or believe? Why? Could the author or sponsor profit from your actions or beliefs?

Second, who might be the target audience? How would you describe the writing style? Is it simplified, conversations, brief, or highly technical? Do readers need extensive technical background knowledge to understand the content?

Third, is the information valid and objective? How does what you find compare with information in other sites or print materials? Do you find evidence of bias or are both sides of an issue fairly represented? Does the coverage of information appear to be appropriate based on other information you located? Does it include facts and data or generalizations and suppositions? Does the information appear to be original or are references or links to other information included? Has the accuracy of the content been reviewed or edited by anyone? If you have questions or concerns, e-mail the site's owner or author. Finally, consult a librarian at your institution's library or ask your instructor for assistance. *Exercise 9.5 provides practices in evaluating Web sites.*

READ Exercise 9.5

Write to Learn

Respond to the following on a separate sheet of paper or in your notebook: Create a checklist of questions to use when evaluating a Web site's source and content.

Documenting What You Find on the Internet

Plagiarism is theft of another person's words or ideas and presenting them as your own. Everything on the Internet is copyrighted at the moment of its creation (McVay, 2000) whether it contains a specific copyright symbol or not. The content belongs to the person who developed it. This includes information from Web sites or electronic communication (e.g., e-mail, chat rooms, bulletin boards). Therefore, you reference electronic materials just as carefully as you would print materials.

Just as there are different **citation formats** for print materials, there are different citation formats for electronic materials. Ask your instructor to identify the one you should use. You can also consult Internet Web sites that describe how to cite electronic resources (e.g., *APA Style,* www.apa.org; *MLA Style,* www.mla.org, *Columbia Guide to Online Style,* www.columbia.edu/cu/cup/cgos/idx_basic.html).

No matter which citation format you use, you need to indicate the author (if known), the page's title, any publication information available (e.g., sponsor/publisher, date), URL, and the date you accessed the material. *Exercise 9.6 lets you practice documenting information.*

READ Exercise 9.6

Chapter Summary Exercise

Write a chapter summary on a separate sheet of paper or in your notebook.

Chapter Review

Answer the following questions on a separate sheet of paper or in your notebook.

1. Create an analogy that compares either the highways of the Roman Empire or the U.S. Interstate System with the Information Superhighway.

2. What is *Netiquette?* How does it differ from face-to-face etiquette?

3. What electronic form of communication (e-mail, listservs, chat rooms, newsgroups) seems to be used most on your campus? What is it used for?

4. How are listservs, newsgroups, and campus bulletin boards alike? How are they different?

5. Summarize the steps in a search strategy.

6. What's the difference between search engines and subject directories?

7. Why is checking the source of an electronic document more difficult than checking the source of a print document?

8. List the factors to consider in checking the content of an electronic document.

9. When are electronic materials copyrighted?

10. What aspects of an electronic document should be included in a citation?

Terms

Terms appear in the order in which they occur in the chapter.

Internet
Information Superhighway
icons
electronic communication
lurk
flames
plagiarism
citation formats

Exercises

Exercise 9.1   You need to access the Internet to answer the questions. Respond to the following on a separate sheet of paper or in your notebook:

1. Go to your institution's homepage and identify (a) the URL, (b) the host computer or server, (c) the domain or home, (d) the path of the files on the host computer, and (e) the type of domain for the URL.

2. Search for the governor's office in your state and identify (a) the URL, (b) the host computer or server, (c) the domain or home, (d) the path of the files on the host computer, and (e) the type of domain for the URL.

3. Think of a company whose products you regularly purchase or a store at which you regularly shop. Search for the name of the company or store and identify (a) the URL, (b) the host computer or server, (c) the domain or home, (d) the path of the files on the host computer, and (e) the type of domain for the URL.

Exercise 9.2   You need to access the Internet to answer the questions. Respond to the following on a separate sheet of paper or in your notebook:

1. Go to Google.com. Click on the *groups* category. Choose a subject area (e.g., *biz, alt, rec)*. List the subject area you chose on your paper. Click on a topic within the subject area. List the topic you chose. Read at least five posts. Summarize each post with a sentence. What are your impressions about this discussion group?

2. Choose a different category at Google.com and repeat the process. Was your impression the same or different? Why?

3. Go to liszt.com (*Topica*). Choose a topic and list the topic you chose. Examine two newsletters or discussion groups within the topic. List the names and identify the focus.

Exercise 9.3   You need to access the Internet to complete the exercise. Respond to the following on a separate sheet of paper or in your notebook:

Use at least four of the following search tools: Hotbot.com, Google.com, Yahoo.com, Northernlight.com, AltaVista.com, Excite.com. Examine the advanced or power search options for each of the tools you choose. Summarize or list what you find. Which one do you prefer? Why?

Exercise 9.4   You will need to access the Internet to complete this exercise. Respond to the following on a separate sheet of paper or in your notebook: After reading this chapter, you decide to look for information on the Internet about President George Bush or former President Bill Clinton (choose one).

1. Go to *Yahoo.com* or other subject directory tool. Use it to locate information about the president you chose.

    a. List the steps (clicks) you made to locate the information. How did you know which categories to choose?

    b. List the first three URLs you find for your topic. For each site, write a sentence that summarizes the content based on the index information.

2. Using a different subject directory from the first one you accessed (use a search engine to locate if necessary), locate three pieces of information about the president you chose.

    a. List the steps (clicks) you made to locate the information. How did you know which categories to choose?

    b. List the first three URLs you find for your topic. For each site, write a sentence that summarizes the content based on the index information.

3. Use the search function in Google.com or other search engine to locate information about the president you chose.

    a. How many "hits" did you get? List the first five URLs you find for your topic.

    b. Do any of your URLs match those you found in questions 1 or 2? If so, how many?

4. Use another search engine to locate information about the president you chose.

    a. How many "hits" did you get? List the first five URLs you find for your topic.

    b. Do any of your URL's match those you found in questions 1, 2, or 3? If so, how many?

5. Which was easier to use: a subject directory or a search engine? Why?

Exercise 9.5   You need to access the Internet to answer the questions. Respond to the following on a separate sheet of paper or in your notebook:

Search for either *Bill Clinton* or *George Bush.* Locate a site that you think contains authentic information and one that you think contains humorous, critical, or sarcastic information. List the URL for each one. Use the questions you created for the Write to Learn activity in the section on evaluation to analyze the site and confirm your decisions.

Exercise 9.6   You need to access the Internet to complete the exercise. Respond to the following on a separate sheet of paper or in your notebook:

Choose one of the following READ Keys excerpts: Chapter 1, 2, 7, or 10. Select a topic from the excerpt and search the Internet using the search tool of your choice to locate three references for the topic. Provide a citation for each reference that includes the following: the author (if known), the page's title, any publication information available (e.g., sponsor/publisher, date), URL, and the date you accessed the material.

Web Exercise   A variety of information related to evaluating Internet sources is available on the World Wide Web. For this exercise, search using the phrase *Evaluation of Internet Sources*.

Choose one of the sites and respond to the following:

1. What is the name and URL of your source?

2. Do you think this is a credible source?

   a. Who is the author, owner, or sponsor?

   b. When was the last time the page was updated?

   c. Are there any credentials to support the authenticity and expertise of the site's author? What links does it include? Who links to this page?

3. Do you think the content is credible?

   a. What is the purpose of the site?

   b. Who is the target audience?

   c. Is the information valid and objective?

4. Identify three new pieces of information you learned about evaluating Internet information.

READ: Keys

READ: Keys Activity Pretest

Rate each of the following words according to your knowledge of them.

Word	Stage 0 *I don't know this word.*	Stage 1 *I've seen this word but I know nothing of its meaning.*	Stage 2 *I've seen this word and can make associations with it.*	Stage 3 *I know this word.*
1. complex				
2. stereotypes				
3. aggressive				
4. excel				
5. inconsistent				
6. persistent				
7. thrive				
8. gender				
9. counterparts				
10. pursue				

READ: Keys Activity 9.1

Read the following article and keep track of your reading time.

Few Women Reach Top Positions
Tiffany St. Martin
Chief Staff Writer

Luoluo Hong, former director of the Wellness Education and Outreach Services at LSU, left the school in July 2000 under what she called at the time "bittersweet" conditions.

Hong accepted the position of Dean of Students at Shepherd College, a liberal arts school in West Virginia, after the Dean of Students search committee at LSU did not allow her to interview for the position.

"I think a piece of it was because I'm a woman, but it's much more **complex** than that," Hong said.

According to the American Council on Education, in 1995 women made up only 16 percent of CEOs of higher education schools.

That number is typical, especially for large flagship institutions such as LSU, Hong said.

Hong said she was disappointed she did not have the opportunity to interview for the Dean of Students position, but does not have any ill feelings toward the University.

"I respect the search process and believe very much in it," she said. "But if I wasn't going to get an opportunity at LSU, I had to make my own career develop."

She left the University despite her connection to the students because of emotional **stereotypes,** Hong said.

When men in administration express their opinions, people see them as **aggressive** and motivated, Hong said.

But, when women faculty members voice the same ideas, others view them as too pushy and emotional, she said.

Women believe in contributing to society and serving others, and tend to remain faithful that they will someday be rewarded, Hong said.

"It's important to take charge of your own career," Hong said. "You can't sit around waiting for someone to do it for you."

She said as a younger professional in higher education, she is aware of the fact that many people can't get past her age despite her years of experience.

It is something that happens at many institutions throughout the United States, Hong said.

Young men without much experience often **excel** past women at the university level, receiving principal titles and bigger paychecks, Hong said.

"There is the possibility for women to advance, but it's **inconsistent,**" she said. "There is something going on, and it's frustrating."

Although people in higher education are in favor of accepting all people, administrators want people working for them to "pay their dues," Hong said.

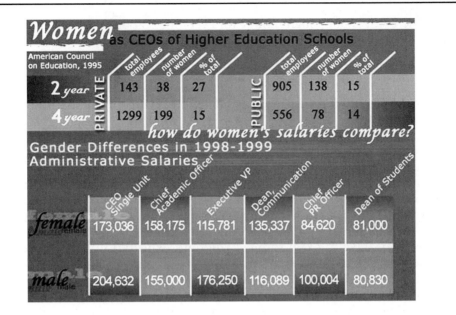

Women as CEOs of Higher Education Schools

American Council on Education, 1995	total employees	number of women	% of total		total employees	number of women	% of total
PRIVATE 2 year	143	38	27	PUBLIC	905	138	15
PRIVATE 4 year	1299	199	15	PUBLIC	556	78	14

how do women's salaries compare?

Gender Differences in 1998-1999 Administrative Salaries

	CEO Single Unit	Chief Academic Officer	Executive VP	Dean, Communication	Chief PR Officer	Dean of Students
female	173,036	158,175	115,781	135,337	84,620	81,000
male	204,632	155,000	176,250	116,089	100,004	80,830

Most faculty members do not want men or women younger than themselves in positions of authority, Hong said.

"You've got to climb the ladder and run the rat race," she said. "You've got to be in control."

Hong cited two LSU administrators in particular who succeeded at the University.

Lynn Jelinski, former vice chancellor for research and graduate studies, resigned from LSU in August 2000 for personal reasons.

She achieved a great deal in her time at the University, Hong said, including demonstrating that women in administration can succeed in higher education.

"She did so much for the school," Hong said. "She showed [women] just how far we can go in our careers."

Another woman in a position of authority at LSU is Doris Collins, associate vice chancellor for student life and academic services.

Collins has been at the University for several years and is an example of how ***persistent*** women can ***thrive*** at LSU, Hong said.

Some women at the University feel as though ***gender*** doesn't matter in higher education.

"We have just as many men leaving as women," said Arlette Rodrigue, vice president of the LSU Woman's Faculty Club and assistant to the dean of the Agriculture College.

People in all positions at LSU are underpaid well behind the national level, Rodrigue said.

Everyone at LSU either needs or wants a raise, but most people make just the amount of money they should, said Geri Staley, secretary of the Woman's Faculty Club and a coordinator in the Agriculture College.

"There just isn't enough money for everyone," Rodrigue said. "It doesn't matter your gender."

According to the College and University Personnel Association's annual administrative survey, females with doctoral degrees received higher salaries than men in 1998–1999 in only 9 out of 54 administrative areas.

The higher-paying positions included library director, humanities dean and chief academic officer.

The survey also showed that female deans of students make $170 more than their male **counterparts.**

Members of the Woman's Faculty Club seem to be satisfied with their careers, even though women as a whole are behind in their professions around the country, Rodrigue said.

Women tend to have higher goals and put more pressure on themselves than men, Staley said.

"Women have to excel to meet the high expectations they've set for themselves," she said. "They're continuing to gain growth [on men]."

Hong left the University to **pursue** a better opportunity in the field she wanted to work in, Staley said.

It had nothing to do with her gender, Rodrigue said.

"I don't feel [a glass ceiling] is really present here as much as other universities," she said. "I feel I can go as high at LSU as I want to go."

From The Reveille and Office of Student Media (June 28, 2001)

834 words / _____ minutes = _____ words per minute

Calculate your reading time by dividing the number of words in the article by the amount of time it took to read it. Then mark your reading time on the chart located on page 338.

READ: Keys Activity 9.2

On a separate sheet of paper or in your notebook, answer the following questions about the article you just read:

1. According to the American Council of Education, what percentage of CEOs in higher education are males?

    a. 16%

    b. 50%

    c. 84%

    d. You cannot tell from the article.

2. According to the article, what is an example of a top position in higher education?

a. Director of Wellness Education and Outreach

b. Dean of Students

c. College Coordinator

d. University faculty

3. According to the article, where does Hong now live?

a. Louisiana

b. Virginia

c. West Virginia

d. Texas

4. Hong describes the conditions when she left as *bittersweet.* What did she mean?

a. It was bitter because she had been laid off. It was sweet because she got another job.

b. It was bitter because LSU was a flagship university. It was sweet because Shepherd was a liberal arts school.

c. It was bitter because she did not get to interview for a job she wanted. It was sweet because she had connections with the students.

d. It was bitter because she was too emotional. It was sweet because she got the job she wanted in another state.

5. According to Hong, which of the following statements is NOT a reason why she didn't get an interview?

a. She was too young.

b. She was the wrong gender.

c. There were too many emotional stereotypes.

d. She did not have a doctorate.

6. Which two administrators did Hong cite as successful examples?

a. Jelinski and Collins

b. Jelinski and Rodrigue

c. Rodrigue and Staley

d. Staley and Collins

7. According to the College and University Personnel Association's annual administrative survey, females with doctoral degrees received higher salaries than men in 1998–1999 _____ of the time.

   a. 1/4

   b. 1/6

   c. 1/8

   d. 1/3

8. According to the article, which of the following individuals is no longer at LSU?

   a. Rodrigue

   b. Staley

   c. Jelinski

   d. All are still at LSU.

9. Which of the following is an example of an emotional stereotype?

   a. When men express their opinions, they appear aggressive but when women express their opinions, they appear pushy.

   b. Hong's departure from LSU was bittersweet.

   c. Hong was disappointed that she did not get to interview for the job at LSU, but she doesn't hold a grudge against LSU.

   d. Hong respects the search process and believes in it.

10. Which of the following is true?

   a. Lynn Jelinski was fired from LSU.

   b. Everyone at LSU is underpaid.

   c. Members of the LSU Women's Faculty Club appear to be dissatisfied with their careers.

   d. Men generally have higher goals and put more pressure on themselves than women.

READ: Keys Activity 9.3

Examine each of the numbered phrases or sentences and complete the following on a separate sheet of paper or in your notebook.

(a) Write the boldfaced, italicized word. Identify one or two words that you can put in the place of the boldfaced, italicized word without changing the meaning of the phrase or sentence and write this synonym or synonymous phrase (words that have the same meaning) beside the word. (b) Identify the part of speech of this word as used in the sentence. (c) Look up the boldfaced, italicized word in a dictionary and write the dictionary definition. How does this compare with the definition from context? (d) List the parts of speech this word can sometimes be. (e) Write a complete sentence with each word.

1. "I think a piece of it was because I'm a woman, but it's much more ***complex*** than that," Hong said.

2. She left the University despite her connection to the students because of emotional ***stereotypes,*** Hong said.

3. When men in administration express their opinions, people see them as ***aggressive*** and motivated, Hong said.

4. Young men without much experience often ***excel*** past women at the university level, receiving principal titles and bigger paychecks, Hong said.

5. "There is the possibility for women to advance, but it's ***inconsistent,***" she said. "There is something going on, and it's frustrating."

6. Collins has been at the University for several years and is an example of how ***persistent*** women can thrive at LSU, Hong said.

7. Collins has been at the University for several years and is an example of how persistent women can ***thrive*** at LSU, Hong said.

8. Some women at the University feel as though ***gender*** doesn't matter in higher education.

9. The survey also showed that female deans of students make $170 more than their male ***counterparts.***

10. Hong left the University to ***pursue*** a better opportunity in the field she wanted to work in, Staley said.

READ: Keys Activity 9.4

In Part A, use the following list of words to fill in the blanks. In Part B, use the information from Part A to complete the analogies.

Part A

chase	complicated	improve	weak
irregular	equal	neuter	unvarying
powerful	follow	labels	subordinate
surpass	sex	hesitant	ignore
originals	determined	decline	simple

Synonym	Word	Antonym
_____	**1.** complex	_____
_____	**2.** stereotypes	_____
_____	**3.** aggressive	_____
_____	**4.** excel	_____
_____	**5.** inconsistent	_____
_____	**6.** persistent	_____
_____	**7.** thrive	_____
_____	**8.** gender	_____
_____	**9.** counterpart	_____
_____	**10.** pursue	_____

Part B

1. gender : _____ :: pursue : ignore

2. _____ : counterparts :: stereotypes : labels

3. complex : simple :: persistent : _____

   4. excel : _____ :: inconsistent : unvarying

   5. pursue : chase :: aggressive : _____

   6. _____ : stereotypes :: excel : surpass

   7. aggressive : weak :: counterpart : _____

   8. _____ : complex :: gender : sex

   9. persistent : determined :: pursue : _____

10. follow : chase :: surpass : _____

READ: Keys Activity Posttest

Rate each of the following words according to your knowledge of them.

Word	Stage 0 *I don't know this word.*	Stage 1 *I've seen this word but I know nothing of its meaning.*	Stage 2 *I've seen this word and can make associations with it.*	Stage 3 *I know this word.*
1. complex				
2. stereotypes				
3. aggressive				
4. excel				
5. inconsistent				
6. persistent				
7. thrive				
8. gender				
9. counterparts				
10. pursue				

Reading Graphics

Chapter Map Exercise

Construct a chapter map from the major headings and subheadings in the chapter.

Objectives

After you finish this chapter, you will be able to do the following:

1. Compare different types of tables.
2. Analyze bar, line, and circle graphs.
3. Demonstrate how to read diagrams and flowcharts.
4. Use timelines to locate information.
5. Read different kinds of maps.

Chapter Outline Exercise

Create a chapter outline from the major headings and subheadings in the chapter.

Each term, you register for your college classes. Perhaps you see a counselor to choose your courses. Your counselor might say this:

> Your English course meets on Mondays, Wednesdays, and Fridays at eight o'clock. You'll have a two-hour break after English class, except on Wednesdays when you have your biology lab. Math will be after your biology lab on Wednesdays. It will be after your two-hour break on the days that you have English but not biology lab. You'll probably want to eat lunch during that two hours, except on Wednesdays. Then you won't be able to eat until after your math class.
>
> On Tuesdays and Thursdays, your first class will be biology. It will start at nine and finish at ten-thirty. Then, you'll have a break for an hour-and-a-half on Tuesdays. Of course, you won't have a break on Thursdays. You have your ROTC lab from ten-thirty until noon then. Your history class will meet right after your ROTC lab on Thursdays. It will meet before lunch on Tuesdays. If you're planning to work, you'll have plenty of time in the afternoons.
>
> You look confused. Let me make a sketch of your schedule. Seeing it on paper may make it easier to understand. (See Table 10.1.)

Table 10.1   Schedule Chart

	Monday	Tuesday	Wednesday	Thursday	Friday
8–9	English		English		English
9–10		Biology	Biology Lab	Biology	
10–11					
				ROTC	
11–12	Math		Math		Math
12–1		History		History	
1–2					
2–3					

Which of these is easier for you to follow? The chart provides a graphic plan of where and when you are in class. It organizes the information your counselor gave you. This makes the schedule easier to understand.

Graphic or visual information organizes and relates information. Such illustrations also explain or make written information more clear. In some cases, graphics provide information that would be hard to explain without their use.

What do you usually do when a chapter includes a graphic? Many students skip graphics because they think it takes too long to understand them. However, reading graphics often takes less time and effort than reading the same information in text.

Comparing Tables

> **There should be a place for everything, and everything in its place.**
>
> —Isabella Beeton
> *Nineteenth century*
> *American home economist*

In a **table,** everything has a place and everything is in its place. Tables order information and show relationships. They organize information into rows and columns. Rows run horizontally across the page (left to right). Columns run vertically down the page (top to bottom). Headings or labels identify content of rows or columns. Steps in reading tables appear in Table 10.2.

Your instructor probably maintains at least two kinds of records for your class in either print (e.g., a gradebook) or electronic (e.g., a database) forms. For example, Table 10.3 shows how an instructor might record absences and grades for a class. You can identify specific details from the table (Galvez was absent on 9/22. Wu's first grade was 64). You can also identify **trends** (directions in which features change) or draw conclusions from the table (e.g., Everyone's grade increased on the second test but decreased on the third test. Levy, Parker, Tomas, and Wu are never absent.) *Exercises 10.1 and 10.2 provide practice in reading tables.*

READ Exercises 10.1 & 10.2

Analyzing Graphs

Graphs symbolically represent information. Graphs show quantitative (numerical) comparisons between two or more kinds of information. The most common types include **bar graphs, line graphs,** and **circle graphs.** Figure 10.1 uses bar, line, and circle graphs to depict college data. Table 10.4 provides a list of steps in reading bar and line graphs. Steps in reading circle graphs appear in Table 10.5.

Table 10.2   Steps in Reading Tables

1. *Read the title.* This tells you the subject or general content of the table.

2. *Identify the type of table.* This helps you to determine the kind(s) of information given. A table tells you the presence or absence of a feature, or it tells you the quantity or quality of a feature.

3. *Look at the labels or headings on the table.* These tell you the items being compared and the features used to compare them. You need to keep the items and features in mind to know when and how the relationships change.

4. *Note any general trends.*

5. *If you are looking at a table as part of the surveying step of SQ3R, stop your examination.* Continue previewing the chapter.

6. *When you read the section of the text that refers to the table, identify the text's purpose before turning to the table.* Does the author want you to note specific facts, draw conclusions, or identify trends?

7. *Use the purpose set by the text to look at specific areas of the table.*

8. *Reread the section of the text that referred to the table.* Make sure you understand the points and relationships noted by the author.

Table 10.3   Record of Grades and Attendance

	9/15	9/17	9/19	9/22	9/24	9/26	9/29	9/30	10/1
Galvex, J	88	91	x		x	0		0	83
Levy, N	72	85	x	x	x	81	x	85	94
Nichols, A	0	56	x	x	x	52		60	68
Parker, K	91	92	x	x	x	89	x	97	98
Tomas, L	87	89	x	x	x	83	x	89	91
Vogt, M	0	0		x		0		62	65
Wu, X	64	70	x	x	x	68	x	74	77

Figure 10.1   Central Community College Enrollment Data

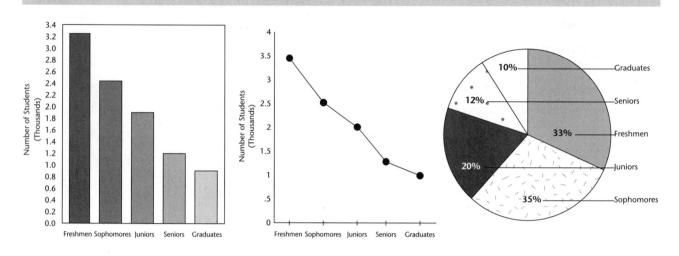

Bar Graphs

Bar graphs compare and contrast quantitative values. They show the amount or quantity an item possesses. Although the units in which the items are measured must be equal, they can be of any size and can start at any value. If the units are large, the bar graph indicates an approximate rather than an exact amount. Bar graphs are sometimes called histograms. Labels or a key shows the contents of each bar.

Line Graphs

A line graph shows quantitative trends for one set of data compared with another set of data. Each line on the graph represents one item. Each point on the line shows a specific relationship between items in each set. For example, a line graph could show relationships between height and weight. Or, it could show the relationship between outdoor temperature and month of the year. If more than one line is used for comparison, labels or keys identify the contents of each line. Line graphs are often considered more accurate than bar graphs. However, accuracy depends on the unit size.

Circle Graphs

A circle graph shows how a whole unit is divided into parts. Because a circle graph focuses on the relationships within one unit, a single circle graph represents a single unit. The parts of a circle graph are expressed

Table 10.4   Steps in Reading Bar and Line Graphs

1. *Read the title, heading, or caption.* This identifies the general group of objects being compared.

2. *Look at the labels or headings for each item or unit.* Identify the specific objects being compared or contrasted.

3. *Identify the units used to measure the items in a bar or line graph.*

4. *Note any general trends.*

5. *If you are looking at a graph as part of the surveying step of SQ3R, stop your examination.* Continue previewing the chapter.

6. *When you read the section of the text that refers to the graph, identify the text's purpose before turning to the graph.* Does the author want you to note specific facts, draw conclusions, or identify trends?

7. *Use the purpose set by the text to look at specific areas of the graph.*

8. *Reread the section of the text that referred to the graph.* Make sure you understand the points and relationships noted by the author.

Table 10.5   Steps in Reading Circle Graphs

1. *Read the title, heading, or caption.* This identifies the unit represented by the circle.

2. *Look at the labels or key for each part of the circle.* Identify the specific components of the circle.

3. *Note relationships among the parts of the circle.*

4. *If you are looking at a graph as part of the surveying step of SQ3R, stop your examination.* Continue previewing the chapter.

5. *When you read the section of the text that refers to the graph, identify the text's purpose before turning to the graph.* Does the author want you to note specific parts or relationships within the circle?

6. *Use the purpose set by the text to look at specific areas of the graph.*

7. *Reread the section of the text that referred to the graph.* Make sure you understand the points and relationships noted by the author.

as percentages or fractions. This is because all the parts equal the whole unit or 100 percent of the unit. Circle graphs deal with fractions instead of units on a continuum, so reading circle graphs differs from reading other graphs. Because a circle is commonly recognized, it is easy to approximate or estimate percentages and see how the percentages combine to form the whole.

READ Exercises 10.3 & 10.4   *Exercises 10.3 and 10.4 provide practice in analyzing graphs.*

Write to Learn

On a separate sheet of paper or in your notebook, estimate the average number of hours you spend daily in each of the following activities:

_____ time spent in class
_____ time spent at work
_____ time spent at home or in personal activities
_____ time spent sleeping
_____ time spent relaxing
_____ time spent studying

On a separate sheet of paper or in your notebook, construct a bar or circle graph to display this data.

Reading Diagrams and Flowcharts

Have you ever heard someone say, "A picture is worth a thousand words?" In texts, authors often use special pictures called **diagrams** (see Figure 10.2). Although most diagrams include words as well as

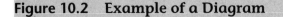

Figure 10.2   Example of a Diagram

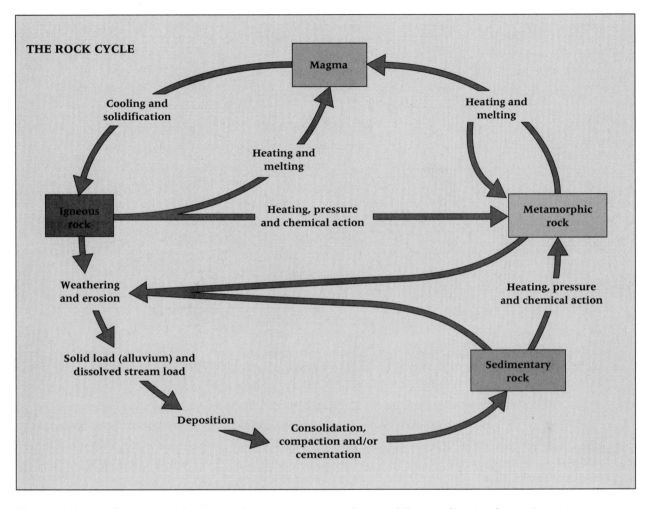

The Rock Cycle: "No trace of a beginning, no prospect of an end," according to the eminent British geologist James Hutton (1726–1797).

From R. E. Gabler, R. J. Sager, D. L. Wise, & J. F. Petersen, *Essentials of Physical Geography,* 6th ed., Figure 14.12, page 385. Fort Worth, TX: Harcourt, 1999.

visual images, they explain complex concepts that would be difficult to understand using only words. Authors use them to help you picture events, processes, structures, or sequences.

If you've ever watched a fountain, you know it directs the path of water in specific ways. Whatever is in the fountain "goes with the flow." Likewise, authors often want you to "go with the flow" when the concept they're explaining is difficult. To simplify the process,

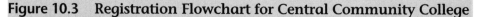

Figure 10.3   Registration Flowchart for Central Community College

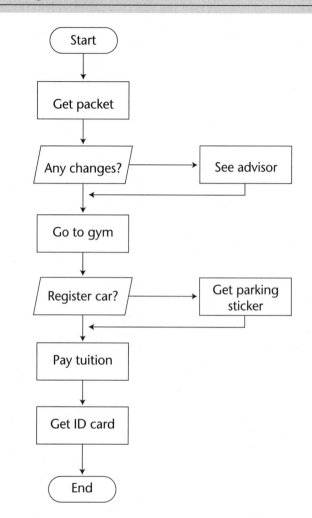

they create an abstract representation of the process. This is called a **flowchart** (see Figure 10.3). Flowcharts also indicate arrangement and show degrees of relationships. Such flowcharts often depict chains of command within organizations. Thus, the information forms a hierarchy, rather than steps in a process. Table 10.6 lists steps in reading diagrams and flowcharts. *Exercises 10.5 and 10.6 give you practice working with diagrams and flowcharts.*

READ Exercises 10.5 & 10.6

Table 10.6 Steps in Reading Diagrams and Flowcharts

1. *Locate and read the title.* This tells what process is being clarified or explained.

2. *If the graphic is a diagram, look at the process as a whole before examining individual parts.* Try to determine how and why the parts contribute to the whole.

3. *If the graphic is a flowchart, look at the beginning and ending points.* Note directionality of arrows. Determine if flow ever goes in more than one direction. Determine meaning of different shapes. For example, diamonds or trapezoids sometime show that a decision is required at that point. In some flowcharts, shapes do not contribute to meaning. In such visuals, the choice of shape depends on the preferences of the graphic artist.

4. *If you are looking at the graphic as part of the surveying step of SQ3R, stop your examination.* Continue previewing the chapter.

5. *When you read the section of the text that refers to the graphic, identify the text's purpose before turning to the flowchart.* Does the author want you to know specific facts, generalizations, or trends?

6. *Use the purpose set by the text to look at specific areas of the graphic.*

7. *Reread the section of the text that referred to the graphic.* Make sure you understand the points and relationships noted by the author.

> **Time has no divisions to mark its passing.**
>
> **There is never a thunderstorm to announce the beginning of a month or a year.**
>
> —Thomas Mann
> *Twentieth century German novelist*

Using Timelines

Although nature has no mechanism for marking special events, authors do. They use **timelines** to show you the order in which events happened. This sequence, or chronology, graphically outlines or describes the history of a topic (see Figure 10.4). A timeline provides a means of organizing and summarizing important dates or events. Steps in following timelines appear in Table 10.7. *Exercise 10.7 gives you practice working with timelines.*

READ Exercise 10.7

Write to Learn
On a separate sheet of paper or in your notebook, construct a timeline chronicling 10 of the most important events in your life.

Figure 10.4 Central Community College Academic Calendar Summer Term

June	1	Dorms open
	3	Orientation for new students
	4	Registration
	5	Classes begin
	12	Final day to add class for credit or to change sections
	24	Last day to drop course without getting a W grade
	29–30	Preregistration for fall term
July	4	Independence Day holiday
	5–7	Midterm exam period
	8	Midterm grades due in Records Office
	22	Last date to resign from the college
	29	Last day of class
	30–31	Final exam period
Aug.	6	Summer commencement

Table 10.7 Steps in Following Timelines

1. *Read the title.* This tells you what time period is being covered.

2. *Find the beginning and ending times on the line.*

3. *Notice any trends.*

4. *Notice any breaks in trends.* If the data seem to change abruptly or if there is a long gap between events, this might be significant and worth your attention.

5. *Make inferences.*

6. *If you are looking at a timeline as part of the surveying step of SQ3R, stop your examination.* Continue previewing the chapter.

7. *When you read the section of the text that refers to the timeline, identify the text's purpose before turning to the timeline.* Does the author want you to note specific facts, generalization, or trends?

8. *Use the purpose set by the text to look at specific areas of the graphic.*

9. *Reread the section of the text that referred to the timeline.* Make sure you understand the points and relationships noted by the author.

Reading Maps

Every place has a specific location, each with its own specific and special characteristics. These locations and characteristics are placed on globes or maps. Locations are shown on globes in three-dimensional form and on maps in two-dimensional form.

Maps constitute the only practical way to show large amounts of space. Because maps show much information, they are more effective than written accounts. Such text would be lengthy and confusing, at best. Thus, maps serve two functions. First, they reduce an area to a size that can be shown on one sheet. Second, they show only those features of interest.

Maps appear most often in social studies texts, although they can also be included in science, math, or literature texts and recreational reading books. Maps help you clarify the text. Thus, map-reading skills aid your understanding.

Even though maps come in various types and have differing features, you use the same steps to read them. Reading maps requires you to use context, draw conclusions, scan, and find main ideas. Maps, then, provide practice for critical reading. Table 10.8 identifies the steps in reading maps.

> There are places I remember all my life, though some have changed— some forever, not for better. Some are gone and some remain.
>
> —from *In My Life*
> John Lennon &
> Paul McCartney
> *Twentieth century British musicians*

Table 10.8   Steps for Reading Maps

1. *Locate and read the title to decide what geographical area is shown.* Identify the type of information that is being given about the area.

2. *Examine the map to get an idea of what it's about.* Locating direction (north, south, east, and west) may be helpful.

3. *When given, note the date of the map.* This indicates the accuracy of information.

4. *Read the key or legend to identify symbols used on the map.* Check the scale to get an idea of how much area the map covers.

5. *If you are looking at a map as a part of the surveying step of SQ3R, stop your examination.* Continue previewing the chapter.

6. *When you read the section of the text that refers to the map, identify what information you need from the map.* Does the author want you to note the main idea of the map or a specific detail?

7. *Scan the map to find this information.* Make inferences about the material on the map. Make sure you understand the author's purpose for including the map.

Map Characteristics

A **scale** of distance shows the relationship between the distance of a place located on a map and this distance in real life. Scales can be shown in the following three ways:

Fraction	1": 100 miles
Written Statement	1 inch equals 100 miles
Graphic Scale	I_____I_____I_____I
	0 100 200 300 Miles

Symbols on maps represent natural (mountains, rivers, lakes) or constructed (cities, roads) details. Reading a map requires a thorough understanding of these symbols. When used, a key or legend on the map shows which symbols are used and what each one means.

Types of Maps

A **political map** (see Figure 10.5) shows the location of constructed features. The only physical features on a political map are oceans, mountains, large lakes, and rivers. Political maps indicate capital cities. They also show the boundaries or international borders between countries. These borders consist of either straight lines plotted by surveyors or wavy lines that follow natural features.

A **physical map** (see Figure 10.6) provides information about the surface features of a place. Surface features include hills, valleys, streams, and lakes. They also provide data about vegetation, elevation, and other physical features.

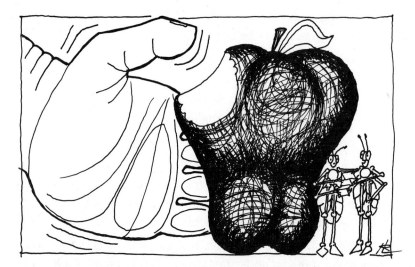

*"Let's see that map again. I was sure that apple
was on the other side of the pie."*

Figure 10.5   Example of a Political Map

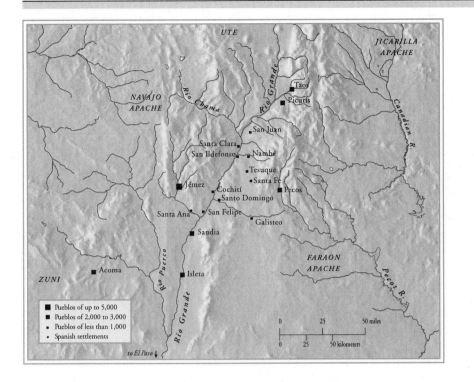

Left: New Mexico, California. 1680. From *American Passages: A History of the United States.* (Map 3.2, p. 84), by E. L. Ayers, L. L. Gould, D. M Oshinsky, and J. R. Soderlund. Fort Worth, TX: Harcourt, 2000.

Below: Maps of the major world ocean currents, showing warm and cool currents. From *Essentials of Physical Geography,* 6th ed. (Figure 6-5, p. 139) by R. E. Gabler, R. J. Sager, D. L. Wise, and J. F. Petersen. Fort Worth, TX: Harcourt, 1999.

Figure 10.6   Example of a Physical Map

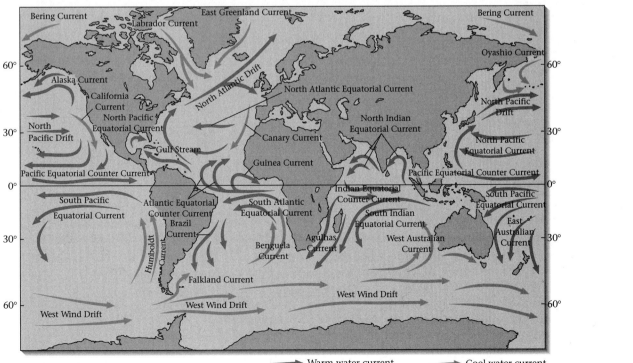

Figure 10.7 Example of a Special Purpose Map

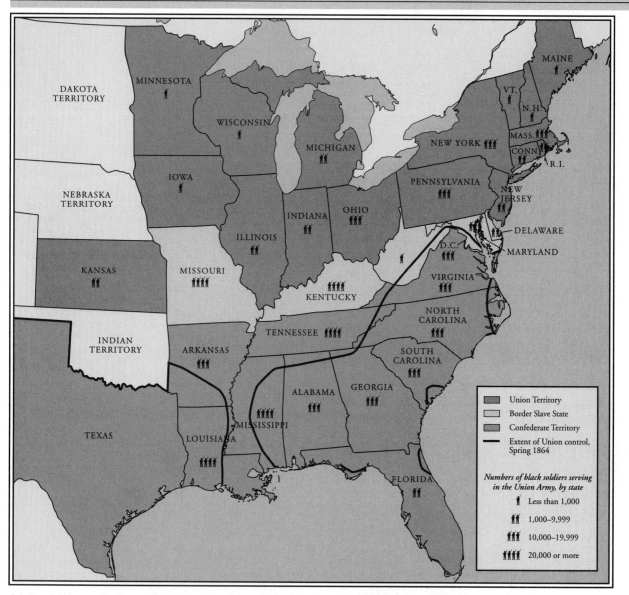

Origins of African American Soldiers. From *American Passages: A History of the United States.* (Map 15.3, p. 511), by E. L. Ayers, L. L. Gould, D. M Oshinsky, and J. R. Soderlund. Fort Worth, TX: Harcourt, 2000.

A third kind of map is a **special-purpose map** (see Figure 10.7). These maps highlight some specific natural or constructed feature, such as changes in a river's course or changes in population.

Practice working with maps in Exercises 10.8 and 10.9.

READ Exercises 10.8 & 10.9

Write to Learn

On a separate sheet of paper or in your notebook, construct a map depicting the route from the place you live to this class. Include at least three physical features and three political features.

Chapter Summary Exercise

Answer the following questions on a separate sheet of paper or in your notebook.

Chapter Review

Answer briefly but completely on a separate sheet of paper or in your notebook.

1. What is the purpose of tables?
2. How do tables differ from graphs?
3. What is the purpose of graphs?
4. How do circle graphs differ from other kinds of graphs?
5. How are diagrams and flowcharts alike? How are they different?
6. Construct a timeline for the due dates of assignments and exams in this course.
7. How do political maps differ from physical maps? How are they alike?
8. What do trends tell about tables or graphs?
9. What is the purpose of a key on a graph or map?

Terms

Terms appear in the order in which they occur in the chapter.

table
trends
graphs
bar graphs
line graphs
circle graphs
diagrams
flowchart
timelines
scale
symbols
political map
physical map
special-purpose map

Exercises

Exercise 10.1   Use the READ Keys excerpt in Chapter 1 ("Credit Management") to answer the following questions. Record your answers on a separate sheet of paper or in your notebook.

Refer to Table 1 and Figure 1 for the following questions.

1. Write the sentence that provides the reference to Table 1.

2. According to Table 1, if a payment is made each month and no additional expenses are charged, how many years will it take to pay off the credit card balance?

3. If the total amount paid consists of the cumulative interest plus the amount owed, what is the total amount of money that will be spent to pay off the credit card balance?

4. The first payment is $68. How do you think the total number of payments would change if $68 payments were made each month?

5. What trend do you find for interest owed?

6. At what point in the table does the amount of principal repaid become more than the amount of interest owed?

7. Why do you think the amount of the payments changes between payment 12 and payment 120?

8. Why isn't the amount of the payments the same each month?

9. Use Figure 1 to create a two-column chart that compares each item in the figure with a logical outcome. Summarize the item in column 1. Identify as many possible outcomes as possible in column 2.

Example:

Item	Possible Outcome(s)
#1 Overspending because you think you will get a raise or higher-paying job.	You don't get the raise/job. Raise/salary doesn't cover spending. Unexpected expenses use funds.

Exercise 10.2   Use the following table to answer the questions on a separate sheet of paper or in your notebook.

Some Missions to Explore Mars

Name	Years at Mars	Type	Description
Mariner 9	1971–72	Orbiter	1st Orbital Surveillance
Viking 1 and 2	1976–1980	Orbiter and lander	Set up weather station, did soil analysis; color images from surface and orbit
Pathfinder	1997	Lander and rover	Tested rover, analyzed rock composition
Global Surveyor	1997–	Orbiter	High resolution images
Nozomi	1999–	Orbiter	Explores interaction of atmosphere and magnetosphere with solar wind
Climate Orbiter	1999–	Orbiter	Studies of Martian weather
Polar Lander	1999–	Lander	Landing near south polar ice cap
Athena	2003	Lander and rover	Collect samples for return to Earth
Mars Airplane	2003	Airplane	Demonstrate powered flight on Mars
Sample Return	2008	Lander and return capsule	Return samples to earth (arriving 2008)

From *Voyages to the Planets,* 2nd ed. (2000). A. Franknoi, D. Morrison, & S. Wolff. Ft. Worth, TX: Harcourt. Table 9.3, page 199.

1. How many orbiters have been sent to Mars?

2. What does the dash (–) after some of the dates indicate?

3. In what decade have most missions occurred?

4. What is unique about the Mars Airplane mission?

5. Which completed mission appears to be the shortest?

6. Which missions focused on Martian weather?

7. How many missions were two type missions?

8. What was the longest time between missions?

9. How many missions have not yet begun?

10. Name one mission that focused on the geology of Mars.

Exercise 10.3   Use the READ Keys excerpt in this chapter (*1960 to 1999*) to answer the following questions. Record your answers on a separate sheet of paper or in your notebook.

Use the bar graph on the Vietnam Conflict to answer the following questions:

1. How many people in the armed services served during the Vietnam conflict?
2. What military branch has the greatest number of participants?
3. What military branch has the smallest number of participants?
4. What military branch had the smallest total number of deaths?
5. What military branch had the smallest number of deaths during battle?
6. What is the total number of people who were wounded but not killed?
7. What military branch had the fewest people to die in battle or by other causes?
8. What is the total number of individuals killed either in battle or by other causes?
9. Do you think the majority of the war was fought on land, sea, or in the air? How do you know from the graph?

Use the bar graph concerning farms to answer the following questions:

1. What trend do you notice in the number of U.S. farms?
2. Approximately how many farms existed in 1850?
3. The greatest decline in farms occurred between _____ and _____.
4. When did the United States have the greatest number of farms?
5. If the trend of the twentieth century continues, what do you predict happened to the number of farms in 2001?

Use the line graph concerning farms to answer the following questions:

1. In what year was the farm population the highest?
2. Approximately how many people lived on farms in 1920?
3. How would you describe the general trend in farm population between 1880 and 1991?
4. Approximately how much acreage was farmed in 1900?
5. In what year was the number of people living on farms and the amount of farm acreage as a percentage of the U.S. total approximately the same?
6. How would you describe the general trend in amount of farm acreage between 1880 and 1991?
7. If the trends in farm population and acreage continued, what do you predict occurred in 2001?

Use the circle graphs on National Expenditures for Health Care, 1960–1994 to answer the following questions:

1. In 1960, approximately what fraction of total expenditures for health care was privately funded?

2. How would you describe the trend for the fraction of costs paid privately for total expenditures for health care?

3. How would you describe the trend for the fraction of costs paid by public-federal funds for total expenditures for health care?

4. How would you generally describe the trend for the fraction of costs paid by public-state funds for total expenditures for health care?

5. In what year was the total expenditures per capita amount paid by public-federal funds 500 billion dollars?

6. In the total expenditures percent distribution, what percentage of health care costs were paid by public-state funds in 1994?

7. In *five-year* increments, the largest increase in the national health expenditures percent of GDP occurred between 19____ and 19____.

Exercise 10.4   Use the READ Keys newspaper article in Chapter 9 ("Few Women Reach Top Positions") to answer the following questions. Record your answers on a separate sheet of paper or in your notebook.

1. How does the percentage of total employees that are female at a private two-year schools compare with the percentage of total employees that are female at public two-year schools?

2. How does the percentage of total employees that are female CEOs at private four-year schools compare with the percentage of total employees that are female at public four-year schools?

3. How does the total number of employees at private and public 2-year school compare?

4. How does the total number of employees at private and public 4-year school compare?

5. What is the difference in salary between a male and female CEO of a single unit?

6. In terms of comparison, list the positions in which females have higher salaries than males in the same positions.

7. How much more money does a male Executive VP make than a female Executive VP?

8. If you totaled the administrative salaries for males and females, what would be the difference between them?

Exercise 10.5 Use the diagram in Figure 10.8 and the following excerpt to answer the following questions on a separate sheet of paper or in your notebook.

Figure 10.8 Geographic Information System

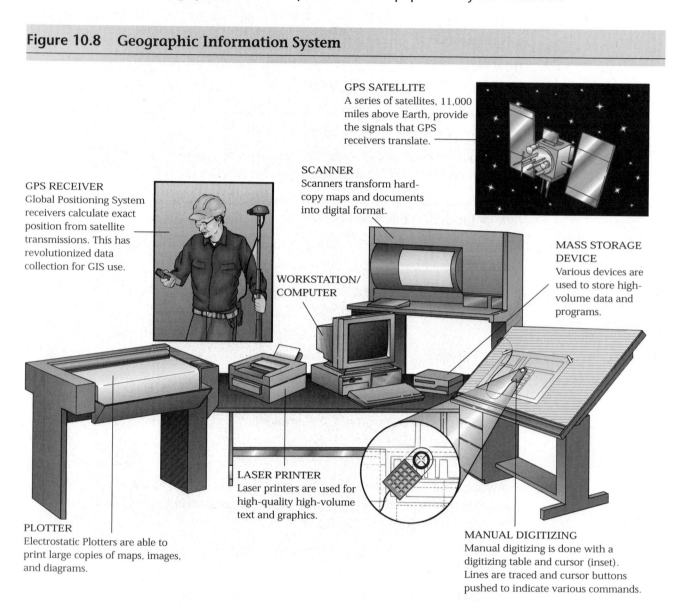

GPS SATELLITE
A series of satellites, 11,000 miles above Earth, provide the signals that GPS receivers translate.

GPS RECEIVER
Global Positioning System receivers calculate exact position from satellite transmissions. This has revolutionized data collection for GIS use.

SCANNER
Scanners transform hard-copy maps and documents into digital format.

MASS STORAGE DEVICE
Various devices are used to store high-volume data and programs.

WORKSTATION/ COMPUTER

PLOTTER
Electrostatic Plotters are able to print large copies of maps, images, and diagrams.

LASER PRINTER
Laser printers are used for high-quality high-volume text and graphics.

MANUAL DIGITIZING
Manual digitizing is done with a digitizing table and cursor (inset). Lines are traced and cursor buttons pushed to indicate various commands.

The Components of a Geographic Information System

A GIS consists of several subsystems: (1) input systems, which provide spatial data into the GIS through the use of scanners that optically convert paper images into a digital format; manual digitizing that is generally used to update maps; and the Global Positioning System, which can feed locational coordinates directly from the field to computer storage in digital format; (2) data storage systems, such as CD-ROMs, computer floppy disks, and hard drives; (3) computer hardware and software systems for data management, access, analysis, and for updating the database (computer hardware and software also facilitate temporary display on the computer screen); and (4) output systems like printers and plotters (which have the ability to generate large hard-copy maps and images). In addition to these four basic subsystems of a GIS, access to many kinds of spatial data (maps, photographs, satellite imagery, digital elevation data) is important. However, it is often said that people are the most important part of a Geographic Information System.

From R. E. Gabler, R. J. Sager, D. L. Wise, & J. F. Petersen, *Essentials of Physical Geography,* 6th ed., Figure 2.29, page 60. Fort Worth, TX: Harcourt, 1999.

1. What does the abbreviation *GIS* stand for?

2. According to the excerpt, how many subsystems does a GIS have?

3. What kind of plotter is used to print large copies of maps, images, and diagrams?

4. What does the abbreviation *GPS* stand for?

5. How are hard-copy maps and documents transformed into digital format?

6. What is considered to be the most important part of a GIS?

7. What is the source of the signals that GPS receivers translate?

8. What is shown on the inset for manual digitizing? How is this component used?

9. Identify three forms of spatial data.

10. Name two types of data storage systems.

Exercise 10.6   Use the diagram in Figure 10.9 (on next page) to answer the following questions on a separate sheet of paper or in your notebook.

1. List the two pathways in which stressors are interpreted.

2. What three parts of the brain react to the Reticular Activating System?

3. Which gland secretes Thyroxine?

4. What is the effect of Thyroxine on organs and tissues?

5. What two glands are activated by the Pituitary Gland?

6. What secretes Adrenaline and Noradrenaline?

7. What gland is part of the kidneys?

8. What two options are available when the body is ready for direct, decisive, physical action?

9. What is the result when physical action is taken?

10. What is the result when no physical action is taken?

Figure 10.9 The Stress Response

From Walt Schafer, *Stress Management for Wellness,* 4th ed., Figure 4.4, page 85. Fort Worth, TX: Harcourt, 2000.

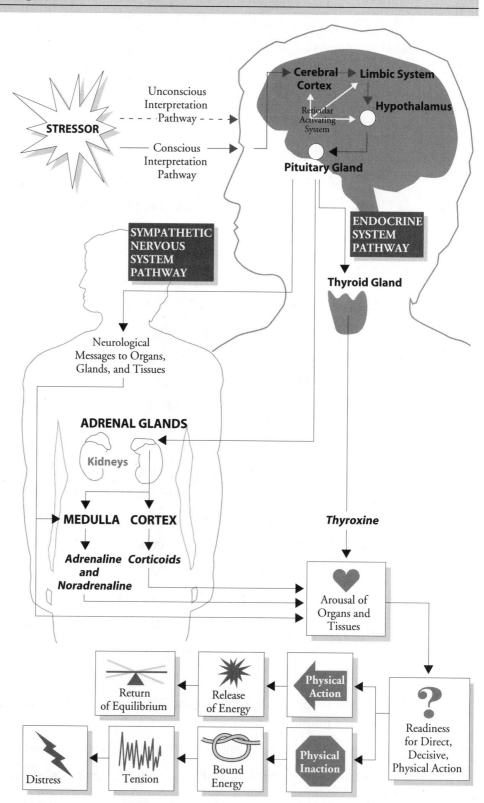

Exercise 10.7   Use the timeline found in the READ Keys excerpt in this chapter (*1960 to 1999*) to answer the following questions. Record your answers on a separate sheet of paper or in your notebook.

1. What are the beginning and ending points on the timeline?
2. In which decade did the most political events occur?
3. In what decade did the fewest social and cultural events occur?
4. In what decade did the fewest economic and technology events occur?
5. Identify three events that occurred in 1973.
6. When was Ronald Reagan elected president?
7. In what year did the movie *Titanic* set a box office record for receipts?
8. When did Iraq invade Kuwait?
9. According to the timeline, what was unusual about 1971?
10. When did the Apollo moon landing occur?

Exercise 10.8   Use the map in Figure 10.10 (on next page) to answer the following questions. Record your responses on a separate sheet of paper or in your notebook.

1. Name two colonies found on the map.
2. Which colony had more towns?
3. What does the dashed line indicate?
4. What do the solid lines indicate?
5. What river empties into the Long Island Sound?
6. Which river passes through both established colonies?
7. Which colony had more Indian villages?
8. What do Deerfield, Groton, Warwick, and Dartmouth have in common?
9. What type of settlement is Mount Hope?
10. Name one town found on an island.

Figure 10.10   New England at the Time of Metacom's War, 1675–1676

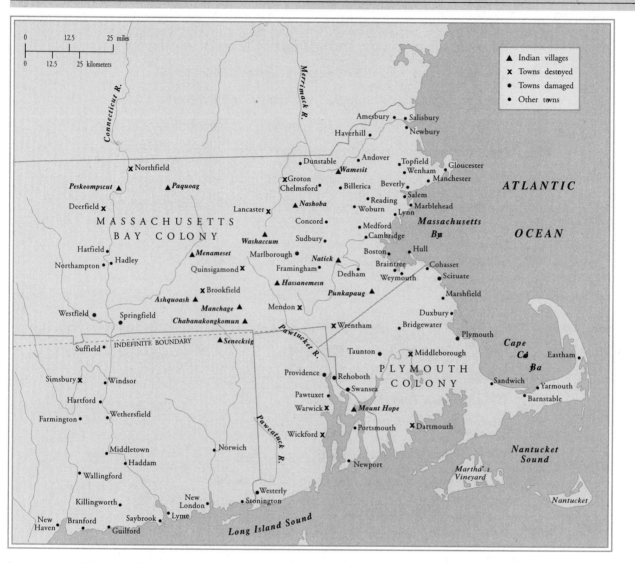

From *American Passages: A History of the United States.* (Map 3.1, p. 79), by E. L. Ayers, L. L. Gould, D. M Oshinsky, and J. R. Soderlund. Fort Worth, TX: Harcourt, 2000.

Exercise 10.9   Use the map in Figure 10.11 to answer the following questions. Record your responses on a separate sheet of paper or in your notebook.

1. In what part of the United States do you find the greatest concentration of highways?

2. List the interstate highways that pass through the state in which your college or university is located.

3. In general, how do the route numbers for highways that run east/west differ from those that run north/south?

4. Which two highways end in Miami, Florida?

Figure 10.11   The National Highwy System

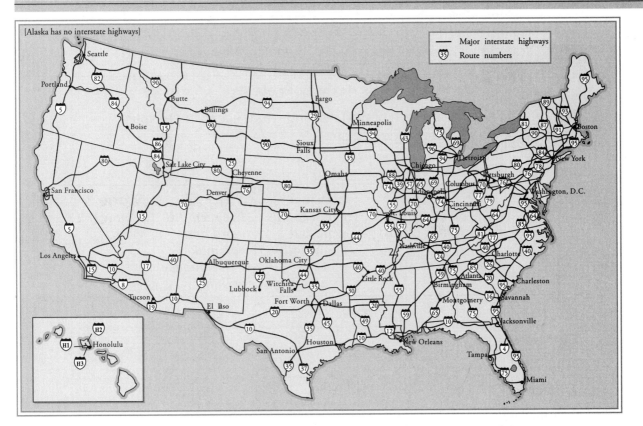

From *American Passages: A History of the United States.* (Map 28.1, p. 983), by E. L. Ayers, L. L. Gould, D. M Oshinsky, and J. R. Soderlund. Fort Worth, TX: Harcourt, 2000.

5. According to the map, if you started in San Antonio, Texas, and traveled north on I35, what would be the last major city on your route?

6. Which interstate runs from Seattle, Washington, to Los Angeles, California?

7. Which highway takes you to Lubbock, Texas?

8. Which highways intersect in Cheyenne, Wyoming?

Web Exercise

A variety of information related to the topics in this chapter is available on the World Wide Web. For this exercise, access MapQuest at http://www.mapquest.com and answer the questions on a separate sheet of paper.

1. Describe the kinds of information about maps found at this site.

2. Locate the town where you were born. What symbols and information do you find?

3. Locate a city you've never visited, but wish to see. What places do you find on the map?

READ: Keys

READ: Keys Activity Pretest

Rate each of the following words according to your knowledge of them.

Word	Stage 0 *I don't know this word.*	Stage 1 *I've seen this word but I know nothing of its meaning.*	Stage 2 *I've seen this word and can make associations with it.*	Stage 3 *I know this word.*
1. tumult				
2. spawned				
3. militant				
4. optimism				
5. articulated				
6. subversion				
7. confrontation				
8. guerilla				
9. unprecedented				
10. prosperity				

READ: Keys Activity 10.1

Read the following excerpt and keep track of your reading time.
Note: Underlined, italicized words are used in Chapter 6, Exercise 6.11.

1960 to 1999

Who could have predicted the turmoil and tragedy of the 1960s? The previous decade, after all, gave scant warning that trouble lay ahead. Filled with powerful milestones, such as the National Highway Act and *Brown v. Board of Education,* the 1950s seemed to reflect the optimism and stability of a confident nation—a place of widely shared values and little public complaint. All was well in prosperous postwar America, or so it appeared.

The **tumult** of the 1960s came suddenly, without letup or relief. It began with the jailings and beatings of civil rights workers in the South, which turned many activists against the philosophy of nonviolence. The civil rights movement, in turn, **spawned** a woman's movement, and then a student movement, which further challenged the *status quo*. Meanwhile, the escalating Vietnam War eroded the credibility of American officials and divided the nation in dangerous ways. Against the backdrop of increasing bloodshed in Southeast Asia, the United States endured a horrifying cycle of home-grown violence in the 1960s, including inner city riots, **militant** campus upheavals, and the assassination of prominent public figures like President John F. Kennedy, his brother Robert, and the Reverend Martin Luther King.

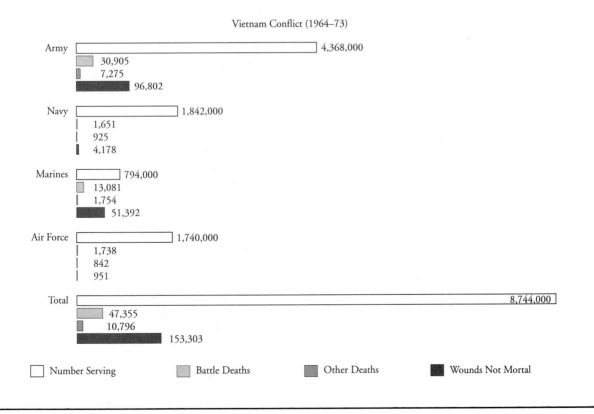

Vietnam Conflict (1964–73)

Army: 4,368,000 / 30,905 / 7,275 / 96,802

Navy: 1,842,000 / 1,651 / 925 / 4,178

Marines: 794,000 / 13,081 / 1,754 / 51,392

Air Force: 1,740,000 / 1,738 / 842 / 951

Total: 8,744,000 / 47,355 / 10,796 / 153,303

Number Serving   Battle Deaths   Other Deaths   Wounds Not Mortal

The 1970s brought little relief. An American president resigned from office for the first time in the nation's history. The North Vietnamese communists took over South Vietnam. Americans faced gas shortages, high unemployment, and staggering inflation. They watched with anger and embarrassment as their embassy in Iran was attacked and 52 Americans were held hostage for more than a year.

Republican Ronald Reagan won the 1980 election by promising to reverse the nation's apparent decline. Mixing personal charm and **optimism** with the darker politics of resentment, he attracted mainstream voters by vowing to strengthen family values, reward hard work, and increase respect for America around the world. At the same time, he reinforced the notion among white working-class voters (known as "_Reagan Democrats_") that the party of Franklin Roosevelt had deserted their interests—that the real enemies of working people were no longer big business and the very rich, but rather big government and the very poor. During the 1980s, the Reagan Administration's policies regarding taxes, wages, unions, banking, and antitrust produced one of the most dramatic redistributions of wealth in American history, with the top one percent seeing its yearly income rise by 75 percent, while the rest of the nation experienced almost no gain at all. Nevertheless, Reagan remained popular president, a politician who **articulated** the fears and dreams of Americans with extraordinary skill.

Through all the tumult of these decades, one certainty remained—the specter of international communism, centered in Moscow. Although the fear of domestic **subversion** stirred up by Senator Joseph McCarthy had largely subsided by 1960, the anxieties generated by Soviet power and influence remained solidly in place. During the 1960s, the United States and Russia _tangled_ over Berlin and Cuba, where the placement of offensive missiles, ninety miles from the Florida coast, led to the most dangerous **confrontation** of the entire Cold War. In Vietnam, meanwhile, American officials defended the growing involvement as a test of will against Soviet-inspired aggression. The larger goals, they insisted, were to halt the spread of world communism and to maintain American credibility around the globe.

The 1970s brought an apparent thaw in U.S.-Soviet relations. The two sides signed a momentous agreement limiting nuclear weapons known as SALT I. President Nixon also visited the Soviet Union as well as Communist China, raising hopes for serious dialogue or _détente_. It didn't happen. As Nixon freely admitted, his visit to China was intended, in large part, to drive a wedge between the Russians and the Chinese, the world's two leading communist powers. Furthermore, the very idea of negotiating with the Soviet Union over issues such as human rights and arms control offended hard-line anti-communists who believed that American military power must largely determine the outcome of the Cold War. In the 1980 presidential campaign, Ronald Reagan promised a much tougher stand against communism in the future.

The Reagan administration dramatically increased the nation's defense budget. It also funded military campaigns against leftist rebels and Marxist governments in Africa, Asia, and Latin America. In one instance, it funneled money from a secret arms deal with Iran to illegally finance a right-wing **guerilla** army in Nicaragua. President Reagan made no apologies for this activity. The Soviets had created an "_Evil Empire,_" he declared, and it had to be destroyed.

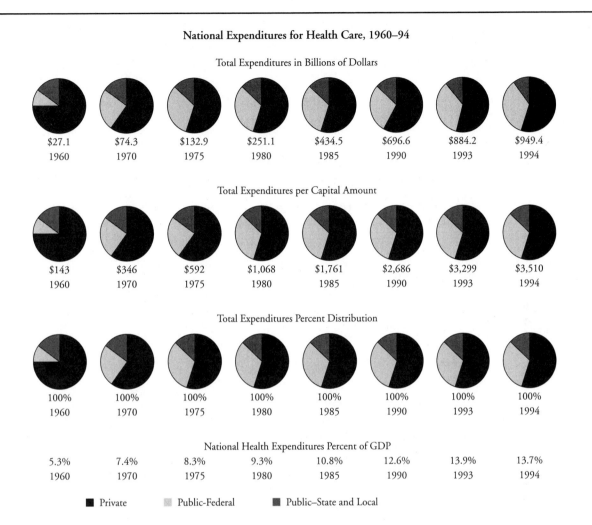

National Expenditures for Health Care, 1960–94

Total Expenditures in Billions of Dollars

| $27.1 | $74.3 | $132.9 | $251.1 | $434.5 | $696.6 | $884.2 | $949.4 |
| 1960 | 1970 | 1975 | 1980 | 1985 | 1990 | 1993 | 1994 |

Total Expenditures per Capital Amount

| $143 | $346 | $592 | $1,068 | $1,761 | $2,686 | $3,299 | $3,510 |
| 1960 | 1970 | 1975 | 1980 | 1985 | 1990 | 1993 | 1994 |

Total Expenditures Percent Distribution

| 100% | 100% | 100% | 100% | 100% | 100% | 100% | 100% |
| 1960 | 1970 | 1975 | 1980 | 1985 | 1990 | 1993 | 1994 |

National Health Expenditures Percent of GDP

| 5.3% | 7.4% | 8.3% | 9.3% | 10.8% | 12.6% | 13.9% | 13.7% |
| 1960 | 1970 | 1975 | 1980 | 1985 | 1990 | 1993 | 1994 |

■ Private   ▨ Public-Federal   ▨ Public–State and Local

In fact, that empire was already in trouble. Assuming power in 1985, Soviet Premier Mikhail Gorbachev well understood the problems his nation faced. Believing that communism must become more democratic and market-oriented in order to survive, he encouraged the policies known as *glasnost* (openness) and *perestroika* (restructure). In trying to save communism, however, Gorbachev set in motion the very forces that would bring it down. A wave of protest swept through Eastern Europe, demanding more freedom and closer contacts with the West. Unlike Hungary in 1956 and Czechoslovakia in 1968, the Soviet Union did not rush troops to restore order. On a trip to West Berlin in 1987, President Reagan encouraged the Protesters by demanding: "Mr. Gorbachev, tear down this wall." In 1989, the **_communist governments in Eastern Europe fell like dominoes_**—Hungary, Poland, Czechoslovakia, East Germany, Romania. It was one of those rare instances, noted *Time* magazine, "when the tectonic plates of history shift beneath men's feet, and nothing after is quite the same."

In 1991, the Soviet Union collapsed, and Russians began the painful transition to democratic politics and a free market economy. For the United States, meanwhile, a new set of challenges emerged. As the world's only

1960   1968   1970   1978   1980

POLITICS & DIPLOMACY

1960: John Kennedy elected president
1961: Berlin Wall erected
1962: Cuban missile crisis
1963: President Kennedy assassinated
1964: President Johnson elected by record margin
Landmark Civil Rights Act passed
1965: U.S. troop levels exceed 100,000 in Vietnam
Malcolm X assassinated
1967: Anti-war protests multiply
1968: Tet Offensive
Martin Luther King assassinated in Memphis
Robert Kennedy assassinated in Los Angeles
Richard Nixon elected president

1970: U.S. troops invade Cambodia
1972: President Nixon visits mainland China
Watergate burglary
1973: Vice President Agnew resigns
1974: President Nixon resigns
1975: South Vietnam falls
1976: Jimmy Carter elected president
1977: Panama Canal treaty
1978: Camp David accords
1979: Hostage crisis in Iran

1980: Ronald Reagan elected President
1981: Reagan survives assassination attempt
Sandra Day O'Connor becomes first woman appointed to Supreme Court
1982: Democrats gain seats in Congressional elections
1983: Strategic Defense Initiative (SDI) proposed
Invasion of Grenada
1984: Geraldine Ferraro becomes first woman to be nominated for vice president by major party
Reagan wins sweeping reelection

SOCIAL & CULTURAL EVENTS

1961: Freedom Rides
1962: Students for a Democratic Society formed
1963: Betty Friedan publishes *The Feminine Mystique*
1964: Beatles tour the United States
1965: Race riot in Watts
1966: National Organization for Women formed
1967: Haight-Ashbury "Summer of Love"
1968: Cesar Chavez leads California grape strike
Anti-war protests disrupt Democratic National Convention
1969: Woodstock music festival

1970: College protesters killed at Kent State and Jackson State
1973: Abortion legalized
1974: Anti-busing protests in Boston

1981: AIDS epidemic begins in United States
1982: Vietnam War Memorial dedicated in Washington
David Letterman show premiers on NBC lat night
1983: Sally Ride first American woman in space
1984: Summer Olympics in Los Angeles

ECONOMICS & TECHNOLOGY

1960: Oral contraceptive marketed
1962: John Glenn orbits the earth aboard *Friendship 7*
1969: Apollo moon landing

1973: Arab oil embargo triggers energy crisis
1979: Nuclear accident at Three Mile Island

1981: Reagan tax cut package adopted
Air traffic controllers strike
1982: Recession ends
Budget deficit exceeds $100 billion for first time
1983: Social Security Reforms adopted
1984: Macintosh computer introduced
1985: President Reagan signs Gramm-Rudman-Hollings act to reduce government spending

1985   1990   1993   1996   1997   1999

1985: Mikhail Gorbachev becomes leader of Soviet Union

1986: Democrats regain control of Senate

Iran-Contra Scandal begins

1987: Nomination of Robert Bork to Supreme Court defeated

1988: George Bush wins presidential election over Michael Dukakis on "no new taxes" pledge

Berlin Wall torn down

1990: Iraq invades Kuwait

Bush abandons "no new taxes" pledge

1991: Persian Gulf War brings Iraq's ouster from Kuwait

Clarence Thomas-Anita Hill controversy erupts

1992: Bill Clinton defeats George Bush and Ross Perot in presidential race

1993: Branch Davidians besieged in Waco, Texas, which results in fiery confrontation

Clinton's deficit-reduction plan passes Congress by a single Democratic vote in Senate

1994: Republicans regain control of House of Representatives for first time in 40 years

1995: Bombing in Oklahoma City kills more than 160 people; fears about militias aroused

Republicans force government shutdown

Settlement of Bosnian conflict reached at Dayton, Ohio

1996: Clinton and Bob Dole wage presidential contest

Clinton reelected to second term

1997: Balanced budget agreement reached

1998: Clinton sex scandals break

President impeached by House of Representatives in December

1999: Clinton acquitted by Senate

NATO launches air war against Serbia over treatment of Albanians in Kosovo

School massacre in Littleton, Colorado sets off debate about violence and gun control

Air war against Serbia ends successfully

1985: Rock Hudson dies of AIDS

1986: *Challenger* Space Shuttle explodes

1987: Scandals engulf televangelist ministry of Jim and Tammy Faye Bakker

1988: Anti-depressant drug Prozac introduced

1989: Actresses Bette Davis and Lucille Ball die

Oil tanker Exon Valdez goes aground in Alaska causing environmental damage

1990: Hubble Space telescope launched

1991: Basketball star Magic Johnson reveals that he is HIV positive (AIDS virus)

1992: Vice President Dan Quayle attacks single mother premise of sit-com *Murphy Brown*

1993: Author Toni Morrison wins Nobel Prize for literature

1994: O.J. Simpson murder trial grips nation

Death of Jacqueline Kennedy Onassis

1995: Simpson's acquittal sparks national furor

1996: Jazz singer Ella Fitzgerald dies

Virginia Military Institute admits women

1997: Movie *Titanic* sets all-time box office record for receipts

Princess Diana killed

Spice Girls group has top pop album "Spice"

1998: Singer Frank Sinatra dies

Slugger Mark McGwire hits 70 home runs for all-time record

1999: Death of baseball star Joe DiMaggio

Michael Jordan (basketball) and Wayne Gretzky (hockey) retire from professional sports

Star Wars, Episode I, The Phantom Menace opens to long lines and critical panning

1986: Tax Reform Act passed

1987: Stock market closes about 2000 on Dow Jones, but loses 508 points on the index in October in a single day

1988: U.S., Canada arrive at free trade agreement

President Bush approves $300 billion plan to bail out savings and loan industry

1990: American dependence on foreign oil reaches historic high

1991: Economy enters recession that will last until late 1992

1992: Unemployment reaches 7.8 percent, the highest since 1983

1993: United States and Europe agree on new terms for General Agreement on Tariffs and Trade (GATT)

Clinton administration proposes national health care plan

North American Free Trade Agreement (NAFTA) approved in Congress

1994: Clinton health care plan dies in Congress

1995: Budget battle in Congress produces closing of Federal Government in December

1996: Congress passes sweeping welfare reform bill

1997: Unemployment rate in May falls to 4.8 percent, the lowest since 1973

Budget surplus reported and future surpluses are projected

1998: Dow Jones average closes above 9,000 in April

1999: Dow Jones hovers around 11,000 in May

United States has strongest economy in world as 20th century draws to a close, but stability of world financial system is still a concern

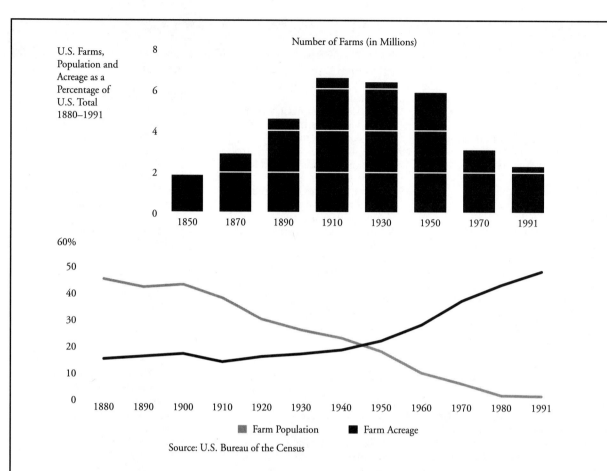

U.S. Farms, Population and Acreage as a Percentage of U.S. Total 1880–1991

Number of Farms (in Millions)

Farm Population   Farm Acreage

Source: U.S. Bureau of the Census

remaining "super power," it now faced a post–Cold War era marred by ethnic violence in the Balkans, tribal warfare in Africa, military aggression in the Middle East, nuclear proliferation in India and Pakistan, and continuing human rights violations from Latin America to China. In addition, a booming world birthrate and the specter of global warming raised serious environmental concerns, while the rapid spread of technology and the information linked people together in truly remarkable ways. During the 1990s, the president who faced these issues, Bill Clinton, saw the economy achieve ***unprecedented*** levels of ***prosperity*** and the lingering problem of the budget deficits eased dramatically. Yet good times at home did not mean political calm. The Republicans regained control of the House of Representatives in 1994 for the first time in four decades and a second term for Clinton seemed doubtful. Yet he won again in 1996, only to face **impeachment** charges arising from a sex scandal in 1998. Despite his acquittal in 1999, his presidency ended under a cloud. Peacekeeping in the Balkans, rising tensions with China, and violence at home were all concerns that would face the next president in 2001. As the millennium approached, America's leadership remained crucial in a rapidly changing world.

From *American Passages: A History of the United States* (2000) by E. L. Ayers, L. L. Gould, D. M. Oshinsky, and J. R. Soderlund. Ft. Worth, TX: Harcourt.

_____ words / _____ minutes = _____ words per minute.

Calculate your reading time by dividing the number of words in the article by the amount of time it took to read it. Then mark your reading time on the chart located on page 338.

READ: Keys Activity 10.2

On a separate sheet of paper or in your notebook, answer the following questions about the excerpt you just read:

1. According to the excerpt, which of the following occurred before 1960?

    a. assassination of Robert Kennedy

    b. resignation of an American president

    c. National Highway Act

    d. inner city riots

2. Which of the following shows the correct order for the development of movements in the 1960s?

    a. student, woman's, civil rights

    b. woman's, civil rights, student

    c. student, civil rights, woman's

    d. civil rights, woman's, student

3. Which of the following events and time periods is correctly matched?

    a. *Brown v. Board of Education,* 1960s

    b. gas shortages, 1970s

    c. SALT I, 1990s

    d. collapse of the Soviet Union, 1980s

4. Who called the Soviet Union an "Evil Empire?"

    a. Nixon

    b. Reagan

    c. McCarthy

    d. Clinton

5. What were the two leading communist powers in the 1970s?

   a. North and South Vietnam

   b. China and the Soviet Union

   c. Cuba and Russia

   d. China and Vietnam

6. What country held 52 Americans hostage for more than a year?

   a. Pakistan

   b. Iran

   c. Cuba

   d. China

7. What did Ronald Reagan promise to attract mainstream voters?

   a. end the Vietnam war

   b. strengthen family values

   c. pass a national highway act

   d. control global warming

8. What was SALT I?

   a. an agreement to limit nuclear weapons

   b. a Russian satellite

   c. a military campaign

   d. a secret arms deal with Iran

9. What concerns were raised as the result of global warming and a booming world birthrate?

   a. economic

   b. political

   c. environmental

   d. religious

10. Which presidential administration produced a redistribution of American wealth?

    a. Roosevelt

    b. Nixon

    c. Clinton

    d. Reagan

READ: Keys Activity 10.3

Examine each of the numbered phrases or sentences and complete the following on a separate sheet of paper or in your notebook.

(a) Write the boldfaced, italicized word. Identify one or two words that you can put in the place of the boldfaced, italicized word without changing the meaning of the phrase or sentence and write this synonym or synonymous phrase (words that have the same meaning) beside the word. (b) Identify the part of speech of this word as used in the sentence. (c) Look up the boldfaced, italicized word in a dictionary and write the dictionary definition. How does this compare with the definition from context? (d) List the parts of speech this word can sometimes be. (e) Write a complete sentence with each word.

1. The ***tumult*** of the 1960s came suddenly, without letup or relief.

2. The civil rights movement, in turn, ***spawned*** a woman's movement and then a student movement . . .

3. Against the backdrop of increasing bloodshed in Southeast Asia, the United States endured a horrifying cycle of home-grown violence in the 1960s, including inner city riots, ***militant*** campus upheavals, and the assassination of prominent public figures . . .

4. Mixing personal charm and ***optimism*** with the darker politics of resentment, he [Ronald Reagan] attracted mainstream voters . . .

5. . . . Reagan remained a popular president, a politician who ***articulated*** the fears and dreams of Americans . . .

6. Although the fear of domestic ***subversion*** stirred up by Senator Joseph McCarthy had largely subsided by 1960s, the anxieties generated by Soviet power and influence remained solidly in place.

7. . . . the United States and Russia tangled over Berlin and Cuba, where the placement of offensive missiles, ninety miles from the Florida coast, led to the most dangerous ***confrontation*** of the entire Cold War.

8. In one instance, it funneled money from a secret arms deal with Iran to illegally finance a right-wing ***guerilla*** army in Nicaragua.

9. During the 1990s, the president who faced these issues, Bill Clinton, saw the economy achieve ***unprecedented*** levels of prosperity . . .

10. During the 1990s, the president who faced these issues, Bill Clinton, saw the economy achieve unprecedented levels of ***prosperity*** . . .

READ: Keys Activity 10.4

In Part A, use the following list of words to fill in the blanks. In Part B, use the information from Part A to complete the analogies.

Part A

uproar	generated	conflict	activist
concluded	wealth	hopefulness	ally
obedience	expressed	poverty	conformist
pessimism	mundane	rebel	unique
peace	unspoken	rebellion	harmony

Synonym	Word	Antonym
_____	**1.** tumult	_____
_____	**2.** spawned	_____
_____	**3.** militant	_____
_____	**4.** optimism	_____
_____	**5.** articulated	_____
_____	**6.** subversion	_____
_____	**7.** confrontation	_____

_____   **8.** guerilla   _____

_____   **9.** unprecedented_____

_____   **10.** prosperity   _____

Part B

1. guerilla : _____ :: confrontation : peace

2. _____ : subversion :: mundane : unprecedented

3. tumult : harmony :: articulated : _____

4. prosperity : poverty :: _____ : ally

5. unspoken : _____ :: optimism : pessimism

6. spawned : _____ :: unprecedented : unique

7. wealth : prosperity :: tumult : _____

8. confrontation : _____ :: spawned : generated

9. subversion : rebellion :: tumult : _____

10. militant : _____ :: articulated : expressed

READ: Keys Activity Posttest

Rate each of the following words according to your knowledge of them.

Word	Stage 0 *I don't know this word.*	Stage 1 *I've seen this word but I know nothing of its meaning.*	Stage 2 *I've seen this word and can make associations with it.*	Stage 3 *I know this word.*
1. tumult				
2. spawned				
3. militant				
4. optimism				
5. articulated				
6. subversion				
7. confrontation				
8. guerilla				
9. unprecedented				
10. prosperity				

Sample Chapter

Opportunities to Work in the Theater

There are more producing groups in the United States today than ever before. Although a large proportion does not provide a living wage, there are many avenues open for theatrical talent. Still, the professional theatre can absorb relatively few of those who seek employment. Fortunately, there are other rewarding possibilities in community, theater, education, and elsewhere.

Theater as an Avocation

Most students who study theatre in colleges do not enter the theatre as a profession. For many, theatre is an avenue for acquiring a humanistic education, just as English, philosophy, or history are, or it is a supplement to study in some other field. Nevertheless, after graduation many continue an <u>avocational</u> interest in theatre either as audience members or through involvement in production. Audiences are, of course, always necessary, both in professional and nonprofessional theatres. There are also many opportunities for working in the theatre as an avocation, because most nonprofessional theater organizations rely on volunteer personnel. The demand for actors is great, and with the interests in scenery, costumes, lighting, properties, makeup, sound, dance, or music, one can usually find opportunities to express them. There is also a need for people to work in public relations, publicity, house management, and other nonperformance areas.

Theatre in Education

Perhaps the largest number of paying theatre jobs is in education. Persons with theater training are usually employed in schools for two purposes: to teach and to stage plays. Sometimes it is possible to specialize in directing, costuming, lighting, or some other area, but to be assured of employment one should be prepared to undertake multiple assignments.

The educational theatre may be divided into levels: theatre for children and youth, secondary-school theatre, and college and university theatre.

Theatre for Children and Youth

Theatre for children and youth may operate within three frameworks: professional, community, or educational. Its distinguishing characteristic is its intended audience.

A related area is creative (or developmental) drama, although technically it is a theatrical activity. Using creative drama techniques, children are stimulated to improvise dramatic situations based on stories, historical events, social situations, or mathematics and science. Creative drama is used to help children feel their way into traditional and real-life situations, to make learning more concrete, to allow children an outlet in the classroom for their responses and feelings, and to stimulate imagination. It is an educational and developmental tool rather than a product intended for an audience. Normally, the classroom teacher, who should have specialized training in its techniques, handles creative drama.

Theatre as such is seldom taught in elementary schools. Children are instead offered plays through a variety of channels. The recreation program in most large cities includes a unit that produces plays for children and young people; many community theatres, high schools, colleges, and universities produce plays for children and youth; some regional professional companies offer occasional productions for children and adolescents, and several professional organizations specialize in plays for children and young people.

There is a significant demand for persons with some training in theatre for children and adolescents and in creative drama. Some colleges and universities employ specialists in these areas; school districts may hire a person who can demonstrate and supervise creative drama; some community theatres employ a director whose sole responsibility is the production of plays for children and youth; and public recreation programs often employ a specialist in this area. In addition, there are now approximately sixty professional troupes that perform for child and adolescent audiences.

Workers in theatre for children and youth need the same basic training required by any other theatre worker. In addition, they should receive some specialized instruction in child and developmental psychology and in the specialized problems of theatre for children and adolescents.

Secondary School Theater

Almost every high school in the United States produces one or more plays each year. Still, many do not offer courses in theater and drama, and <u>plays</u> sometimes are directed by persons with no theatre training at all. On the other hand, some secondary schools have excellent theatre programs. Productions are cast from high school students and are performed for an audience made up primarily of other high school students, parents, and others from the <u>immediate</u> community.

Secondary school teachers should understand the adolescent and may need to be certified to teach subjects other than theater, such as communications or English, because often teachers are not allowed to devote their full time to teaching theatre.

Undergraduate Colleges and Universities

Most colleges and universities in the United States offer some coursework in theatre. In most cases, theatre courses are included in the liberal arts curriculum, whereas the production program is treated as <u>extracurricular</u>, with participation open to all students.

Teachers in a liberal arts college may have an opportunity to specialize in such areas as directing or designing, but often they must teach and supervise several areas of production. Undergraduate programs offering the <u>bachelor</u> of fine arts degree in theater usually admit students to that degree program only after auditions, interviews, or portfolio reviews have established students' talent and commitment. Because these programs are usually oriented to the professional theatre or to preparing students for additional training at the graduate level, instructors should be able to set high standards through their own work. In these specialized programs, participation in production is often restricted to <u>majors</u>.

Graduate Schools

The graduate school, designed to give specialized training, requires a staff of experienced specialists, and employment is usually available only to those who have demonstrated ability in specialized aspects of the theatre. The graduate school is crucial to the theatre, because most practitioners now receive their basic training in colleges and universities. Graduate schools also train those who will become teachers, <u>dramaturges</u>, theatre historians, critics, and scholars in the field.

University Resident Theatres

Some colleges and universities support resident theatre companies. Many of these companies are made up of students; some <u>mingle</u> students and professionals, and a few are wholly professional. Typically, each group produces plays of many types and from many <u>periods</u>.

The majority of those in such companies are actors, but a director, a few technicians, and sometimes a designer are included. Each year companies belonging to the University/Resident Theatre Association (U/RTA) hold <u>joint</u> auditions for admissions to the companies and/or to the graduate training programs with which they are affiliated. The number of students from each school who are permitted to audition is limited. University resident companies that use only professional actors usually hold auditions in New York and a few other locations.

The Community Theatre

Almost every town with a population of more than thirty thousand has a community theatre. Many of these theatres are operated entirely by volunteers; others pay the director of each play and may provide a small sum for the designer and other key workers. Typically, a community theatre employs a full-time director who supervises all productions. The more <u>prosperous</u> groups also have a full-time designer-technician, and some hire a director of theatre for children and youth as well.

Because of their purpose, community theatres usually do not hire persons other than in supervisory capacities. The primary function of community theatre—in addition to providing theatrical entertainment for local audiences—is to furnish an outlet for the talents of adult volunteers.

Those who seek employment in the community theatre, therefore, need to be leaders. They should be <u>diplomatic</u>, able to cooperate with diverse personalities, and know a great deal about public relations.

Summer Theatres

There are many summer theatres scattered throughout the country. They usually perform from June until September. There is much variety in summer theatre. Some groups present a different play each week or every two weeks; during the run of a show, one or more upcoming productions are usually being rehearsed. Some companies perform a single work for the entire summer. Some specialize in plays by a single playwright, most frequently Shakespeare. Some perform only musicals. Still others employ only a <u>nucleus</u> company and import well-known motion picture, television, or stage actors to play leading roles. Occasionally, summer theatres try out new plays.

There are many kinds of summer companies. Some are entirely professional and hire only professional actors, designers, and directors. Others mingle professionals and nonprofessionals. (Actors Equity classifies companies according to the number of professional actors employed, minimum salaries, and working conditions.) Companies employing professional actors may hire designers and directors who are not union members. Some summer theatres are operated by educational institutions and give college credit for participation.

Many summer theatres have intern programs. Interns may receive room and <u>board</u> and even a small weekly salary; the pay is seldom more than enough for living expenses. Some organizations ask interns to pay a fee, but this practice is generally frowned upon.

Most hiring for professional and semiprofessional summer theatres is done in New York and a few other large cities. A few summer theatres send a representative to major theatre-training programs to hold auditions. Summer theatres run by colleges usually hold auditions on their own campuses. Whatever the arrangement, summer theatres provide only seasonal employment.

Not-for-Profit Professional Company

There are now about three hundred not-for-profit professional theatres in the United States. (Most theatres beyond Broadway are organized as not-for-profit, a status that makes them eligible for assistance from arts organizations, foundations, and corporations; to be granted this status under tax laws, an organization must be able to establish its purpose as cultural and community service-oriented rather than as profit making.) Most not-for-profit theatres belong to the Theatre Communications Group (TCG), whose office in New York is a major <u>clearinghouse</u> for information about job openings and opportunities in the theatres affiliated with it. These not-for-profit theatres include the many regional companies outside New York as well as many Off-Broadway and Off-Off-Broadway theatres in New York.

Not-for-profit theatres are divided into categories according to their budgets and working conditions. Actors Equity controls the contracts for professional actors throughout the country and prescribes the percentage of actors in each <u>company</u> who must be Equity members. It also sets minimum wage scales.

Not-for-profit companies obtain their personnel in various ways. Most employ an artistic director and managing director on long-term contracts. Other staff (including designers, technicians, publicity directors, and box-office managers) may work on a continuing basis and may remain in their jobs for many years, but usually they can be let go on short notice. Such personnel are usually hired on the basis of portfolios, interviews, recommendations, and demonstrated aptitude or achievement. Actors are frequently hired for a single production, although some may remain for additional shows. Smaller companies, as well as large companies in sizable population centers, may hire many of their actors locally, but many still do the majority of their hiring after holding auditions in New York, Chicago, Los Angeles, Seattle, or elsewhere. Some use the services of Broadway and casting directors. Some companies will audition applicants from colleges and universities but usually only if applicants have been carefully screened in advance.

There are now more persons employed in not-for-profit professional companies than in for-profit theatres.

For-Profit Professional Theatres

The jobs most difficult to get are those on Broadway, not only because there are few opportunities but also because of union control. Some of these conditions apply elsewhere, but seldom so fully. Las Vegas has also become a major employer, especially for performers in musical reviews and for design/technology positions.

Directors

Directors are employed by the producer. The director must be a member of the Society of Stage Directors and Choreographers, which has standard contracts to specify the director's rights and working conditions.

Actors

Most fully professional actors belong to Actors Equity Association. In New York and other right-to-work states, actors who can prove that they have earned a set amount of money performing over a given period of time can apply for and receive an Eligible Performer's Card. This card allows non-union professionals to audition for union-governed productions without restricting the performer to working solely in union houses. Nevertheless, most professional actors (including dancers and singers) must belong to Actors Equity Association. Actors Equity requires producers to devote a minimum number of hours to open interviews or auditions for each show. This screening may be done by an assistant, and few of the applicants may actually be permitted to try out. Casting directors may also handle much of the preliminary work. Many actors obtain auditions through agents, and others are invited by the producer to try out.

Stage Managers

Stage managers must also belong to Actors Equity. Most begin as performers and for extra pay take on the job of assistant stage manager; a large show usually has several assistant stage managers. If assistant stage managers prove reliable, they may subsequently be employed as principal stage managers. After the show opens, the stage manager may rehearse the cast as needed. Therefore, training or experience in directing may be an asset to the would-be stage manager.

Designers

Designers are employed by the producer. All must belong to the United Scenic Artists Union, the most difficult of all stage unions to gain admission to. Applicants must pay an examination fee and, if they pass the rigorous exam, a sizable initiation fee. This union also controls design in television, films, opera, and ballet. Designers may be admitted to the union as scenic, costume, or lighting designers, or they may qualify in two or all of these areas. All contracts must meet the union's minimum requirements. Many younger members of the union work as assistants to well-established designers.

Scenery, Costume, Lighting, and Property Crews

Members of the various crews that run shows must belong to the International Alliance of Theatrical Stage Employees. Crews are carefully separated, so that no one will perform more than one function. This union restricts admission to make sure that most of its members will be employed. Acceptance depends as much on knowing the right persons as on having training.

Others

Each production must have a company manager and a press agent, who work directly with the producer. The manager aids in letting contracts, arranges for rehearsal space and out-of-town tryouts, and handles the payroll. The press agent is concerned principally with selling the show. Both must be members of the Association of Theatrical Press Agents and Managers.

Any theatrical worker may have an agent, whose job it is to market the client's services. An agent can be crucial in getting a hearing for clients who might otherwise never be able to display their talents. For these services, an agent is paid a percentage of the client's earnings on each contract negotiated. Agents customarily must be approved by the client's union.

The number of job opportunities in New York is very small in relation to those seeking employment. Usually fewer than one-fourth of the members of Actors Equity are employed at one time; fewer than twenty-five designers in each of the fields of scenery, costume, and lighting design all of the shows seen on Broadway each year; and a small number of directors direct the shows. Most designers and directors work on no more than one show each season.

Many people try to discourage would-be professionals from going to New York, but nothing can keep many from doing so. It has become common, nevertheless, for aspirants to look to theatres beyond Broadway as alternatives.

Special Employment Opportunities

In addition to the opportunities already discussed, others are available in related areas. Television and motion pictures offer additional opportunities. It has become increasingly common for actors to move from the theatre into television and film. Without these possibilities, many professionals would lead a difficult life indeed. But, because these supplementary fields have their own unemployment problems, they can merely relieve some of the pressures.

Some industrial and commercial firms stage special shows to publicize their products. Frequently, these productions are lavish, and some tour major cities. These shows normally play for invited audiences only; they pay well but provide little further recognition. Most are cast in New York.

Many municipal recreation departments employ persons trained in theatre. To be eligible, one must usually also have had some training in health, physical education, and recreation.

Theatre for the aging is an emerging field. As life expectancy increases, the potential of this field will probably expand.

Theatre by and for the handicapped is a growing field. As awareness has grown of the special problems of the handicapped, theatre has sought ways to serve the needs of this group.

Theatrical techniques have been adapted for nontheatrical uses. For example, they are now used therapeutically with the emotionally disturbed. To work in such fields, training in psychology as well as in drama and theatre is needed.

When the variety of theatrical activities—in both the nonprofessional and professional theatre—is considered, there are many employment opportunities. Though there are fewer jobs than applicants, especially in the professional theatre, there is always a demand for talented and dedicated persons. The future of the theatre depends on those select few.

From Brocket, Oscar Gross, and Ball, Robert, *The Essential Theater,* 7th ed. Belmont, CA: Wadsworth, 1999.

Answers to Chapter Maps

Chapter 5 Map

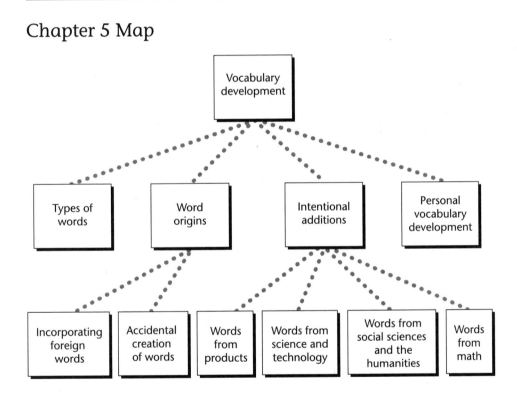

Chapter 6 Map

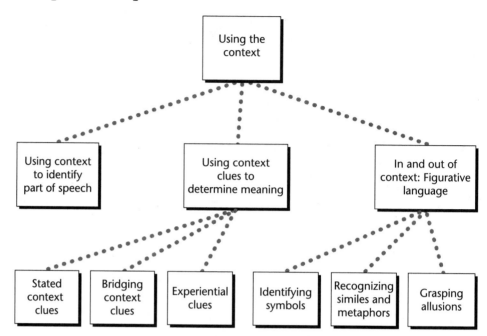

Chapter 7 Map

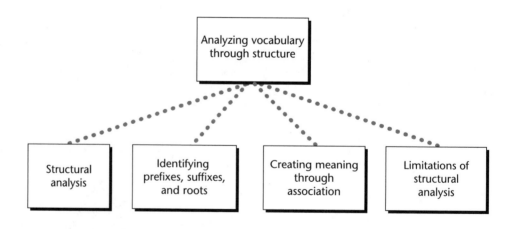

Chapter 8 Map

Chapter 9 Map

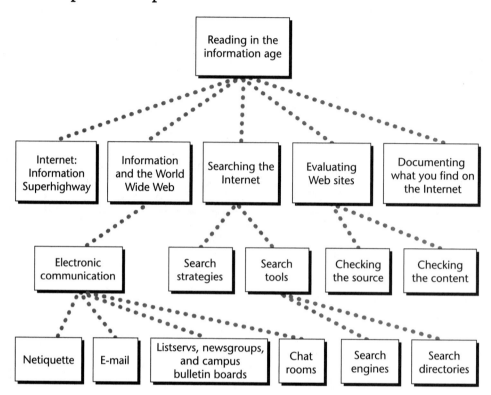

Chapter 10 Map

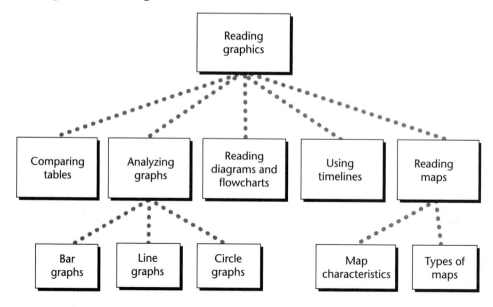

How to Compute Words-Per-Minute

To determine a general reading rate, words-per-minute, you divide the number of words read by the amount of time it took in minutes. Once you know your rate, you can record it as well as your comprehension score on the graph on the next page.

Example:

$$\frac{\text{No. of words}}{\text{No. of minutes}} = \text{WPM}$$

4000 words read in 5 minutes

$$\frac{4000}{5} = 800 \text{ WPM}$$

If you want to know an *exact* words-per-minute figure, convert your total reading time into seconds, divide the seconds into the number of words read, and then multiply the figure by 60 to change it back to minutes.

Example:

$$\frac{\text{No. of words in article}}{\text{No. of seconds}} \times 60 = \text{WPM}$$

2000 words read in 4 minutes 10 seconds

(4 min, 10 sec. = 250 seconds)

$$\frac{2000}{250} \times 60 = 480 \text{ WPM}$$

Rates and Comprehension Progress Graph, Chapters 1–10

	1	2	3	4	5	6	7	8	9	10
Date										
Rate										
Comp										

R
A
T
E

W
P
M

RATE WPM		COMPREHENSION
1,000		100
950		
900		90
850		
800		80
750		
700		70
650		
600		60
550		
500		50
450		
400		40
350		
300		30
250		
200		20
150		
100		10

Glossary

A

acronyms words formed from the first letter or the first few letters of several words.

acrostics memory techniques that consist of phrases or sentences made from the first letter or first letters of the items on a list.

adult comments the part of a person that controls the child voice through logic; the part of you that explains the reasons for completing a dull or boring task.

affix one or more letters attached to the beginnings or endings of bases or words to alter the meaning of a base or word; prefixes or suffixes.

allusion an idea expressed in shortened form referring to works of literature, history, and the arts.

analytical a learning preference of the brain for verbal, logical, and organized thinking.

assumption an inference made with the use of given facts and global knowledge.

B

background knowledge the sum total of a person's language and global knowledge; everything you already know about a subject, including facts, feelings, and experiences.

bandwagoning a propaganda technique in which a person, product, or concept seems desirable because it is popular with others.

bar graph a chart that shows the frequency of data; shows quantitative comparisons; a histogram.

base the part of a word that provides essential meaning; a root.

bias prejudice or favoritism.

bridging context clues words within the text to signal the kinds of conclusions to draw about the meaning of an unknown word.

C

cause/effect pattern   an organizational text pattern that either states or implies an association between result or outcome and the condition that made it happen.

child comments   the part of a person that wants to have fun, and have it now; the part that does not like to do dull or boring tasks.

circle graphs   graphics that show how whole units are divided into parts.

citation formats   organizational standards for referencing information.

clichés   overused similes or metaphors.

comparison clues   word or phrase signals that indicate that two or more things are similar or alike.

comparison/contrast pattern   an organizational text pattern that shows likenesses or differences between objects or concepts.

conclusions   decisions, judgments, or opinions that are reached by reasoning.

context   the surrounding words that suggest the meaning of an unknown word.

contrast clues   word or phrase signals that indicate the opposite meaning of an unknown word; signals that can be used to define that word.

cramming   frantic, last minute memorization; this method of study lacks permanency.

critic comments   represents a person's beliefs about self; sabotages motivation by telling you that success can never be attained, and suggesting that you not even try.

critical thinking   thinking logically about information, people, and choices to make reasonable, informed decisions about learning, relationships, and life.

D

definition text-based clues   punctuation marks that indicate that the meaning of an unknown word follows directly.

details   pieces of specific information that support or give information about the main idea of a paragraph or passage.

diagrams   special pictures used to explain complex concepts that would be difficult to understand using only words; used to help readers picture events, processes, structures, or sequences.

dominant   a preferred or strong learning style.

E

elaboration   memory activities that connect new meaning to background knowledge.

electronic communication   contact or messages such as e-mail, listservs, chat rooms, and newsgroups that are conveyed through computer access to the Internet.

etymology   the study of the origins of words.

euphemisms   forms of figurative language that use words or phrases that are less expressive or direct but that also are less distasteful or offensive.

eustress   the type of stress that brings out a person's best performance.

example clues   word or phrase signals that indicate given example(s) of an unknown word. These examples can be used to define that word.

experiential context   no specific written clues. Rather, the reader must examine the context and use background knowledge to draw conclusions about the meaning of unknown words.

expert opinions   judgments of those who have knowledge and skill in a particular subject.

external distractions   distractions that are physically outside of a person, like noise or temperature.

F

facts   statements of truth based on direct evidence.

figurative language   written or spoken words that use sensory images to create pictures in the mind's eye.

flames   rude or hateful electronic messages.

flowchart   a drawing that shows the steps in a complicated process.

G

general vocabulary   common, everyday words whose meanings are the same in all subjects.

global   a learning preference for subjective, visual, and spatial thinking.

glossary   an alphabetical listing of terms in a text.

graphs   symbolic representation of information that show quantitative comparisons between two or more kinds of information.

I

icons   small images or symbols that are links from one webpage to another.

image advertising   a person, product, or concept that is associated with attractive types of people, places, sounds, activities, or symbols.

Information Superhighway   Internet nickname.

Internet   a global network of computers that facilitates the transfer of electronic information and communication.

intrachapter guides   text markers found within a chapter that help readers find their way through a chapter; include headings, subheadings, terms in context, boxed information, different typefaces, graphics, or marginal notes.

K

kinesthetic perception   sensory experience derived from bodily movement and tensions.

L

learning style   brain preferences for acquiring, processing, and using information.

line graphs   graphics that show quantitative trends for one or more items over time.

linking verbs   verbs that link predicate adjectives and predicate nouns to the subject of a sentence; *being* verbs.

list/sequence pattern   an organization of text ideas, arranged in either a random or structured order.

literal   directly and clearly stated information; not inferred or suggested.

loaded words   words that generally make people, issues, and things appear worse than they might really be.

location   mnemonic technique that occurs when you link a concept with a place.

logical inferences   conclusions that cannot be avoided; for example, if a = b and b = c, then a = c.

lurk   when subscribers to electronic listservs or newsgroups read the comments of others without responding.

M

main idea   the central thought or meaning of a paragraph or passage that can be either implied or stated. The most important point the author makes about the topic.

maintenance   in learning, simple repetition of information to achieve memory storage.

mapping   creating pictures that show relationships among concepts and express patterns of thought; provides a quick means to visually determine the plan of a chapter.

mental imagery   mnemonic technique that requires you to form a picture in the mind of what is needed to be remembered.

metacognition   the ability to think about thinking.

metaphors   forms of figurative language that compare two objects without the use of *like* or *as*.

mnemonics   devices used to improve memory and recall.

mnemonigraphs   the drawings of mental images made physical.

multisensory   the combination of two or more senses (sensory preferences).

N

name calling   a propaganda technique that makes one person, product, or concept seem more attractive by using unpopular terms to describe the competition.

narrative text   written information in story form with elements of fiction including plot, character, setting, and so on.

O

objective   a type of text question in which a student selects the answer from several choices provided by the instructor. Included among these are multiple-choice, true-false, matching, and fill-in-the-blank questions; factual, literal.

opinions   judgments or viewpoints.

organizational patterns   various orders in which the sentences in a paragraph or paragraphs in a passage are written.

outline   a short organizational list that shows a pattern of ideas.

overlearning   in learning, a technique that reinforces information through practice.

P

paraphrase   to restate information in your own words.

parodies   mnemonic devices that use humor to copy serious works or phrases.

part of speech   one of eight grammatical categories into which words have been grouped: nouns, pronouns, verbs, adjectives, adverbs, conjunctions, prepositions, or interjections.

physical imagery   a mnemonic that requires you to draw a mental image.

physical map   a map that shows the natural features of a country or region.

plagiarism   taking someone's writing and presenting it as your own original ideas.

plain folks   a propaganda technique in which a person, product, or concept seems more common or natural through the use of everyday people or situations.

political map   a map that shows the location of man-made features.

postchapter guides   text features at the ends of chapters that help the reader summarize and synthesize text content through the use of summaries, review questions, terms, or suggested readings.

prechapter guides   text features at the beginnings of chapters that introduce the reader to chapter content through the use of the title, introduction, pre-reading questions, terms, outline/map, or objectives.

prefixes   one or more letters attached to the beginning of a base or word to alter the meaning of the base or word.

previewing   surveying to get the main idea about something that will be read later.

prime study time   the time of day at which a person is physically and mentally most alert.

problem-solution pattern   an organization of ideas that identifies a problem and a remedy or remedies for it.

propaganda   a form of persuasion.

punctuation text-based clues   punctuation marks (commas, brackets, parentheses) that indicate that the meaning of an unknown word directly follows.

puns   humorous use of words or phrases to suggest more than one meaning.

R

review   the basis for critical understanding; organizing and synthesizing information for greater understanding; practicing information for learning depth and permanence.

root   the part of a word that provides essential meaning; a base.

S

scale   a representation of size or space on maps; indicates the relationship between the distance of one place located on a map and the distance in real life.

signal words   words or phrases that show the organizational pattern of a paragraph or passage.

similes   forms of figurative language that compare two dissimilar objects with the use of *like* or *as*.

spaced study   consists of alternating short study sessions with breaks.

specialized vocabulary   common words that have a new and different meaning in specific subjects.

special-purpose map   a map that highlights some specific natural or man-made feature (i.e., changes in population).

SQ3R   a reading/study plan developed by Francis Robinson; steps are survey, question, read, recite, and review.

stated context clues   written clues (words or punctuation) to the meanings of unknown words.

stereotypes   standardized mental pictures of someone or something.

stress   a physical or emotional factor that causes tension; anxiety.

structural analysis   splitting words into affixes and roots to discover meaning.

study groups   having partners in the review process to discuss information and make learning active. Listening and explaining information to each other helps group members use their auditory, visual, and physical senses in learning new material.

subject-development pattern   text organization that introduces, discusses or summarizes a topic.

subjective   a type of question in which a student must provide an original written answer; a type of test question in which the instructor provides no choice of answers; included among these are essay, short answer, and some fill-in-the-blank questions.

suffixes   one or more letters attached to the ending of a base or word to alter the meaning of the base or word. The suffix also can alter the part of speech of the word.

supplementary materials   readings or other information that support a primary text in course content.

surveying   the first step in SQ3R, which involves getting an overview of the entire chapter by looking at the chapter title, headings, subheadings, bold-faced words, key sentences, and so on.

symbols   ideas or concepts that stand for or suggest another idea or concept by means of association or relationship.

synthesis   a personalized system of associating relationships between details and main ideas from a variety of sources. A process of forming a single body of information by associating and relating data from various sources (notes, text, and so on) is a synthesis.

T

table   a systematic listing of information in rows and columns.

technical vocabulary   words that are specific to a content area and have no meaning outside of that area.

test anxiety   a physical or emotional factor that causes tension before, during, or after an exam; stress.

testimonial   a propaganda technique in which a famous person recommends or supports a product or concept.

text labels   notes written on printed materials which restate or translate information found directly in the text. They help you draw conclusions, make generalizations, or show how information can be applied in different situations.

timelines   graphic outlines of sequenced information; a chronology of important dates or events.

topic   the subject of a passage or paragraph.

topic sentence   the sentence that expresses the main idea in a paragraph or a passage.

trends   directions in which features in a graph or chart change; common, contrasting, or unusual features.

W

weasel words   a promise that is implied but not definitely stated.

word games   rhymes, songs, puns, parodies.

References

Anderson, R. C., and Pichert, J. W. (1978). Recall of previously unrecallable information following a shift in perspective. *Journal of Verbal Learning and Verbal Behavior,* 17: 1–12.

Balint, S. W. (September, 1989). Campus comedy. *Reader's Digest.*

Bloom, B. (1956). *Taxonomy of Educational Objectives, Handbook I: Cognitive Domain.* New York: David McKay.

Bower, G. H. (1970). Analysis of a mnemonic device. *American Scientist,* 59: 496.

Brandeth, G. (1980). *The joy of lex.* New York: William Morrow.

Bryson, B. (1990). *The mother tongue: English and how it got that way.* New York: William Morrow.

Cyveillance, 2000, www.cyveillance.com, November 3, 2001.

Dale, E. (1958). How to know more wonderful words. *Good Housekeeping,* 146: 17+.

DeBono, E. (1992). *Serious creativity.* HarperCollins: New York.

Feldman, S. (1998). "Web Search Services in 1998: Trends and Challenges," SEARCHER, June, 1998, www.infotoday.com/searcher/jun/story2.htm.

Gower, R. (1991). Klinsmann contemplates life without soccer. *Soccer America,* p. 20.

IDC: *Analyze the future.* www.idc.com, November 3, 2001.

McArthur, T. (ed.) (1992). *The Oxford companion to the English language.* Oxford: Oxford University Press.

McVay, M. (2000). *How to be a successful distance learning student: Learning on the Internet.* Needham Heights, MA: Pearson Custom Publishing.

Noel, L., Levitz, R., Saluri, D., and Associates. (1987). *Increasing student retention.* San Francisco: Jossey-Bass.

Tenney, J. (March, 1986). *Key word note-taking system.* Paper presented at the 19th Annual Meeting of the Western College Reading and Learning Association, Los Angeles, CA.

Tomlinson, L. M. (1997). A coding system for notemarking in literature: Preparation for journal writing, class participation, and essay tests. *Journal of Adolescent & Adult Literacy,* 40(6): 468–476.

Index

Boldface numbers indicate tables or figures